Marlene Kangas
New York
November 2004

BY THE SAME AUTHOR

Autobiography

A Postilion Struck by Lightning
Snakes and Ladders
An Orderly Man
Backcloth
Great Meadow

Novels

A Gentle Occupation
Voices in the Garden
West of Sunset
Jericho

Correspondence

A Particular Friendship

A SHORT WALK FROM HARRODS

DIRK BOGARDE

VIKING

VIKING

Published by the Penguin Group
Penguin Books Ltd, 27 Wrights Lane, London W8 5TZ, England
Penguin Books USA Inc., 375 Hudson Street, New York, New York 10014, USA
Penguin Books Australia Ltd, Ringwood, Victoria, Australia
Penguin Books Canada Ltd, 10 Alcorn Avenue, Toronto, Ontario, Canada M4V 3B2
Penguin Books (NZ) Ltd, 182–190 Wairau Road, Auckland 10, New Zealand

Penguin Books Ltd, Registered Offices: Harmondsworth, Middlesex, England

First published 1993
1 3 5 7 9 10 8 6 4 2
First edition

Typeset by Datix International Limited, Bungay, Suffolk
Filmset in 11½/14 pt Monophoto Bembo
Printed in England by Clays Ltd, St Ives plc

A CIP catalogue record for this book is available from the British Library

ISBN 0-670-85151-5

For

GARETH AND LUCILLA

With very much love

'. . . at sixteen the height of my ambition was to construct a cage . . . for a pet linnet. ' Sussex, May 1937

Author's Note

When I finished writing *Backcloth* in 1985 I was absolutely sure that I would never write another book again, let alone another volume of autobiography. I had been overtaken by events far beyond my control. However, the only thing which is certain in life is that we can never be certain of anything. Here then is my eleventh book and sixth volume of autobiography.

For obvious reasons I have altered a number of proper names and some place names, but the events are as they were and as I recall them without the aid of diaries or journals. Alas, the area of France about which I write has now been drastically altered, almost beyond recognition. This, then, is a tribute to the patch of it which I was privileged to own and which I greatly loved.

It is also a tribute to the memory of a valiant and courageous man who loved it with an equal passion. My love and my thanks to my editor, Fanny Blake, who encouraged me and supported me whenever I foundered in the 'remembering', and, as always, to Sally Betts, who once more has had to cope with my 'inserts' and 'corrections' with patience and rapidity.

D. v. d. B.

List of Illustrations

Frontispiece: Constructing a cage for a pet linnet
Beginning the *porte d'entrée*, 1973
Finished. Autumn, 1973
November 1968
September 1977
The house after the conversion, July 1968
The Long Room, 1985
The chimneyplace, 1968
The chimneyplace, 1985
Starting the kitchen extension, 1974
Finished. May 1974
Le Pigeonnier, August 1979
The start of the Big Fire, August 1986
The moon country
The first Christmas, 1969
The terrace, 1985
Last photo of the terrace, 1985

Chapter 1

Sitting here, as presently I am, the nicotiana is higher than my head. Well. As high as. The scent is overwhelming, drifting out into the still evening air. I suppose that I should try and find a word other than 'drifting'. But that is exactly what scents do on still summer evenings; it's what this scent is doing. So it remains. Drifting. It's all part of building up an illusion of peace and calm. I planted the things out in April, earlier than advised, but I did it anyway, and did it so that I should be able to sit one evening quite embowered by blossom and suffocated by heavy scent.

And so I am.

A sort of peace descends. It would appear, from all outward signs, that stress has faded.

Only 'appear'. I still jump like a loon if a book falls, a door bangs, the telephone rings. That's rare. Rarer than falling books or banging doors. The telephone hardly ever rings. And never between Friday afternoon and Monday afternoon.

People go away.

Sometimes, on Sundays, if it gets really grim, I walk to the station to buy a newspaper I don't need, or want, and talk to the very friendly chap who runs the paper stall. His mate runs the flower stall. We speak of the weather, local football (about which I know nothing, but I nod and listen), and it breaks the silence.

Heigh ho. A fat bee nudges rather hopelessly among the fluted white trumpets. If you could talk to a ruddy bee I'd tell it that it was out of luck. You won't get any pollen from that lot, the trumpet is far too narrow.

But it's not after pollen. Nectar. That's the word. And it won't get that either. A hopeless, fruitless search.

Talking aloud to oneself, or trying to engage a bee in conversation, or discuss the state of the day with a portrait, or the wallpaper, is an almost certain sign of incipient madness and, or, senility.

I don't honestly feel that I have reached either of those stations of the cross; but I have checked it out with others who live alone and living alone, they assure me, gets you chatting up a storm.

To no one.

Well, it fills in the silences. Sometimes they are good, the silences, but at times they do get a bit heavy. Music helps, of course. I listen to more music now than I ever did before.

The evening sun is warm on my face, the terrace tiles still hot under my bare feet, hot from the glory of the day. It really is a kind of contentment. The bee, the nicotianas, the stillness and, high in the tree beyond, the kestrel.

He arrived like a silent dart a few moments ago; sussed me out, snapped his head round, fixing me with huge golden eyes. Steady. Below, on the close-mown grass, two wood pigeons waddle about like a couple of blowsy bag-ladies. Aware, with the extraordinary vision which they possess, of the danger above but disinclined to fly until death swoops, they continue to waddle. Very British.

The tree frills in a slight breeze which arrives suddenly like a sigh. The kestrel sways gently, eyes still on me. The nicotiana, the white and yellow daisies, the magenta bells of the fuchsia rustle and swing and suddenly, as if the breeze had been a signal, the kestrel takes off in a long low swoop, glides across the lawns, flustering the bag-ladies, planes upwards over the trees on the boundary and is lost to sight.

All is still. The breeze has dropped as suddenly as it arrived. A crow across the garden cries out in raucous worry; its mate, squatting on a rickety platform of twigs, calls back two or three times; the bag-ladies shake ruffled feathers and nose and bob, cooing in relief.

Danger has passed.

The garden is still, fading gently into evening. The ice in my whisky chinks, almost convincing me with the serenity of its delicate sound that there is nothing for me to do, or nothing which has to *be* done. But I know very well that there is.

The nightly watering chore has to commence. I do find it exhausting, carting gallons of water about and trying not to bump into the furniture on the way. Dusk is falling slowly, my ice melting; through the fretwork of the tree the elegant shape of Peter Jones looms, flags limp now in the breezeless air, sleek, proud, clearly bent on a collision with the Royal Court Theatre across the square.

Lights spring up somewhere on the top floor, an ambulance siren wails, a window is slammed shut, traffic mumbles distantly, a voice calls out, a woman laughs and feet clack-clack-clack along the pavement.

I am back full circle. I'm where I started out on my journey at the meek and wondering age of seventeen.

Consider: at sixteen the height of my ambition was to construct a cage from garden-bamboo for a pet linnet. Which I did, only to find that I had misjudged the widths of the bars, through which the bloody bird sped. Story of my life you might say. But you'd be quite wrong.

At seventeen, refusing education of a higher kind, refusing university, refusing all chances of becoming an office boy, or a runner, at *The Times*, Printing House Square, refusing, in fact, to follow my exceedingly clever father into his post as art editor, I agreed, fairly ungraciously I have been told, to a place at art school in Chelsea Polytechnic. At seventeen, just turned, I was a year too young but apparently showed 'interesting talent' so they took me on. Unaware of my lack of education and my cavalier method with measurements or anything requiring thought. (Check with bamboo bird cage above.)

However, there it was: I went. And sitting here I can almost see the spire of St Luke's church, which was not so far from the school. Which is why I can say that I am back full circle. For this was my area, my manor if you like. I knew it, and loved it, well.

So.

At seventeen an art student, at nineteen I was scrubbing out the pans and pots in the tin wash at Catterick Camp. At twenty-seven, after a good bit of voyaging, I was back again, became a 'film star', and at forty-eight, deciding to take stock and readjust the seasoning of life, I left England for Provence and sat up on a mountain among my olives and sheep very contentedly until I was sixty-seven. When the heavens all of a sudden fell.

So I came back here. To the area in which I had begun to grow up; or, if not that exactly, to set down tentative roots, and commence an adult life. It was familiar territory, I walked among ghosts, pleasant ones, and felt not so strange, and people were initially very kind, until I decided, quite by myself, that solitude was better by far than being 'in demand'. So I cut adrift and went on my way. A dinghy bobbing along happily in the fog of unfamiliarity.

Being 'in demand' simply meant that you were presentable enough, not an unspeakable bore, that you could talk left and right at a dinner or luncheon table, be agreeable, amusing (moderately), and, above all, that you were unattached. That was the most important thing of all: no wife or mistress to trail about, just you yourself. Free, *available,* the desperate hostess's dream. You had become a 'spare pair of trousers'. It is not as disagreeable as perhaps it sounds. You get your supper free – you just have to do a bit of singing for it. Not difficult. Merely tedious.

The deadliest thing of all was the agonizing sameness of it. After over two decades away I had grown far distant from the chatter and behaviour of the people with whom I now dined or lunched. I did my best to bone up, as it were, on London events by reading a great many daily newspapers. I could talk about, for example, plays and films and books which I had never seen or read simply because I had studied their critics. *All* of them, so that I could work out for myself how things were in that performance or production or book. I read about politics, something I had hardly ever bothered to do in France; even got into American politics through the pages of the glossy news magazines. Nervously I went to my dinners if not in a black tie, which I did not possess and refused to wear anyway, at least moderately well armed with general information. What bugged me most was that I was not at all *au fait* with the local politics of the neighbourhood. I had no idea who was sleeping with whom, who had gone off with a wife or husband, boyfriend or lover, and where they had all hidden. I didn't know who was 'in' or 'out', and was amazed, above all, to discover that the only thing which really had not changed over the years was the speech pattern of the guests at these unquestionably perfect, elegant, beautifully presented and, ultimately, dull evenings.

Generally speaking my hosts, hostesses and their guests were all, to my silent consternation, merely marking time. A long-forgotten roar from my regimental sergeant-major at Aldershot drifted often into my mind while I toyed with a slim Baccarat wine glass: '*On your marks! Slow march!*' And this is exactly what they were doing, apparently quite unaware and uncaring. Perhaps it was all too late for them anyway? It seemed to me that they were digging themselves into a hole of their own making. Trapped hip deep in the past. Their scenario was sepia, thumbed and tattered.

I had, personally speaking, chucked my copy away years ago when I left the grey-white cliffs of Dover for a new life. But now on returning I discovered, to my dismay, I had to dig it out again, dusty and faded by the years, and play it over once more. Or, rather, replay it, without the confidence and knowledge that once I had possessed. It was very worrying really, but, I suppose, better than boiling up one of those deathly plastic bags, or crumbling Carr's water biscuits into a tin of heated-up soup over the sink. I couldn't do more, frankly. Boiling an egg had become either 'victory' or 'disaster'. Even with an egg-timer from the Reject Shop. It was extremely insular and (a name the papers decided to lumber me with) 'reclusive' to hang in just with myself. I really couldn't complain that the telephone never rang, because I was fast becoming a deadly, unsociable boor. My own fault. Therefore I decided to accept the invitations which did come my way from generous and affectionate friends from way-back-when. To go out and discover life among the living! Not to sit there alone in my room, to go where the music played . . .

Okay. But did it? Let me describe an average evening. You can make up your own mind. It was a far cry from my life before. I had known Victoria for years, since my earliest days in the post-war theatre. She had a very pretty house in Charles Street filled with minor treasures. Flowers, silks, good paintings, good furniture. It was not by any means an 'arrogance of good taste'; it was extremely comfortable, pleasing and very expensive. She had arrived from America years before with a glorious figure with which to carry her clothes and a glorious figure with which to purchase them from the great houses and to please her bankers and her future, pretty useless but titled, husband. In short, Victoria survived radiantly, and by the time I met her, after my first big West End success, she was intent on launching me into Society. I didn't desire that, and there really wasn't much 'Society' flying about by that time, 1947–50. What was left after cruel decimation in the war and vicious taxation didn't amount to very much. Victoria's world was crumbling like an Alka Seltzer. Only she, and her guests, didn't dare face the fact.

One happily peaceful evening she telephoned me. Her voice, light, warm, only very slightly inflected by distant Philadelphia, coaxed me. 'Now, sweetie, *don't* be tiresome. Put this down in your little book. The 17th. Supper here, eight-thirty, come about 7.45. There will be eight. So exciting that you are back *at last*! What an abberation that all was! A peasant farmer in the hills! *Madness.* Abroad is so "alien", don't you think? Not black tie. I have two Socialists coming. They write books but aren't at all vegetarian, which has pleased Mario enormously. Oh! It's exciting that you are back again! A delicious "spare pair of trousers". You'll be *swamped* with offers. But I have got you first, haven't I? What huge fun it is to have you home!' I didn't in all truth feel elated.

Sheraton table gleaming, silver, crystal winking in soft light. An air of comfort and old-fashioned elegance and riches. Served superb food by three sullen Filipinos. It always was at Victoria's. Whatever else you might have to put up with, the food was glorious. Mario was the best private chef in London at the time. Eight of us at table, the silk-covered walls spread with Piranesi engravings, Colefax and Fowler swags at the windows, candles sparkling in Georgian silver. I sat between Phyllida and Margot. Margot had informed us in the drawing-room that she had called a taxi one evening to go to the Savoy and, in her anxiety not to be late for dinner, crashed straight into a lamp-post, smashing her nose. She now, in consequence, was forced to wear a black frilly lace mask. It was very becoming. I wish to differentiate here between Margot with a mask and without one. *With* was far more acceptable.

Across the table, separated tactfully, were the two book-writing Socialists. Perfectly acceptable as it would appear: she in sprigged voile with puffed sleeves, her hair braided across her head like a Viennese loaf, he in, predictably, a red tie worn with a white suit and a very high collar in the manner of Tom Wolfe. She was quiet, rather nice, asked if I missed France and did I ever make jam from my figs? I said no. He said that the theatre should be an 'event'. Last from nine a.m. until eleven p.m. Not just 'a pathetic two hours with arrogant, overpaid property developers and their women only longing for the interval and the bar'. It should be for the working man. Elevating, enriching, a form of subsidized 'feeding for the mind'. Pretty unworkable, I should have thought, but I said nothing.

Between them poor Constance Pullinger sat toying wistfully with a little silver box. 'My pilly-pill-pills.' She opened and closed the enamel lid with one finger, urgently. Smiling sadly across at me, she rattled the box like a castanet. 'I'd be lost without these. *Too* awful to be sent to prison or a concentration camp and not be allowed them. I'd *willingly* die then.'

Margot suddenly turned from her partner, a plump middle-aged man called 'Bunny' Dilford-Pryce, prodded my arm to deflect me from Constance opposite. 'High as a kite,' she hissed in a whisper, and then aloud said, 'Bunny says you now live permanently in London?' She was what she would have called 'twinkling' encouragingly behind her froth of black lace. 'Sold up in France? Too sad . . . although I simply *loathe* the French personally, but one has to remember Elizabeth David and Cézanne and that clever Mister Proust, and all . . . but even so. You *will* be in demand! Where are you exactly? Victoria said a flat?' I told her, she crumbled a piece of her bread roll, nodded agreeably, head bent towards me listening. 'I know! I know *exactly*. Nanny has a dentist there. Perfectly acceptable . . .'

Obviously I had passed some sort of private test which she had set, for she was still smiling, lips pursed in a roguish smile. 'Not *quite* SW1 but not far off and only a short walk from Harrods. *Wonderful* for you!' Satisfied that she had filed me away in her memory bank, plus my district, she returned to 'Bunny' on her right.

Constance, meanwhile, still listening blankly to 'Tom Wolfe', quietly opened her little silver box, took a pill, swigged it down with a gulp of Sauternes and shuddered as if she had bitten into cyanide. Which as far as I could tell, she might have done. Catching my curious, kindly eye, she smiled across, hand to throat. 'Sometimes they catch in one's gullet. At the bendy bit. Did you know? And don't *quite* go down. So they don't take effect for simply ages. Not the idea at all. *Instant* oblivion is all I ask. I dote on oblivion. Did Margot say Harrods?'

'She asked where I lived now. I told her and she seemed pleased for me that I was just a short walk from the place. I gather that's a good area in which to be?'

'I simply wouldn't know. I never go to Harrods now. Really impossible, all those guided tours with miserable Americans and bespectacled Japanese, and dreadful young women spraying one with the maid's scent. *Perfume*, they call it! Who wants to shop in a souk, after all? Too fraying. I think my little pill went down. Peace descends.' She smothered a tiny yawn, blinked, smiled at me, turned away to listen to 'Tom Wolfe', wearily.

Bunny Dilford-Pryce suddenly leant across Margot's wide bosom and whispered to me as if we were in some conspiracy together. 'I saw you on the box the other day! Simply dire. Did you see it? Terrible bunk . . . something about India? I know there was an elephant. Ages old. You were *indecently* young. Black and white, of course.'

I assured him that I never watched myself on television. The Filipinos had started to remove the first course and re-lay for the second. Victoria busily repinned her Cartier clips at her breast, eyes darting about her table. 'Fascinating!' she said, I supposed to Bunny. 'I so adore really *ancient* films like that. We were all so naïve then. And what fun it all was. *Was* there an elephant?'

'Never watch yourself? Really?' Bunny probed diligently. 'Not *ever*? Surely yes?'

'No, never.'

'Well normally *I* don't. Ever. Detestable thing, television. Should be in the staff quarters. Written and made by, and for, housemaids. That's where I saw it. Just a peek. My man was doing the silver, so I took a look. Too *eerie*. You were so boyish!'

'It was a long time ago,' I murmured helplessly. I mean, what do you say to that kind of idiot chatter? But he suddenly cackled with delight, finger raised so we should all attend. 'Ah ha! Ah ha! I know! Only a dog returns to its own vomit! That it?'

'Something like that,' I said.

Bunny squealed with delight at his quip and Victoria very speedily came to my rescue, adjusting her little black veiled hat (always worn at her dinner parties), smiling sweetly to defuse any possible irritation.

'Bunny dear! *Not* at my table. Frightful word to use before one's food. Vomit! *Really!* And look' – she placed a very firm restraining hand on my arm – 'Here come those delicious little quails' breasts that Mario does so superbly. Brilliant! What a *lovely* evening you are all giving me!'

The room was suddenly noisy with the clatter of dishes and service. 'Tom Wolfe' was barking with laughter. Constance was happily blank.

I realized, with some amusement, that far from coming out to join the living, as I had thought, I was actually sitting among the living dead. I made a silent vow there and then at Victoria's table never again to put on a dark suit to dine in a cemetery.

★

In a pretty short time I gave up that sort of exhausting frivolity, preferring my own company and a large Scotch. Or two large Scotches. I didn't have to shave and struggle into a clean shirt at seven o'clock, to drag myself off and be bored witless, lost and floundering. No demands were made on me on my own. Nothing was taken from me. I could just please myself. It was rather attractive. Whatever energy still remained to me was not dispersed and exhausted by talking inanities with the lost. So I hung the dark suit up in the wardrobe and let it be known, gently but firmly, that I was no longer about to give 'evening performances'. Simply 'matinées'.

And it worked. I began to enjoy being by myself and to that end, trying to revert to the shade of a life long ago ended, I bought a cheap pair of jeans, a pair of trainers, never wore a tie and hunched myself comfortably into my worn, and pretty filthy, anorak. I felt all at once happy *dans ma peau*, a French saying which means exactly what it says: 'in my skin'. To exercise, which I now had to do twice a day at least, I made extremely brave efforts to walk quite long distances in order to stretch my ailing leg and to get plants and things for my terrace, which now had to become my summer living-room. There was also the vexed question of food, food that didn't need cooking. Because of my not being able to at first. So that meant marketing for one. A worrying business. One chop? One cod fillet? One piece of steak? I had not the least idea what to do with the things, should I buy them. In supermarkets, I was quick to discover, things were usually packaged for two or more. And had sell-by dates so that one was forced to wear glasses just to buy a tub of yoghurt . . . No cooking. Nourishing. Easy. Like tinned soup.

At home in France, marketing was easy. You could always buy one slice of pâté, a leek, a carrot, one potato to bake. A *tranche* of ham was served and wrapped with as much respect and reverence as if one had ordered breast of peacock. But that was in the market. Not a pre-packaged, neon-lit immensity of harassed women clattering trollies about. I pretty soon learned that hanging around in the check-outs was not a good idea. I was, amazingly and disconcertingly, recognized a good deal. There was a lot of '*Yes it is!*' and '*No it isn't. He's getting bald*', or '*You ask him. Go on . . .*', and I got a bit tired of being asked if I '*used to be someone famous, whatchermacallit?*'

So I gave up supermarkets and kept to the smaller, less frightening shops. Some of which I had found close to hand because anyway I was unable to walk very far. But now, exercising determinedly, I managed to get out on longer journeys. Once I actually got halfway up the Kings Road, scuttling along quite quickly for me, like an apologetic turtle, hunched, head down in the anorak collar to avoid recognition. But it didn't help much.

From a table in the courtyard of the Pheasantry I was hailed by a shout above the traffic. 'Durk! Durk! I do not believe it. I just do *not*! I am in awe!' It was Mae-Ellen, a half-remembered friend from long ago in Los Angeles. I didn't really want to remember her. She was all right, but exhausting. She hugged me with obvious pleasure, insisted that I walk back with her to her place. 'It's just right here. Sydney Street. Oh, come on . . .'

I said that I really was a bit jaded, had walked enough, was lame and all that stuff. She insisted, and I buckled and gave in. 'It's right here! If you got this far you can get to my little house.' If I collapsed in the street, my name and address and telephone number were in my wallet. It was always possible that whoever picked me up, if anyone should stoop to do such a thing, might not remember who I used to be. Mae-Ellen had a dusting of freckles, red hair cut in what she termed 'a bang', wore white stockings, which seem to be a favourite with certain kinds of American women who lean towards intense intellectualism, which gave her legs the unhappy impression of up-ended milk bottles thrust into neat little lace-up shoes. She wore wire glasses, a Madras cotton skirt, a too-big Aran sweater and a rope of various tropical seeds strung on a thread round her neck. She was very warm and welcoming when we reached her place off Sydney Street, offered me herbal tea, which she said she was just about to infuse because I'd interrupted her cup at the Pheasantry, but I declined this offer, and sat in a creaking wicker chair while she hurled about with a kettle and teapot.

'I just can't *believe* bumping into you like that! So weird! When was the last time? At Ruthie's place on Doheney? Aeons ago. My, how time flies. And here I am in Europe again! Can you believe? You haven't changed. Really. Well, we all get old, inevitably, but you look just great. It suits you. I'm with the embassy now. First Washington, now London. I'll be here for a while then I get to go to Frankfurt, Germany. It's so worth while.' She poured hot water into her pot. 'I am a counsellor. You know that? To army wives on the bases. I can't say exactly where, but you know . . . they are real lonely those wives. They suffer.'

I was beginning to suffer myself. She was being kind but boring, I felt trapped and wanted to pee anyway. I had felt instant claustrophobia the moment she shut us into the narrow hall of her dark little house. 'You want a cracker? Candy?

This isn't my place, you know, I just borrow it from my friend Cindy. She's great. She's in Uttar Pradesh or some place . . . If there is a famine, a war or an epidemic, Cindy's *off*! She is so caring! Sure you won't have some peppermint tea? It's refreshing.'

The dingy little room looked out over St Luke's churchyard. Bamboo and cane furniture, dragged blue walls, a dusty bunch of faded pink larkspur bound with twine in a twig basket. Mae-Ellen was stirring her tea with a pencil. 'What I am doing is reely important, I just go along and talk with these women and they talk right back. They are just lonesome for conversation. They call me their new Avon lady! Isn't that adorable? It releases them: conversation. They are stuck on the base, with their kids, and then there are hos-tle women just outside, in tents and things, with placards, 'Yanks Go Home!', and worse. It's not friendly, and they feel vulnerable. Lonely. They have the PX, sure, they get movies, there are the padrés, a rabbi as well, can you believe? And they get wonderful medical treatment for the kids. But they still feel lonesome. Stuck on a base. It's spooky. Unnatural. And with those awful hos-tle women . . . well . . .'

I nodded. I was busting for a pee and would have to ask her where to go. I sat still containing myself because she was off again. 'I say to them, look, I say. There are just wonderful compensations. You have your husbin, you have your children. That is so right, so traditional, so American. The Family. Right? Together, united. They love you and that is one helluva deal today. To have a loving family around you. *Love*. You want proof of that love. Well: the very first proof of that love is the very first gift which your child will offer you. You, the giver of life. You, its mother. And you know what this gift is? It is shit!' She sat back in her chair, her glasses glittering with triumph. I asked her where the lav was and she looked bewildered. 'Oh! That! The john? It's right up there, on the left. Okay?'

When I returned she was refilling her mug. 'Defecation . . . To continue . . . defecation is the very first "Thank you" from your child. It is just automatic. I think it is kinda marvellous, don't you? Uplifting. Of course in our terms we would say it was just an automatic reflex, but I say no! It is a deep psychological desire, buried way deep down in the subconscious of the new-born, that just insists on giving thanks for its life. I tell my women that: somehow I feel that it helps them. Comforts them. It gives them a new angle on their lives. Are you sure you won't take some peppermint?'

But I managed to get away. Slightly overwhelmed. I didn't get this kind of stuff on the hill. Perhaps being back in London was going to be altogether rather exhausting? I hadn't seen Mae-Ellen for years. And then only twice at parties in Los Angeles. The risk of collision in the Kings Road was worrying. I had hoped not to see her again. Breathing air, however much it was polluted, was better by far than sitting in her dreary little room.

The Kings Road was still the same road that I had first walked in wonderment at seventeen and now, at seventy, it still had the same effect in spite of quite disastrous architectural changes and the ones which had taken place among the people who now thronged and jostled in it. But it all *felt* the same, and I still *felt* seventeen. I was surrounded by 'familiars', altered, of course, but still recognizable. I have said, earlier, that I walk with ghosts. And so I do. Not all of whom I knew or ever met. But they must still be about. Their shades?

Comforting me. Oscar Wilde coming from Tite Street, Lily Langtry going up to the Cadogans', Carlyle walking slowly to his tobacconist, Augustus John in sagging dressing-gown and slippers off to the Five Bells. My parents were here too – when they were young and I just born. Off they went to the Good Intent, or to the Embankment to the Blue Cockatoo. Henry Moore bought his packets of vine charcoal from Green and Stone's, and Kathleen and Graham Sutherland, elegance and beauty beyond anything I had ever witnessed in my life before, and known among us students at the Polytechnic as 'The Beautiful People', long before that phrase (coined then) was so debased later for far less glorious creatures. But they had all been here. And Danuta! She *must* be around somewhere. Heavy Polish breasts bouncing under her cheese-cloth shirt, broad feet in lattice-leather sandals, striding with swinging Percheron hips into the little studio which she rented in a crumbling Regency house where the fire station stands today. I well remember her removing my virginity there, before a plopping gas fire on a runkled rug, and casting it, and finally myself, aside as contemptuously as an old jacket. In 1939 she went home to Krakow for the summer recess. And that was that.

So I am not unfamiliar with my area. Bewildered perhaps, but it fits me. Even though the players on the stage have altered beyond recognition, the play, as it were, remains much the same. Same format. Different sets and players. There are black faces now among the white. Bedraggled girls in Doc Marten's, black tights, black velvet pull-on hats, flowing black shifts to their calves. In mourning for youth? Shaven-headed young men in leather and floral prints, headbands or baseball caps, arrogantly astride glittering motorbikes the size and splendour of Cadillacs.

There is a stink of greasy food now, of mushy pasta and pizza, of cheap coffee and pot, the thump thump thump of heavy metal music from the open doors of tacky shoe shops. All around, the nasal whine of adolescent life, wandering idly up and down, sucking ice creams, chewing gum or hamburgers, laughing, and squawking like apprehensive parrots. All on the edge of things. Waiting. Moving. Oddly different in so many ways, but *familiar*. Different from the people that we were at their age. But, remember, at their age I was making a bird cage for a linnet.

My local grocer's is still open. I take a wire basket and wander in wondering what to eat for my supper. A fraught business. A tin of soup? Easy. No mess. One dish to wash. Perhaps some ham? Cold ham and boiled potatoes. Perhaps with a bit of chutney. I was, I realized, muttering aloud to myself. One reaches such a state when approaching a pressing decision on one's own. And, because I had momentarily deflected myself through my anxious preoccupation with supper, I tripped over one of those blasted shopping-trollies, usually tartan, which elderly ladies drag behind them in supermarkets. The woman, in a plum-cloth coat and pudding basin hat, glared at me as if I had attempted to snatch her bag, shrugged off my apology and turned back to her companion, a thin woman in a knitted beret. 'You was saying?'

'Well. I said to 'im, well then I said, what's that lump doing there? Wasn't there lunchtime. Very nasty it looks. Very nasty. You watch your bleedin' mouth 'e says to me. Don't meddle! Well, I says, you go to Boots cash chemist and get something to put on it. Get lorst! 'e says. Silly old cat. My own child! Own flesh and blood. Flabbergarsted I was.'

Considering ham or pie at the counter, listening with curiosity to the conversation behind me, I was all unaware of mounting irritation from the woman next to me. She started to push hard at my wire basket with her own.

'Do you *frightfully* mind?' Her voice was cold with disdain.

We had crossed the Great Divide. This was no lady from the Dwellings, this one was bent on battle. There would be no democratic encounter here between her mushroom hat, well-cut silk dress, tight grey hair and my aged anorak, dirty jeans and trainers. I was ready for the sacrifice, and armed with this reassurance she pressed forward.

I did not budge. Not a millimetre. I willed her to have another bash at my basket and this she did, swinging at mine like a demolition ball and chain.

'I did ask you to move. I am trying to shop.'

'And I, madam.'

'Here before you. And I know exactly what I want. So.'

'And I do. Exactly.'

A youth hovered about behind the glass counter. She raised a jewelled fist to summons him.

'Young man! Smoked salmon. Scottish not farmed. Eight ounces.'

She turned to me once again and demanded that I move. I said that I would.

When I had been served.

This unseemly, trivial squabble had reached the point where I thought she might see fit to swing her basket at my head, her eyes burned with such dislike and contempt; but at that instant Mr Collinson, crisp in white apron, eyes sparked with mischief behind thick glasses, was quite suddenly in attendance.

'Ah! M'lord! There you are. What can we do for you today? Gala pie?'

The mushroom hat and the silk dress moved swiftly away. She stared at me, white with hostility.

Mr Collinson, beaming at a minor victory, clasped his hands. 'The tongue, m'lord? Of course. Can I tempt you to three slices?'

Behind me in the queue a woman's voice said, 'Oh my dear . . . Gerald and I had to dine with them at their place on Tuesday. They really won't do, you know. I mean, Christmas cards from Kensington Palace stuck all over the room. *In June!* Quite impossible . . .'

Takes all sorts in my manor. A goodly mix, as my father would say.

At the check-out plum-coat had beaten me to it.

'My own flesh and blood, Chrissie. Did you ever?'

Walk up to my square, sunlight freckling through the plane trees.

But no dogs leaping in idiot welcome, no scent of freshly cut hay, no scuttering lizards on the stone walls, no quick 'plops!' from suddenly disturbed fish in the pond. No pond. No voice from the terrace calling, 'Were the London papers in yet?'

Emptiness sighs. Perfectly all right. No problem.

How the hell did I get here?

Chapter 2

Memory seems to come to me in snatches: I suppose because one suppresses so much that was untenable. Is it that? Or is time somehow altogether too vast to hold in detail? Or am I merely getting old? The latter most probably.

I can remember that evening pretty clearly. I cannot pinpoint much in the immediate days before it. But that evening, that last dreadful evening, is as clear to me now as if it was yesterday evening. Clearer in fact. But apparently etched on to glass. It has a strange transparency about it, like a Lawrence Whistler goblet. Vision, through space, to vision.

It was about six. The time when, normally, I'd be pouring my first glass of wine and, depending on the season, settling into the big chair by the stove or my 'place' in the deep striped chair on the terrace under the vine. But this particular evening was unlike any others. Time was wrenched.

Elizabeth said quietly, 'He's late.' Meaning the taxi from Nice.

She was standing at the edge of the terrace, toes hooked over the rim, looking down across the little lawn, beyond the terraces to the gate in the lane. The gate was wide open. We would see the roof of the taxi glittering in the last of the sun running past the hedges, flickering through the olives.

I think that I said, 'Yes. He said six o'clock precisely. But maybe the traffic was heavy . . . he has to come right across the town.' Something like that.

Forwood was sitting perfectly still in one of the big striped chairs, his stick with the greyhound's-head between his knees, hands clasped over the handle. He was perfectly still, contained, except that one foot trembled gently.

Up the track towards Titty-Brown Hill, in the orange light of the evening sun, Christine and Alain had wandered away from us. She was playing with a sprig of rosemary she'd pulled from the hedge. They were being mercifully tactful.

I went into the Long Room to the corner cupboard where I had, purposely, left half a bottle of Haig and a litre of Evian and some little mustard glasses. I took a brimming glass and downed it. Lost my breath, refilled, added a little water.

Apart from the fact that there were no flowers, no green plants, no pictures, no books, the room was still recognizably mine. As it had been for over twenty years. Christine and Alain had bought nearly all the furniture.

A cushion on one of the big arm-less chairs I'd bought in Milan bore a body dent. I automatically took it up and 'plumped' it. A perfectly idiotic gesture. It was no longer my cushion to 'plump'. Or my chair. Or my room. I'd never see it again in my life.

On the terrace Elizabeth went over to her modest pile of luggage, checked it. I looked at Forwood, he looked at me. We smiled.

'Having your drink?'

'Sun's over the yard arm.' Banality. I'd only ever laughed at people who actually said it.

Elizabeth called, 'Here he is. Awfully late . . .'

Up at Titty-Brown Hill, Alain and Christine had seen him too. They turned and came slowly, reluctantly, down towards us.

Forwood eased himself up from his chair, I put the glass

back in the bar cupboard. I did not look round again. Elizabeth had slung her shoulder bag over her arm.

The wheels of the taxi crunched into a swerve as he took the corner of the drive beyond the *porte d'entrée*, a door slammed. I called out, 'Jacques?'

'*Oui, monsieur. Ouf . . . mon dieu! Le traffic . . . à l'aeroport. C'est complètement fou.*' He lifted the lid of the boot, we started loading up.

Christine was standing in the centre of the terrace, the vine leaves casting trembling shadows like torn lace across her face, her hands twisting the sprig of rosemary.

Suddenly she burst into agonizing tears, buried her head in her hands, bent forward sobbing. I hurried to her, put my arms round her shoulders.

'Don't cry! Please don't cry. I should be crying, not you. Don't cry, for God's sake, on the first evening in your new house.'

I shook hands with Alain in silence. We got to the car. I helped Forwood into the front, which he preferred. Elizabeth and I got in at the back. Jacques slammed the boot. I settled my hand-grip and the bundle of walking-sticks and umbrellas. '*Allez vite!*' I said and we reversed, turned, crunched slowly across the *parking* past the pond, past the bay thicket, left down the track. We none of us spoke or looked back. At the gates I got out, the car eased into the lane, I slammed the gates just as I had slammed them every evening for so many years. But this would be the very last time. Final. Finished. Closed.

The gates clattered together, the chain and padlock swinging, scoring an arc in the waggon-green paint. There was rust on the tin sign. 'CHIENS MÉCHANTS! ATTENTION!' But there were no *chiens méchants* now.

I got back into the car, slammed the door, we moved down the lane slowly past the three big plastic dustbins brimming with junk. A battered brass lamp that I'd never been able to fix, but always meant to, lay in thistles. No one spoke, not even when we got to the T-junction at the main road and turned left up towards the village. There were some people crossing the road going towards the Mini-Market, but I couldn't tell who they were.

Jacques cleared his throat softly. '*A Saint-Paul, eh?*'

'Saint-Paul,' I said.

That's how it ended.

Rather dragging along the lane with two full baskets, I was shoved into the rough grass verge by a rusting Citroën. It stopped with a lurch and groan of brakes, a window was wound down. A grey-haired woman called out in French, 'Do you want help? They look heavy.'

'They are. Thank you. Just to the little calvary.' My French was almost serviceable.

I got in beside her, shoved the bags in the back. It was a jumble of children's toys, towels, baskets, a giant bundle of carnations. She was rather small with grey hair, and could just see over the steering-wheel. A cigarette, with a worrying inch of ash, drooped from her mouth. She didn't remove it during the trip. She was in her early seventies, wore a man's wrist-watch and a grey flannel suit.

'My name is de Beauvallon. I live at Clos des Lilacs.'

We started up, jerked, began to bounce unevenly along.

'*Tiens!* I must have a flat tyre! I thought so in the village. I'll just make it I think . . .'

'It's not far. I live just up the hill from you. I can see your entrance from my bedroom window.'

'My two cypress trees? And my columns?'

'They are very fine, Madame.'

'You notice that one of the balls on a column is lost? My idiot son-in-law ran into it with his Peugeot. Are you staying with Jean-Claude and Jacqueline?'

'No. I live there.'

She turned swiftly to face me, eyes off the road, ash on the cigarette. She squinted through her smoke.

'Live there! Since when? I've been in Paris for three months. *Live* there?'

'I have bought it from Jean-Claude. He's moved to Nice. It is my land now.'

She, thankfully, returned to her driving, rounding a sharp bend, coming out on to the straight. At the far end two enormous cypress trees, fifty feet high, dwarfing two tall stone columns. One minus a stone ball on its top.

'You are English? American? Do you have a name, M'sieur, *par hasard*?'

'English.' I told her my proper name. The 'van' and the 'den'.

'Americans don't speak French very well. They have a hideous accent. How long have you been *propriétaire*?'

'I bought it in November. But I moved in only two weeks ago.'

'July. He never breathed a word. Strange man. You have a wife?'

'No.'

'You will need assistance on that land. It has not been tended for years, the olives haven't been *taillé*, pruned, for years. Disaster.'

We had reached the calvary and the gateway to her house.

My track went up the hill to our left. I started to clamber out, grabbed the bags, thanked her. She said, in perfect English, 'So, we have a new neighbour! I had *no* idea. The families, Jean-Claude's and my husband's, own all the land here. So you will be safe from development. But the place is a ruin.' The ash suddenly fell from her cigarette, spilling down her jacket. She paid no attention, the butt hung on her lip.

'You speak wonderful English. I wish I could speak French so well.'

'I was at a convent near Watford. As a girl. Before the First World War.'

She started her car again; it rattled. 'I shall have to limp down to the house. The tyre is old, so is the car, so am I. Good luck. One day we must have a meeting. The electricity board demand to put up an enormous post right here. On our land and right in your eye-line. Unless you don't care about that . . .?'

'I care very much indeed.'

The car shuddered and she started to limp lopsidedly between the cypresses.

'I'll speak to you.' She waved a hand vaguely out of her window and went off in little puffs of pink dust.

I turned and clambered up the hill. At the entrance, so to speak, for there was no gate apart from one in my active imagination, there was a battered tin post-box on a thick wooden post. To my surprise, there were some letters. Real letters at last. Someone had found out where I'd got to. More importantly, the sorting office, I supposed in town – Nice? – had discovered me.

I was not completely abandoned in the midst of rural France. I had a telephone and a postman knew that I lived at the farm. Progress was being made!

Forwood was doing something to the car. I don't know exactly what he was doing because I don't know anything about cars. After a horrendous accident in monsoon rain in Calcutta when I had, wretchedly, killed a couple of people by driving into them (not my fault, I hasten to add: during the unpleasant trial which followed I was completely exonerated), I never drove again. Never will. But I could sense a problem: the doors were all open, bonnet raised, engine running. He was blowing something hard which he held in his hand.

'Found what's wrong? Why I had to lug all this down to the village and back?' I set down my baskets.

'Dirt. In the plugs . . . I think.' He held something up to show me. 'This is a plug. Got it? The car won't run without plugs. I used a spare. Okay?'

'Yes. If we don't have a car up here, we'll be done for. That is a *very* long walk to the village . . .'

'All downhill.'

'*Up*hill from the corner with the nasty little caravan.'

'One day I'll have to get a mower. They have plugs too. Perhaps a scythe? Look at the height of the grass. Feet. Tough as a wire broom.'

I took up the bags again and went up to the cellar door. 'It'll have to be a scythe. Haven't got the money for a mower, for God's sake!'

He switched off the engine, slammed the doors, closed the boot.

'Should you have thought of that before you signed the deeds, perhaps?'

'Well, how was I to know there were acres of savannah here? We weren't even allowed on to the terrace. Almost. I didn't know the place was a ruin, the land flooded. The olives dying.'

'Waving goodbye, in fact. You are lumbered. Four hundred dying olive trees, "the youngest of which is two hundred years, the eldest one thousand", according to the deeds.'

He picked up the yellow plastic bucket in which he kept his spanners and a strip of dirty rag, pushed the old plug into its package.

'You keep on muttering about having a car up here. You've *got* a car. Only you can't drive the thing.'

'I know. *Entendu*. That's why you agreed to come here: to drive the car.'

He pulled the rag from a clatter of tools, started to wipe his fingers. 'Unpaid chauffeur. I don't mind for a bit. But how will you cope when I decide to pull out? I only agreed a year, remember?'

I took up the straw basket. 'Sure. Fine. Okay. I remember. I'll learn to drive again. Much easier out here: less traffic, no zebra crossings, buses, mad cyclists. Someone down at the garage will teach me. No problem.'

Forwood chucked the oily rag into the bucket, which he hung on a hook high on the wall. 'I am constantly amazed by your implicit belief in your own dishonesty. God! Now, did you remember the two kilos of bullock's cheek? Dog food, Dirk?'

'Ah! *That's* what it was. I knew there was something. It was nagging . . . Hell . . .'

'That's what you went down there for. Manage on your own. Sure?'

'Perfectly. Never fear. Perhaps you'd go down, then, and get the cheek, now you have a nice clean plug? Otherwise I'll boil up some rice. I know I got the rice.'

'Terrific. You'll have an awful lot to learn in a year, chum.' He sat down on an old packing-case left over from the move. It had a wine glass and an umbrella stencilled on the side. Began cleaning his nails with a bit of stick.

'Well, perhaps you'll enjoy it here?' I said, picking up the second basket, weighing them both without much thought. 'I mean, decide *not* to return to the UK after all? I might have to do a film again one day. For the money. For a mower, the kitchen roof . . . You'd have to deal with that, wouldn't you? Contracts, script approval . . .'

'Would I?'

'Well, yes . . .' He was starting to make me feel slightly uncomfortable. He had a habit of doing that. Calm, reasoning, very pleasant. Firm. Perhaps he would clear off? In a year. He had never absolutely promised to stay on once I was 'settled in'. I swung the baskets gently, to and fro.

'You have dealt with every film, every contract, the tax, all that jazz, for over twenty years. Every tax return. How could I do all that?'

'As you will with your driving. And how to change a plug. If you can drive a car, change a plug, and start *and* push the mower, you'll be able to deal with the contracts and the tax. No problem.'

I set the baskets down, feeling a little uneasy. 'Well, I shall. I know all about plugs, for God's sake. Plug-hole, earplug bath plug, Rawlplug – I'm not a complete idiot.'

He rose, hitched up his jeans, started towards the cellar steps. 'You are giving a quite brilliant impersonation, that's all. And mind your head on this beam.' He tapped it with an oily hand.

'Well, it could grow on you here? What on earth would you *do* back in the UK? At your age? Who would you manage? You said yourself it was all changing, the time now of the dialects and the uglies . . . not your scene. And there will be a mass to do here: mowing, driving, the garden. And if I *did* have to make a film here, for the loot only, you'd be essential . . .'

'Thank you.' I heard the edge of dryness in his voice. 'We'll see how it goes. Okay? I'm not totally convinced . . . remember what I just said? About this beam here?'

'You said, "Duck."'

He cocked his head lightly to one side, grinned at me. 'Got it. Very good. Then do.'

I collected my baskets.

We went up the stairs from the windowless cellar into the kitchen – a dark pit: hooded stove in one corner, chipped stone sink in another, a smell of stale grease. I set the baskets on the table, unloaded. A six-pack of beer first.

'Fat-head. That's what weighed you down. The beer.'

'I need the beer.'

'Need a dislocated spine as well?'

He was washing his hands at the sink; the water was running so I did not feel obliged to answer. There were a bag of rice, six candles, some leeks, carrots, a green net-sack of potatoes, a pack of brown sugar with a parrot on the cover, a *cartouche* of Royal Longues – cigarettes which someone who did not smoke had assured me were made from dried lettuce and therefore harmless. I counted the change, spread it on the table among the leeks and carrots.

'Not cheap, France. That's the change from five hundred francs.'

Forwood was drying his hands on a piece of kitchen paper.

'Beer and cigarettes cost. Luxuries. We *need* the food.'

'There is also some mail. The sorting office in Nice, or somewhere, seem to have found us. The second batch in three weeks.'

'Anything urgent looking? And where's the bread?'

'In the basket. A *complet.* Nothing urgent-looking. No official signs, or OHMS.'

I found a glass, opened a bottle of beer and went down the slate stairs into the Long Room below. I called up about Madame de Beauvallon, the car, the flat tyre, the concrete post which was apparently about to be stuck right in the view down to La Napoule.

'Ask them to paint it green,' he shouted. 'Won't see it so much. I'm off to the village now . . .'

'By car?'

'How else?'

'It didn't work . . .'

'It does now. I can't stand the Ben Nicholson and sundry *faux* old masters sliding about the wainscoting any longer. What's the French for "picture hooks"?'

On the terrace, under the vine, in a spiking of self-sown hollyhocks of varied hue, I sat on a white-painted tin chair from Monoprix (end of season sale) while a thousand bees nudged and shouldered into the frilly red and pink discs.

It was calm, cool, under the vine, the savannah ahead trembled and wavered in the heat. The car came wobbling slowly over the ruts from behind the house. Stopped. I raised my glass in a salute, a window wound down. 'Won't be long. I'll get the dog meat. Did you get a London newspaper?'

'No. Not in when I was there. Careful of Madame de Beauvallon, she's lethal with that Citroën – can't see over the steering-wheel. Can't steer anyway. But she *is* well disposed.'

'Understood.' At that moment Labo the wild stray-dog I'd picked up in Rome, tore across the terrace, having heard the car, screaming with delight. Car-mad, he was scooped up, dumped in the back. They bounced slowly off again over the ruts in the track deep and hard as frozen plough.

We'd have an awful lot to do to an awful lot of things. In time. For the moment I watched the listless dust rise and fall in fading clouds behind the inching car, fished a struggling bee out of my beer, flicked it into the hollyhocks with contented carelessness. I wasn't fifty yet. There was plenty of time for drowning olives, rutted tracks and the unopened mail in the kitchen.

My chunk of France lay almost dead-centre of a triangle of villages. Well, one proper village, Saint-Cyprien, up behind my land, Le Pré to the west, and Saint-Sulpice to the east. Le Pré straggled along the main road: a bar, some shops, two garages – an Elf and a Shell – a café with a juke-box, and a modest restaurant which served all right-ish food. Occasionally. Saint-Sulpice was not much more than a crossroads, a monument to its liberation by the Americans on August the 21st, 1944, a row of ageing mulberry trees, a wide *place* where the annual fair and circus was held and, along the road up towards Saint-Cyprien, the olive mill with its enormous wheel. Above the crossroads, on a modest hillock, stood the church with its Provençal flat roof, surrounded by olive trees and cypresses. There were some scattered houses, a churchyard sliding down the hill, the monuments and marble angels looking like a tilting chess set, and at the bottom of all this, neat and trim, the *bureau de poste*. The *bureau de poste* was to play a vastly important part in my life, although I was unaware of that fact in my early weeks – as unaware as I was that, just up the road beyond it, glittering in chrome and plate glass, the Mini-Market, opened in the week I took up my residency, would almost become my pivot.

The mayor of Saint-Sulpice, Etienne Ranchett, a fierce little man with a face like a loganberry, was rumoured to keep a young (and disagreeable) mistress in a hideous little modern villa on the edge of the village. To make life more tolerable for his wife, and avoid gossip, he permitted the erection of the Mini-Market on the old vegetable garden of the house which belonged to his mother-in-law. His wife, a warm-eyed, splendid figure of a woman, Florette Ranchett, became the owner. It shut her up: she turned a blindish eye to the mistress on her doorstep and threw herself with alacrity into the role of shopkeeper in this unlikely modern box set among the olives and rough-walled vegetable garden of her mother's house.

The trouble was that, even with the imposing awning in brown and orange with *Mini-Market* in gold all along its scalloped edge, the glitter and the hum of the freezer, the sparkle and shine of the brilliantly tiled floor (mashed carrot and spinach), in spite of all these attractions no one very much came into the place. Its very glamour put them off and inhibited them. They much preferred the cold, cruddy, dark little shop which had apparently originally stood in its place, run by Madame Ranchett's mother. It was comforting, it had worn linoleum, I was told, fly papers, good bread, and gave credit. In the new shop a new and alarming machine rolled out your bill, all figures and signs, and at the end, after *Thank You for Shopping Here* (in English) there was a more alarming note which, hastily translated, simply said NO CREDIT.

No good French peasant could put up with that for long. And they didn't. They went elsewhere, even if it meant taking the local bus, and Florette Ranchett sat stoically behind her counter, among mountains of lavatory rolls, kitchen paper and serried rows of Harpic, Tide and Omo, on her own. Sometimes, very occasionally, someone would hurry in for something they had suddenly found themselves to be short of, and tourists parked to buy stuff for picnics to take down to the beaches or up into the hills. Otherwise the tins and bottles gathered dust, the stall of vegetables outside under the awning wilted, and Madame Ranchett read *Nice-Matin* from cover to cover six times a day.

I think that the first thing I ever bought from her was a tin of Kiwi dark brown. Her warmth and gratitude was such that I had the distinct impression that I had, by mistake, bought up her entire stock of champagne. She handed me change from my twenty-franc note and explained that the machine was American and that she really couldn't help what it printed on the receipt. Of course she gave credit! In an agricultural village how could she not? They were not millionaires here, depending on the *rose de mai*, jasmine and olives for a living, and sometimes the corn for feed. She was convinced that with patience she could sit it out and that business would become brisk. After all, they all knew and liked her, the mayor's wife and all. Give them time, she'd say, they are as suspicious as goats, and as silly. She was right of course: in time people did begin to drift back – the added bother of the bus, the extra money for the fare, the red pencil ripped through NO CREDIT (a modest suggestion of mine) made it easier, and pleasanter, to run down the hill, across the road, or walk up from the crossroads to do the shopping. Also she had a varied selection of things. She was brave, wise and very handsome. We got on extremely well together, and as soon as she found out that I was a *propriétaire*, had already applied for my *permit de séjour*, and intended to remain in the area for the rest of my life, we eased into a close and affectionate friendship. She never came to my house, I never went to hers. That is not the way in France – a failing of many English people who are neighbourly, if not nosey, and simply don't understand the laws of French family privacy. It works splendidly if you do: you eat together in restaurants but seldom, if ever, dine or break bread at their table. Sensible and a great saving for the cook.

Stuck on a shelf behind the till, with a strip of Sellotape, there was a battered photograph of Madame Ranchett, hair piled high, arms thrown round a dusty American sergeant, laughing with delight. A really pretty woman, enjoying herself on Liberation Day. It was no wonder that Etienne Ranchett had married her, but extremely odd that she had ever married him. However, power comes with the office of mayor, and perhaps that was in the air then. I never asked. But she did admit, one day when I took a closer look at the photograph, that, frankly, the war hadn't been a problem in the village. Until *we* started mucking about down at La Napoule and sending tanks and planes all over the place. They were very handsome, very correct, kind to the old and especially to children. Madame Ranchett had no complaints about the Germans at all.

The Americans, when they arrived, were *far* worse: drunk, stole the chickens as well as the eggs, behaved incorrectly with the young women and cut down the most fruitful olive branches for tank camouflage. They were glad to be free, because it meant that *all* France would be free, but they were quite glad to see the back of the liberators when they finally left.

'Perhaps', I ventured mildly, 'it was different up north?'

She shrugged, sighed. 'Perhaps. But I was not there. I believe in Paris it was bad. Very bad. No food. Deportation. Down here it was easier. They left us alone. Of course we had the Resistance . . . but *they* caused a lot of trouble too, really. If they blew up a bridge, well . . . how could the farmer get to his stock . . . the sheep and goats, the harvest? And then, and then! They would take hostages, the Germans. If you live with the hornet you don't poke sticks into his nest!'

'Well, anyway. It's finished.'

'Thank God. It was bad in England too? Bombs . . . the mayor and I went to England. Once.' She shuddered pityingly. 'Never again.'

'Oh. I'm sorry! Why?'

'Look. The ferry was late. It was dark. No signs to London after Ash-Furd. We got lost in some development called Addy-Coombe, I will always remember the name, no one would help us, they looked at us as if we were mad and went away. It was awful. Awful. Then we saw a sign that said *Hotel* . . . no food. We were too late. Too *late* at *nine o'clock*! We had to find a café in the dark and we had some white chicken like rubber, and frozen peas like emeralds. And as hard. It was a disaster. A disaster. We drove back to the ferry the next morning. We had to sleep in a terrible place one of your policemen told us about. Bed and Breakfast. Horrible! But there was a big bed. I cried myself to sleep, the mayor drank half a bottle of Scotch he bought on the ferry. In the morning we came back to France. You understand me? I understand why you came here to live. Intolerable! Intolerable! Those peas. My God! I wouldn't even string them on a nylon thread as a necklace. I'll never forget them. Never.'

*

On the west end of this enchanted triangle of villages there was a small area called Quartier des Groules. A narrow road wound downhill, lined with stone plaster-faced houses. Each had a mounting-block of solid limestone just outside the front door, making it easy for the occupants to mount their ass or donkey, or horse very often, but making life almost out of the question for motorists. The only reason that I mention this is that I had to go to the Quartier every two weeks to take and collect the laundry, for my laundress (and that was her permanent job) lived in a three-storeyed house right at the end. So the hazardous narrow road, bristling with mounting-blocks which would easily have wrecked a tank, had to be negotiated with extreme prudence.

In the first years the Simca Brake just made it; Forwood's Maserati (a fearful bit of showing-off which he loved keenly) never made the first yard, but, later on, the sturdy Peugeot just, by extremely skilful navigation, managed to get down to Madame Mandelli's pretty little terrace. Every two weeks a vast basket of 'dirty' was hauled out of the car, and an equally vast basket of 'clean and ironed' was taken on.

Madame Mandelli laundered like an angel: sheets were ironed and folded into eighteen-inch squares of pristine, crisp splendour, shirts lay flat, ready for stacking. There was a delicate scent of some kind of soap powder, but mainly they smelled of the clean hillside air in which she dried them. At the back of her house, in an area where there was no sign of a flower, rabbit hutch, chicken coop, where no tree existed, where only the blue nylon ropes and coloured pegs reigned supreme, sheets and shirts and pillowcases flew and flapped like bunting at a regatta. Free to the winds of heaven.

In the first months of my life at Le Pigeonnier (that was

the name of my place – I don't think I've mentioned it before), a cherished friend and his wife were determined to be 'the very first guests in your new house'. The appalling fact is that by the time they got to me he was already dying from terminal cancer, and his wife was grey with fatigue and despair, desperate to please him, but terrified.

Nevertheless they came. He was determined – his doctors knew there was no hope: they arrived. But it was folly. Almost as soon as he had staggered off the Train Bleu at Cannes he was only capable of being got into bed. The terrible journey had done for him. So, a doctor: rapidly sought in the telephone book by Forwood, who sensibly picked the one nearest to us.

Dr Poteau was a saint. I suppose that is the cliché word, but it, like all clichés, is true for that is what he was. He sorted things out for Robin, as far as he was able medically, but, and this was the worry, he asked if I was capable of changing a bed *three* times a day? I said that I could, I was pretty good at bed-making, mitring all the corners and so on. But what Poteau actually meant at that time was could I wash the sheets? The patient would need changing twice, if not three times, a day because of raging fever. Pyjamas, everything? Had I the means to accommodate this problem? Of course I hadn't. There was no washing-machine. I could iron teacloths and T-shirts fairly neatly, but that was all. There were absolutely no facilities for a dying man with a pile of sodden sheets.

Dr Poteau gave me *his* laundress, Madame Bruna Mandelli, a gesture of the utmost generosity and goodness: I, the English stranger, was overwhelmed. Madame Mandelli had a washing-machine, could take me on – she 'did' for the doctor, his family (his wife having only one arm she could not manage laundering), the local priest and two exceptionally grand 'old families' in the district – for a short time only. She was quite prepared to deal with two sets, or three, of sheets and pillowcases and Heaven alone knew what other bits and pieces. But, she wanted to make clear, she had her regular clients, a limited amount of time, and when my patient had either died or gone back to England, then she would reluctantly have to close my account. As it happened she never did close it: as with Madame Ranchett and Madame Pasquini at the *bureau de poste* (I'll come to her a bit later), my life was enhanced and made glorious by their kindness and affection. One can't do better in life than that.

Bruna Mandelli was a small, compact woman. Italian, from Cremona, she was a superb cook, an industrious housekeeper, a doting mother of two (a son of four and daughter of two), a loving wife. Her house (actually I only ever got as far as the parlour-kitchen in all the years) was immaculate, sparkling, crammed with china ornaments, flowers and green plants in pots. It was always pungent with the scents of tomato, oregano, basil and freshly made pasta, which she hung in sheets over a broom handle, supported on the backs of two chairs, with a double page of *Nice Matin* beneath: if you could read the small print through the pasta then it was acceptable. Not otherwise.

Madame Mandelli's hair was vivid henna-red, her strong arms were freckled as a rainbow trout, and she carried a pair of eyebrows, carefully pencilled in maroon half-circles, exactly one inch above the place where her real eyebrows (which she seemed to lack) should have been. Thus she appeared to be in a condition of permanent surprise.

The first two weeks of Robin's visit passed slowly, but moderately well, considering nurses, and potions, and the excellent Dr Poteau. I stripped the bed two or three times a day (for his fever would not abate), pyjamas were changed constantly, towels slung into heaps, and I carted everything off to Madame Mandelli in the big willow laundry basket. Her terrace, at the far end of the little street, was crammed with pots and old enamel pans rioting with impatiens, geraniums, white daisies and cascading pelargonium. They were sheltered from the blazing sun by an ancient mulberry which stood, a bit lopsidedly, dead centre.

This particular morning there seemed to be no one about. The sun burned down, casting dark shadows, but there was no sound of the singing, which was usual, if monotonous; no odours from the kitchen, as there always were, no cheeping and chittering from the budgerigar's cage which normally hung on a hook by the front door. No cage.

Ominously, I saw the basket of 'clean and ironed' standing deliberately on the terrace beside the closed front door. The little red exercise book, used for the laundry list and the account, lay on the top of the folded sheets. The bamboo-bead curtain hung still. No rasp and clatter in the morning wind. Maybe she had gone to town? Unlikely at this hour. I set down my basket of 'dirty' and called out. No response. I called again, louder. Forwood leant out of his car window curiously. I shrugged, called again: 'Madame?' I had to pay for the 'clean and ironed' and check with her the list of 'dirty'.

I was about to make a final attempt when a shutter above my head opened cautiously, and through a frill of medlar leaves, looking rather like a gargoyle, an anguished head peered down. The face was drained. Tears fell.

'Disaster!' she murmured. '*Oh! Dio! Oh! Dio! Catastrophe!*' And shaking her head she recommenced what she had obviously been doing until my arrival, indulging herself in most unattractive weeping.

I held up a fist full of francs. 'For last week's stuff!'

She wiped her face with both hands. '*Scusa! Scusa! . . . Momento* . . .' she said and I leant against the mulberry watching a stream of ants swarming up and down its trunk.

The door opened, the bamboo curtain was parted. '*Prego* . . . enter . . .' She did not look directly at me; by the sag of her shoulders she was resigned and hopeless.

'Oh Madame! Excuse me . . . You have such sadness?'

She sat heavily in a chair by the table, head in hands. '*Ecoute moi* . . .' and she was off.

Well, it really wasn't all that much of a disaster or a catastrophe. All that had happened was that her washing-machine had blown up. It was old, out of date, there were no spares, it was unmendable. That's all. But, of course, for Bruna Mandelli, with her clients and large family, it was disaster enough.

Her face was dragged with grief, her eyes red from weeping, her maroon eyebrows smudged into two livid bruises. So distracted had she been that she had even forgotten to remove her pink plastic rollers. I gave her the money she was owed and said that I would instantly go into town and purchase a new washing-machine, modern, with a full guarantee. She uttered a little scream of horror, covered her mouth with her hands, shook her head frantically. 'No! No! *Quelle horreur! Jamais!* Never, never . . .'

I felt as if I had made a fumbled attempt at rape; then of course I realized that I had desperately insulted her as a woman, as a laundress and a person of deep, intense pride. She hiccupped with anger until I explained in my poor French (you really do need a bit more than menu French for this sort of deal) that it was essential for me to get my laundry done, that I would purchase the machine for us all, and that she would do all my washing and ironing absolutely free until such time as she had paid me back. I thought that that made sense?

Gradually, as she unpinned her rollers, she conceded that it *might* make sense to her. Without the machine she'd be pretty desperate herself, and gravely out of pocket. I reminded her that the priest would be in despair too. All those vestments and the altar stuff? Finally, with a flicking of nervous looks, a blowing of her nose, wiping her face with hard-worked hands, she told me the name of the best electrics shop in town, and with a helpless shrug of resignation, but a verbal agreement that she would do my laundry free until she was out of my debt, she went into the kitchen area, brought out the budgerigar cage and hung it on its hook outside the front door.

As we drove away I looked back and saw that she was carefully arranging a teacloth over it to shade it from the sun. A sign, I felt certain, of acceptance. Storms in the Mediterranean are quite often short and violent.

Two days later, after a deal of tipping here and there, and an instant cheque, not a credit card (viewed with grave suspicion in town) a perfectly gigantic German creation, blinding in white enamel and chrome, was delivered, and fitted, in Quartier des Groules. It appeared to do just about everything except the ironing and the sewing on of buttons. Otherwise it was a miracle machine.

One morning, the day after Robin and Angela his wife had finally managed to get taken off to the airport, with oxygen cylinders, care and attention in abundance, and were headed for London and the final clinic, I opened the front door on to the terrace to let the desperate dogs out to do their pee (we had overslept from sheer exhaustion). I almost tripped over a package wrapped up in red and gold paper, a hoarded piece of last Christmas apparently, to judge by the gold stars and holly sprigs. Inside, a boxed bottle of Chivas Regal.

There was no message.

Chapter 3

Everyone knew it as 'the moon country', and that was long before Neil Armstrong set foot on the thing and proved them right. It was a savage, strange landscape, a desolate limestone plateau one thousand metres up. It looked as if a tremendous wall had been pushed over by a giant and had fallen, quite flat, cracked but unbroken, across the mountain top. It stretched for acres, about a half-hour drive from the house, up a sharply twisting road, which gave some people acute vertigo and others what they called 'water brash', so that they were compelled to stare desperately at the back of the person in front and dared not look out of a window or through the windscreen. Coming down, of course, was worse. Usually eliciting stifled moans, swallowing gulps and pleas for a rest. As I didn't suffer either from vertigo or travel sickness, I was fairly soulless.

In the summer months, from May until the end of September, the house became a cheap *pension.* People I had hardly nodded to in a different life suddenly wrote effulgent letters saying that they'd 'be in your area about then, so could we possibly be simply dreadful and ask you to give us a room/bed/board/meal, whatever?' and it was difficult to refuse. Of course, family and friends were quite different, and hugely welcome. But the others were a bit of a pain, frankly. They also cost a good deal. Although, to be sure, some did bring gifts in kind. Like a cheese, bottles of untried wine, fruits or, worst of all, fresh fish from the market in Nice or Cannes or some other port which, by the time they got it to me, had gone off. And anyway, usually (always in fact) their meals had already been planned and catered for, so there was nothing to be done with the fresh 'gone off' fish but chuck it. However, people *did* try.

And, very often, their company on the terrace in the evenings, with a glass of wine and the drifting scent of good tobacco under the vine, was comforting.

However, it was the usual thing to do to go up to the moon country after lunch. Unless it was absolutely blistering (July and August were hellish), they were stuffed into cars and led up the twisting road in order, I always insisted, to aid their digestion. The fact that many longed to throw up the three-course lunch just consumed was neither here nor there. Anyway, to me. The dogs, Labo and a boxer, Daisy, they too didn't give a fig: their screams and shrieks at the mere mention of the word 'motor car'; the very slightest move towards leash and collar turned them into raging tigers.

So we'd set off. Once on top, in the clear, cool air of the plateau, people began to regain their balance and almost quite liked the whole operation. Apart from the descent, that is. However, in the winter it was all very different. The days were shorter, lunch took a little longer, we left the washing-up and went off in that hour or two left just before the light began to fade and the sky drained of colour and the evening star sprang into the pale, clear, winter emptiness as if a switch had been snapped on, heralding the night.

Then we clambered across the corrugations of the honey-combed limestone, the screes of shale and fallen rocks, the low clumps of thyme, box and juniper hiding in crevasses, and round the rims of little sunken fields which had been, literally, scratched, centuries ago, from pockets in the harsh land, raked and tended, each with a cairn of stones and shards ploughed up from the thin earth.

There were no trees at this height – the wind saw to that – just stunted writhen pines, straining to exist, clinging desperately with exposed roots like aged, knuckled fists clutching the steep sides of the scratchings of fallow soil.

In the early spring, clumps of hellebore hung acid-green bells in clusters along the goat tracks, or a wind-wrenched bramble thrust tiny buds against the aching ice-blue sky. In the little fields, or dells, the new barley and wheat were a green gauze, as thin and sparse as a hair transplant. Crows and ravens stalked about grubbing, or seeking twigs and straw for nests. Sometimes, but very rarely and only when the dogs had capered miles away, you might catch a fleeting sight of a wildcat, but they melted into the thyme and rock-hugging juniper and myrtle. And one was never really quite certain that they had been there, otherwise the silence sang, and only the distant tonkle of a goat bell or the very vaguest whisper of trickling water from a hidden spring broke the perfect glory of the silence.

The summer, of course, was quite another matter. Fat green lizards baked on the oven slabs of limestone, vipers swung and curled away into the cracks and crannies, and in the places where the little springs had made modest pools among the tumbled stones, tadpoles wriggled and dived in the crystal, cold water.

However, in the winter these same springs and pools froze solid, looking shiny, like molten glass spilled across the rocks, dragging ragged curtains of icicles where they had started to trickle over ledges, until the frost had stilled them and frozen movement.

But in early spring, and before the day trippers arrived from the coast, on the high plateau the landscape was benign and sweet. Every patch of grassland was sheeted with great drifts of blue and gold crocuses, white narcissi, cowslips, clover, scarlet anemones and, in the sheltered cracks of the rock, clumps of tiny cyclamen: their combined scents on still days was overpowering, the humming of a trillion bees foraging for nectar filled the air.

Sometimes, driving up from the plain, one could be in for a surprise, although very often I was warned ahead. Washing up at the sink, I could see the top of the mountain from the window plumed with cloud, which meant that the voyage up would be hazardous. Zig-zagging up and turning at one of the steep bends, there would suddenly be a solid wall of dank, dripping, drifting fog. Visibility down to a couple of metres, sidelights on; windscreen-wipers squealed and whispered, moisture dripped and beaded and the rare car coming towards one would inch slowly past in the thick gloom, lights faded to amber through the mist, number-plates almost unreadable. The silence was odd. Profound, empty. One felt absolutely alone, isolated, with no connection to the world so recently left behind on the plain below. And then, very slowly, the fog would rip into shreds; it would tear and rend, whirl and fray, melt into tatters and suddenly, within an instant, it had gone, spiralling aloft into a sky as clear and sparkling as polished glass, blue as cornflowers. No clouds. Glittering, brilliant, washed and sharp-edged.

At the top of the pass a new world lay ahead. Looking back, the great bank of fog loomed sullenly, a sombre blanket of boiling cloud, dark and impenetrable, cold, clinging. It always amazed me that we had driven safely through.

The air up there was cool, the distant hills softer, greener, the far mountains of the pre-Alps jagged against the porcelain blue. At the far edge of the great tumble of limestone rock, proper fields, not the scratched little dells in the stone, were lush with serried rows of potatoes, peas, beans, carrots. People worked among the crops, stooping, striding, stacking boxes brimming with 'early' vegetables for the markets down on the plain, exhausted now by the heat. But, in time, even up there at this height, in June and July, all this bounty was shrivelled by the burning sun. The spring flowers went as swiftly as they had arrived and succumbed to the relentless heat in the high, pure air.

Up there the houses, too, altered. No longer Roman-tiled roofs and vines for shelter, no olives: now sharp-roofed chalets, with wooden balconies and log stacks amidst sentinel firs set among beech and poplar trees. A mountain landscape and a mountain people. Provence was always surprising.

Madame Pasquini was the *chef de bureau* at the post office in Saint-Sulpice. A trim little woman, she managed her *bureau* with enormous efficiency, dealt with stamps, pensions, parcels and the telephone cabinet in the corner of her small room from behind a high counter. One of the pleasantest sounds I could hope to hear was the *Bang! Bang! Bang!* as she franked the day's mail ready to be sacked and collected by the yellow mail van for the sorting office. It meant that I had not actually 'missed the post'.

Her office was sparse: apart from the counter, some scales, a pickle jar of wild flowers and the telephone, there was nothing there to make one linger. A deliberate effect: even her little pot-bellied stove for use in the bitter winter was well behind the counter so no one could huddle round it and have a chat. She was far too brisk and busy for that sort of life. When I first got to the village she was, if anything, distant. I was unfamiliar with the cost of stamps and the various bits and pieces of money. I know I often irritated her, but she did her best to say nothing. And it was only when she discovered that I had obtained my *carte de séjour*, allowing me to stay in the area of the Alpes Maritimes for six months, and after my indication that my stay would be permanent, that she eased up on coolness and allowed herself a flinty smile. That vanished, the flintiness, after an encounter we had up in the moon country. Vanished for ever.

She had a little red Renault and a large, hairy dog. I don't know what sort of dog it was . . . a mix-up, but it was aged and she adored it. She felt secure with it curled up on a strip of grubby carpet at her feet. No one would cosh her or rob the till with Joujou about. The fact that Joujou had a sparse allowance of yellow teeth and rheumy eyes and had to be well into late, if not old, age seemed not to have occurred to her. Or perhaps it had? Anyway, she set it aside, as people do, and refused to consider the facts before her.

Driving through the limestone rocks one Sunday afternoon, I saw the red Renault parked far ahead by a stone basin into which a spring gently bubbled. Up on the top of the ridge, hard against the skyline, a tiny figure windmilled frantic arms.

'I think that is Madame Pasquini, waving away up there,' I said.

'Fool of a woman! Run out of petrol probably. Women. Honestly, hopeless about cars . . .' Forwood was always dismissive of women drivers, but he did, that time at least, start to slow down as the figure up on the ridge came scrambling towards us, arms flailing, legs skittering about on the rock and shale.

She was calling out, but for the moment (windows closed, dogs squealing with excitement, the air conditioning belting – it was the first really hot day of spring) she was soundless. I got out and began to clamber up towards her, waving back, I suppose to reassure her that I was on my way? Idiotic the things one does.

As we came together, she looked wretched, untidy. Hair ragged, stockings torn at the knee, one sleeve up, one down. A lady with a problem: a dead body? A sheep? It was quite obvious that *she* had broken nothing, she was so energetic, but her voice was hoarse with desperation.

'Monsieur! Ah! *Grâce à Dieu! Aidez moi.* Help me! I have a terrible catastrophe! Come quickly, come quickly.' She turned round and scrambled back the way she had come. I was bound to follow. It was a perilous journey skidding about on the rock. There were sudden little pits, crevasses, clutches of juniper and box: a fall, a trip even, would mean a fracture or a break.

At the top, lying in blazing sun beside a clump of thyme, was the inert body of Joujou, eyes already glazing, tongue slightly protruding. Clearly dead. Flies on its muzzle.

Madame Pasquini fell to the rocks on her knees and grabbed a foot. 'Can you help? It was a viper! I saw it . . . lying on the rock . . .'

I squatted beside her, opened one of the dog's rheumy eyes wider than it already was, looked at the tongue, felt, idiotically under all that thick hair, for a heartbeat. 'Madame, I regret he is dead.'

Forwood, breathless and irritated, had caught up with us. 'Madame Pasquini's dog has been bitten by a viper.'

'I see. Is it dead?'

'Very.'

Forwood addressed himself to the weeping *chef de bureau* in French, asked: how long ago? About half an hour. She couldn't do anything to help it. It went into a coma almost instantly, it was old. Then Forwood announced the grim news himself. '*Il est mort, Madame. Hélas!*'

For a moment she remained on her knees, the sun beating down on the rocks. She ran a hand through the shaggy hair, shrugged gently, rose to her feet. '*Alors* . . .' she said.

We carried the dead animal down the hill. It was a hefty weight, and Forwood, I knew, was not absolutely delighted: he'd got on an Italian shirt of which he was particularly fond. However, apart from the droplets of blood on the muzzle, there was no mess, and we dumped the corpse, with its lolling head, into the Renault boot and, with a silent handshake all round, watched Madame Pasquini drive away.

Almost from that moment on she and I – well, all three of us really – became very good friends indeed. Nothing was said, there were no particular thanks given: there was merely a flow of pleasant understanding and patience when I bundled about with 'four stamps, airmail for South Africa, ten for Japan, eight normal for Germany, twenty-four for the UK and a fat envelope of manuscript for Hitchin, Herts', where my excellent typist, Sally, was ready to make sense from chaos. This was the usual weekly deal at the *bureau de poste*. Madame Pasquini got very used to the constant fan mail, and the stamp prices and fluctuations, and knew, instantly, that the buff envelope with the manuscript had to be registered, crayon-crossed and labelled '*Exprès*'. '*Tiens!* Another book! Monsieur Dickeens!'

When she went away on her holiday, usually to Brittany, she always sent a card to say that she was having 'pleasing *vacances*, with very good food and just a little wine'. And, one time, shortly after Joujou's death, I bought a small puppy of mixed breed from a gipsy child, who was dragging it about on a rope in the Marché Forville in Cannes, and, cautiously, placed it on Madame's counter beside the jar of lilac and the scales. Her immediate cry of delight, '*Oh! Comme il est beau!* Si *beau!*', and the fact that she took it into her arms right away indicated that, should I suggest she might accept it, she certainly would. And did. And thus was formed a firm bond which was never broken. The creature grew to reasonable size (no giant), was spirited, pleasant, loving and a wild mixture of perhaps a hound and a spaniel – one could never know what breeds had been utilized. And she didn't care anyway, and called it 'Jack' . . . because that was an English name. The logic escaped me, but then most French logic did anyway. However, gradually I was peopling my new life with good friends who would remain with me. And they did.

It was an agreeable sensation for a foreigner in a strange land. A feeling of 'joining', being accepted. More 'belonging'.

One day, checking the list of cleaned and ironed on Madame Mandelli's table in her spotless kitchen, sorting out franc notes for payment, I said something about having to get a wall built at Le Pigeonnier as a shield against the savage mistral which roared straight across the terrace and ripped flowerpots, rakes, brooms and garden chairs across the hill and thrashed the shutters, and made life generally exhausting. I, personally, detest wind: it makes me restless and irritated. It was a phenomenon that no one had bothered to tell me about, this mistral. I mean, I knew it blew, I knew what it *was*; but I had not the very least idea that it came careering down the Rhône valley, which was miles away, turned sharp left when it hit the sea, and raged straight up the valley to blast my house and land, head on, rending the roof tiles into confetti, the trees into tatty feather dusters. Something had to be done pretty quickly about a deflecting wall, a barrier. Bruna Mandelli pursed carmine lips, shook henna-red hair, sighed, and said that she detested the mistral because it made *her* so *fatiguée*, and that her husband Rémy was a splendid *maçon*, and would I like him to come to the house to talk about the idea? She could, she said, hand on heart, recommend him as the best *maçon* in the district, and probably the best entrepreneur and *maçon* between Ventimiglia and Toulon. And he would be 'fair' and had worked at the house with the previous owners. Indeed, he and she had first met there in the stable (now a part of my Long Room) during the war, when they were very young. He knew every stone and tile. He was a suggestion that I simply should not refuse. I am always extremely grateful to the Fates, and Bruna, that I did not.

Rémy Mandelli was pretty large – six foot something – muscular, handsome, with a cloth cap permanently at the back of his head, a Gitane on his lower lip, a flash of gold when he grinned or laughed. His handshake was strong, his accent thick Provençal (unlike his wife he had been born in the area), and his energy was unlimited. He was to prove an excellent *maçon*, as had been promised, and, in the end, a loyal friend. Perhaps his ideas and mine did not always coincide: he was longing to rip out everything that was old and beautiful and stuff the house with factory tiles, chrome and glittery brass, and was constantly bewildered when I discovered a store of ancient tiles in some abandoned farm building, or a battered oil lamp with a ruby-red glass shade in a *brocante*, and he found it hard to come to terms with my insistence that the plaster in the house should be, at all times, rough-rendered, with the brush marks showing. This threw him into a great fuss. '*Malheur!* People will judge my work is careless! That I am a peasant!'

He was even more bewildered, and irritated, when he was asked to strip down all the beams in sight to the bare, glorious, silvered oak. Coats and coats of brown or yellow paint peeled off like potato skins, and his glum look when I praised his work, his shrug, his disgusted pottle of spit into a discreet corner, forced me time and time again, to comfort him with the firm arm of friendship and a chatter of clucking praise.

In the end, after some two years, he began, very cautiously, to come round to my way of thinking, and eventually it was Monsieur Rémy who crowed with delight when, wrecking some old building across the valley, he would salvage things which he would normally have rejected as 'ancient rubbish' for the treasure which I considered them to be. Eventually, his battered truck would bump up the track bearing an ancient beam, a slithering of floor tiles, stacks of roof tiles, or a plate rack covered in dust and thick cream or brown paint which concealed a solid, carved olive wood glory.

He once brought his parents up to have a look. They would, he assured me, be astonished to see that I had re-created exactly what they had spent their lives, and a great deal of money, getting rid of.

'It's like a museum!' he cried, and the parents, aged, gentle, she all in black, he in the church suit, cap in hand, rosebud in his buttonhole, came to Le Pigeonnier and marvelled silently to see the re-creation of an almost forgotten way of life. I hasten to add that at no time did the house ever qualify for the cover of *House and Garden* or the *Architectural Review*. It was simple and undecorated.

They were bemused, his parents, by the fact that there was no television set, no cocktail cabinet; that there were no curtains, only shutters; and that the huge fireplace burned only logs, that the floors were uneven and polished like glass.

Like my own mother before her, Madame Mandelli senior sighed that there was no carpet, that the lamps were mainly oil, that the beams were stripped and on display and not concealed tidily in the ceiling. Anyway, they were extremely polite, and left with many handshakes and nods of apparent approval. '*C'est comme le temps ancien!*' But the nods, I could see, shortly turned to sad, worried shakes of disbelief as they drove away, sitting in the front cabin of Monsieur Rémy's truck. A mad foreigner! Poor fellow. All that drudgery brought back again!

Of course, Monsieur Rémy and I were not, at any time, the only people at work on the place. Forwood took charge of all the outside work, that is to say the maintenance of the terraces, the pruning of the vines, the spraying, the cutting of the hay, the raking, the never-ending cleaning of the land. This was essential by law, for fear of fire. If the land was not cleaned, the fine was instant and costly. Anyway, one's neighbours in the farms about the area were quick to complain if things seemed lax. Their property was at risk too, and if a fire started in the mistral, everyone was in dire trouble. So the cleaning, or the *débroussaillage* never ended. Only in January and February was there a little respite; after that everything started to push up again.

I was never any good at machines, certainly not the grass-cutters with which I had to deal: enormous red things with zig-zag blades that belched and roared, had gears and exhausts, and tore away with me. I might just as well have been driving again. It required all one's strength to guide, control and hold them. We had four of these in varying widths. All German. No other country made anything as tough and vicious. They were tanks, frankly. And they did the job. I stayed, as much as possible, around the house and the modest bit of flower garden, which I hacked out of a piece of field, the overgrown *potager*, where I attempted to grow vegetables and herbs, and the pond area. Otherwise I joined Monsieur Rémy and his Troupe.

The Troupe is worth a slight diversion here. It was led by Monsieur Danté, a stooped, grey-haired man of indeterminate age with a drooping moustache, probably no more than fifty. He hardly ever spoke, never smiled, and carried some profound sadness about with him like a pocket watch. From time to time I would see him stop doing whatever he was doing and consider this sadness, shaking his head slowly, sighing, brushing his eyes with an arm; and then, after a blink or two, he'd continue his work. Monsieur Rémy said he'd had 'a bad war', but he was a good worker. Two Arabs made up the rough-work part of the Troupe. One was vaguely retarded, kindly, silent, thin, very strong and an excellent worker with stone. Him I only ever knew as Fraj. He came from Tunis. The other fellow was very different. About eighteen, medium height, from Sousse, he fancied himself inordinately, glancing from time to time at his reflection in a tiny pocket mirror he carried in his shirt, running a piece of comb through glossy curls, bearing his lips in a wide smile to display remarkable, for an Arab, teeth as white as peeled almonds. He was known to us all as Plum-Bum on account of the purple velvet trousers, hacked off at groin level and skin tight, which he wore at all times during work. He had a pretty little wife, of about fourteen or fifteen, who was as often as not, over the years, pregnant and always dragged a small child by one arm behind her like a toy dog on wheels. It usually had a blue plastic dummy shoved into its mouth and a pink and orange knitted cap with a pom-pom on its wobbling head. She never spoke when she sometimes arrived on the site to bring Plum-Bum a message or a packet of food, but would demurely look down, and twist about on her flip-flopped feet with chipped red toenails. They lived together, with about a dozen other Arabs, in an almost derelict building on the edge of the village, and Monsieur Rémy assured me in a hoarse whisper that they were better off than most of their neighbours because Plum-Bum enjoyed unlimited sex with the ones who were without wives. He delighted, said Monsieur Rémy, in 'jig-jig' for money, and never lacked clients. However, he was a good worker, apparently loved his wife and got her pregnant as often as possible. Monsieur Rémy recounted all this with a degree of awe. '*Malheur!*' he would mutter. 'He is a veritable stallion and only eighteen!'

It is highly likely that Fraj, Plum-Bum and his wife were all 'illegals', that is to say Arabs from Tunisia or Algeria who had managed to slip into France via Marseille and melt, tactfully, into the population. They had no papers, but Monsieur Rémy shrugged that off and said that as long as they worked hard, as his two did, got paid in cash, and there was no record, on paper anyway, of them being employed by him, then *tant pis!* He'd pick up another couple if anything went wrong: there were plenty just hanging about waiting to do any kind of work in order to survive. No one could possibly keep a check on them all. Fraj was the only real worry. He could do nothing but build stone walls, at which he was amazingly good, placing stone upon stone with astonishing accuracy. He was kept busy on my terraces for nearly all the time I lived on the hill. It was rather like painting the Forth Bridge, never ending. Sheep skittering across the terraces leapt a wall and brought down a boulder. Fraj patiently rebuilt it, a trace of dribble on his chin, his dull eyes keen for the size and weight of the stone. The only other job he could manage was sweeping up with a long-handled broom. It took him hours.

However, with the Troupe under the eagle eye of Monsieur Rémy, with me offering my untutored assistance, and Forwood on the terraces, we all managed very well. In time the dark pit with the stone sink in a corner was gutted and transformed into a spanking modern kitchen, a garage built against the north wall, a pond dug where the cesspit pipes had cracked and leaked into a green mossy bog, and the mistral finally deflected, anyway from the front terrace, by a stone and beamed *porte d'entrée* hung with a big oak door salvaged from the original kitchen.

The house, as far as I could see, was secured. All that was needed were some trees. Although I had an hectare of ancient oak wood climbing up the hill at the back, there were no trees round the house itself, save for two old pollarded limes planted to shade the terrace. What I wanted was a frame of cypress trees. I didn't want to wait for them. I wanted instant timelessness.

I got it. The trees were carted up from a nursery in the valley, thirty to forty years old, secure in enormous wooden tubs or, rather, *bacs*. These were then inched towards the pits, dug by Fraj and Plum-Bum and lined deep with manure and heavy gravel. The staves of the *bacs* were eased apart and the trees manually slid into place. I bought three originally. Monsieur Rémy insisted that three was the correct number for a Provençal house. Faith, Hope and Charity – or, if I preferred it, the Holy Trinity. Anyway, they guaranteed luck, health and prosperity, and, as he was quick to point out, with no damp-course, the walls built on living rock, the roof riddled with beetle, and the tiles unfixed, at least I would need the luck.

In time, more cypress trees were planted: a grove of five down the slope of the track, one outside the kitchen window, one at the edge of the pond, so that it was reflected in the still water to remind me of the peace and elegance of Hadrian's Villa outside Rome. All nonsense, of course, and vastly expensive.

In order to achieve all this bounty I had to go off and work again. Two depressingly awful films earned me enough for the kitchen, the pond, the trees and a new electric light system. The *poteau* had at last been stuck down on the boundary between Madame de Beauvallon's land and mine, but the EDF (Electricité Departmente Française) agreed to paint it green to match the olives and it really hardly showed. But we were at least now connected for the first time to the mains. So I bought a refrigerator too . . . And, apart from breaking my self-imposed rule of 'no more movies', no great harm was done. No one ever saw, or remembered, them. I don't think they even made it on to video.

Florette Ranchett pushed a copy of *Nice Matin* towards me: 'You see? Soon I will be behind bars. Like a beast of prey. *Ouf!* What has happened to the world?' A black, banner headline: 'ATTAQUE BRUTALE!' Two youths, masked and on a moped, had stabbed, bashed on the head, and then robbed the postmistress over at Saint-Matthieu, not far away. She was near to death in hospital, the youths had escaped, the countryside was in shock. Naturally enough. If the *bureau de poste* in a tiny hamlet could be attacked, what hope was there for the rest of the area? The age of innocence had finally ended in violence. Within a few weeks (after the unhappy death of the Saint-Matthieu postmistress) every small village shop, every post office, had iron grilles slung along their counters. The simple, easy, trusting village life had finally finished.

Florette Ranchett said sadly, 'Innocence and kindness have gone. This was a village which the world forgot. We were bypassed completely! They nearly forgot to liberate us in 1944 because they were up on the main road and we were down here. And now; after all that, the Germans, the Italians, the Resistance . . . after all *that*, our own begin to destroy us! I know what it is, of course . . .' She got up and went to get an ice-cream for herself, from the freezer. 'It's the fault of television. The kids see all this terrible American stuff. They copy, we have not enough police, *et voilà!* It is the end of familiarity, of friendliness, of trust. You'll see!'

Of course I did. Madame Pasquini down at the post office was equally sad, but, at the same time, resigned. Jack could bark but Jack didn't bite. No longer was it possible to lounge against the counter and chat away about the vines, the snow, the heat or the cold, or just about the cost of seed potatoes. Ordinary politeness remained, of course, but village trust faded. No one was ever encouraged to linger by Madame Pasquini, but she had become very much a friend since Jack and was vastly curious about the letters and packets that kept on coming to my address, even though I had made a valiant effort never to reveal my exact location to anyone apart from family and important business links. I suppose it is fair to say that I was her best client. I was in her *bureau* almost daily and spent a modest fortune. Naturally that was appreciated also.

Across the road, facing the post office, set in an immaculate vegetable garden, stood a hideous little modern villa, Les Sylphides, shaded by a great fig tree. Its owner was a retired postmaster. I never spoke to him. He was always, summer and winter, occupied in his garden. Every year the walls of the villa were a smother of morning glories, his roses were bigger than cabbages, his onions ranged in rows as precise and elegant as the dancers whose ballet had given his house its name. His wife, a tiny creature, with neat little feet, cropped white hair, huge round wire-glasses, wrapped about in a spotless floral pinny, was known to me at least, as Madame Moineau. For a sparrow, plucked, was exactly what she resembled. And she twittered and cheeped, tucked into a corner of the counter at the *bureau de poste*. She and Madame Pasquini were inseparable friends. They both, I was to learn, had a burning passion for the tarot cards. Madame Moineau was the absolute queen of the pack, and people from all about came to consult her, even from as far away as Cannes, Nice or even Avignon. She was famous for her readings.

However, she had not foreseen the disaster about to befall

her way of life in the post office. Now she was on the outside of a great iron grille and poor Madame Pasquini (plus Jack) was locked away behind. Lounging on the counter, idly talking away about the harvest, the price of knitting wool at Monoprix, the dark rumour that a Dutchman had been asking about the empty farm up at Le Foux, all this comforting chitter chatter was now somehow inhibited. If you had a packet to mail it had to go on a revolving plate which took it into the secure part of the office. No longer could you weigh your own goods on the brass scales, stamp the thing, and hand it over to the expert hands of the postmistress. The intimacy had vanished. Madame Moineau still hunched herself into her corner, she was still constantly a presence, but somehow it was not quite the same any longer.

To speak to Madame Pasquini she felt forced now to raise her voice, and this grievously embarrassed her. So she sighed, nodded about at whoever was present, and curtailed her conversations. Her tarot cards had not revealed, either, the enormity of the *real* disaster which lay ahead in her gentle, fragile path.

One day she was not in her corner . . . the next day . . . and the next. I asked if she was perhaps indisposed? On holiday? Madame Pasquini, certain that no one could overhear us (there was only one noisy English tourist in the telephone cabin trying to get a call through to Flaxman. I heard him spelling it out alphabetically in desperation: 'F for . . . *France*, um . . . L for *Londres*, A for, umm . . . *Au revoir* . . .'), said, 'M'sieur is ill. Very ill. They don't know what is wrong. Perhaps a *thrombose*.' This continued for a week and then one day he was whipped off to hospital.

Madame Moineau spent all her days there, tending her

beloved man. The garden slowly became neglected, the dead blooms hung on the morning glory like dirty handkerchiefs, weeds sprang up among the onion rows, the roses budded, opened, were spent and fell, the shutters remained closed.

'Why is she always at the hospital? Does she stay there?'

'Until the evening. Then she comes here to sleep. She has to help the nurses.'

'I don't understand? Doesn't she get in the way?'

'He wants her there. He is very alarmed. She takes her crochet. It comforts him. It is his first time in hospital.'

'Is it grave?'

She shrugged, stamped a pile of tourists' postcards, a job she detested. *Bang! Bang! Bang!* 'I think perhaps it is. They do not say. She helps to change his sheets and so on . . .'

'Change his sheets? Can't the nurses do that? She is so tiny . . .'

Madame Pasquini gathered the cards into a bundle and bunged them into the thick sack ready for the evening collection at five-thirty. 'How can the nurses change his sheets if he is in the bed? Madame gets him out, he trusts her, and sits him on a chair while they do their work.'

'I see . . .' I didn't, of course. French logic. How can they make your bed if you are lying in it? Worrying. But I asked no more, and during the next few days we did not speak about the owner of Villa Les Sylphides, until one afternoon I heard dreadful, wrenching cries coming through the open window of the *bureau*. Madame Moineau was clasped tightly in Madame Pasquini's arms. She was destroyed with sobbing and every now and again uttered terrible howls of grief. I was about to quietly leave but Madame Pasquini called me to please stay. She would take Madame across to the villa.

Perhaps I would telephone Madame Ranchett to come quickly to Les Sylphides – the number was on the wall? . . . And mind Jack?

I was left alone in the post office. I could have robbed the till. Anything. But I called the Mini-Market; Florette Ranchett said she would come down right away, was it *grave*? I said yes. *And* serious. There is a distinction in France.

Fortunately for me, no one came in, no one asked for a stamp, no one wanted to use the telephone or demand their pension. I just sat on a stool beside the dog until, in a few moments, looking pale and naturally distressed, she returned briskly, shut herself firmly behind her cage. She thanked me and said that Madame Ranchett was now in charge, the doctor was on his way with a sedative. Fortunately they had found a bottle of cognac to calm her down. Later on, she said, she would go across and stay overnight in the villa. 'Jack will keep me company. *Hein?* Jack? Guard Maman?'

I asked for the stamps I needed. She tore them out from the stamp-book, pushed them under the grille, did a little sum on a piece of paper. Back to business.

'Twenty-five francs.'

I gave her the money. 'Can I ask you what has happened? Can you say?'

She looked at me sharply, her eyes were red. '*Si. Si.* I can say. It is catastrophic. Catastrophic! Sweet Saviour, give us help . . .' She shut her eyes tight.

'His heart? Has something happened because of that? Thrombosis they said?'

'I told you that. Yes. But it is not so. He is not dead . . . better that he were . . .'

'Not his heart?'

Suddenly she came from behind her counter and cage, crossed the tiled floor, slammed the front door, turned the key, and leaning against it, head down, she said: 'They have cut off his legs. Both his legs!'

'Oh God! But why . . .'

'An error! There was *nothing wrong* with his legs! An error . . .'

'*An error!*'

'They didn't know who he was. The papers were mixed up. They thought he was someone else. There was nothing wrong with his legs!'

She unlocked the door, went back to her counter. '*Voilà!*' she said, now composed.

In a daze of dismay I began to stick stamps on my envelopes.

'You recall? His garden?' she said suddenly. 'He worked in his garden every day, winter and summer. Nothing wrong with his legs. Nothing! An error!' She was collecting my letters in a pile, picking up her franking seal.

Out in the car park I looked across to Villa Les Sylphides. The shuttered windows, the ragged garden, a teacloth and an apron twisting listlessly in the soft wind. From behind me, through the open window, Madame Pasquini was preparing for the evening collection.

Bang! Bang! Bang!

Chapter 4

I remember the moment that I first saw the house. I remember the date, even the precise hour. We drove up into Saint-Cyprien for the first time on a crisp, gusting morning. The trees were turning, leaves spinning up and off into tossing thickets. The sun was high, the sky that intense Ricketts blue of childhood: brilliant, hard, washed clean by the recent mistral, it sparkled like a polished mirror. In the square outside the *mairie*, a tricolour snapped and pulled at its white pole, people clustered round the war memorial; collars up against the wind, hands thrust into pockets, they were joined by a wavering procession from the church. I saw the wreath of blue cornflowers (for the French it is the *bluet*, for us the poppy) for remembrance. Close companions. Round the base of the heroic bronze soldier, the glinting medals on the best suits of elderly men shuffling along behind the priests, sombre in wind-whipped lace and billowing vestments. It was November the 11th.

Unlike the British, the French hold the eleventh hour of the eleventh day of the eleventh month as sacred. A day for remembrance. We just shove everything together on the first convenient Sunday of the month and have an official procession in Whitehall. The personal, family, village and small-town feeling of loss, intimacy and continuity has long been lost to us. Not so in France.

We eased slowly through the procession, running dogs, laughing children, choir boys clattering. The church clock began to strike the hour. We stopped. Moments later, the tinny sound still held, wandering on the air from the final stroke. We sat silent. Then Claire, the agent who was taking us around to view properties, moved on again down a steep lane, slowed her car to inching-pace, and stabbing her finger to the left indicated the next location was below. Through a wood of ancient oaks (with trunks too wide for two men to embrace) hung on the side of a steep rock-faced cliff, I saw, far below, the rippled red-tiled roof of a modest, compact farmhouse, standing four-square to the winds on a green plateau below which spilled terrace upon terrace of great olive trees. Beyond the terraces a little pointed hill crowned by a chapel. Beyond that, a valley. Beyond the valley, golden with fading vines, the jagged line of the Estoril mountains, lilac against the harsh, scoured blue of the sky, and, to the far left, distant, sparkling, dancing in the light, teased by the wind, the mistral-whipped sea, creamed with little flickering waves. I knew then, following behind Claire down the hill, that I must have it. And by the end of December, after many battles, fears, panics and terrors, I got it.

Driving back to Saint-Paul that morning, unwilling to view any other house, I found Simone Signoret at her accustomed place behind the olive wood table in the bar of La Colombe, playing Scrabble. She looked up squinting through cigarette smoke, a Bloody Mary in one hand, a scatter of letters in the other. '*Et alors?* Any luck?' I sat on the end of her bench while she placed her letters on the board carefully. '*U, et E, et T. Voilà! "Taquet"*. A word. I win.' She put the cigarette in an ash tray.

'I've found a house. *The* house.'

She nodded slowly, took a sip of her drink, put the cigarette back between her red lips. 'With land? How much land?'

'Twelve to fourteen hectares. Four hundred olive trees, an oak wood. A well. Isolated.'

'Price?'

'About 75,000.'

Her eyebrows rose an inch. '*Francs?*'

'No. No. Pounds. About.'

'Make an offer. It is agricultural, eh?'

'Agricultural. Yes. In poor condition.'

'An offer. It's been a bad year. Remember the *évènements* in May? That has frightened a lot of the locals. Another revolution. Make an offer: they're probably desperate to sell.'

Three days later I took her to have a look at the place. From the outside only. The owner was selling without having informed his wife and family, and until I had made a definite offer I was not allowed to return to the area. We had been round once: not enough time really to be certain, unless you were as mad as I.

Simone came up the track from the bottom road, and also had a look through the oak trees on the top road, and declared that it was '*Une* vrai *maison*' and that I should make an offer immediately. There were another twelve hectares adjoining, with a crumbling little house, which I could have for a further eighteen thousand quid and a year's option to buy.

I went up to the bar, ordered a beer from Pierrot. He opened it and poured it, watching me thoughtfully. 'You have found a house? Perhaps it's good luck today?'

I said that I had found the house I wanted. Told him where. He grinned and wiped the counter down with a sponge. There was a dull flash of silver, or maybe even pewter, from his rather thin mouth.

'Ah ha! So maybe you will soon be *Monsieur le Propriétaire*? It is possible?'

I said it was possible: I had to make the offer.

'And *then* you give me a little piece of paper. I will ask Maman if it's good for you. It is useful to know and she is never wrong, not once. She was sure about Madame Julia and meningitis, sure about the sheep Monsieur Isoardi lost, sure about the American boy, you remember? Last summer. Dead in the Vallon Rouge and no one knew where, apart from Maman! You give me your paper. I'll find out for you. *Compliments! Compliments!*'

Pierrot, who was somewhere in his early fifties, thin, stocky, balding, gaunt, kind, an excellent barman, heavy handed with the rich tourists, considerate with 'regulars', had an aged mother (with whom he still lived) who was famous in the village, and indeed the whole district, for her predictions. You might have called her a witch, something like that. But she did have an amazing success with her powers, and even the local police, one was assured quietly, had often asked for her help. All you were required to do was write something on a piece of paper, anything at all – a telephone number, a name, a line of a song – and she would hold it in her hand and consider whatever it was you were demanding. And, eerily, she was as often as not correct. So, anyway, I wrote something on a piece of paper and handed it to Pierrot.

I was not superstitious, you understand, merely cautious. But, in any case, after a long session with Forwood, and a longer one with Simone in the evening after dinner, and with a good amount of Estandon Blanc going round the table, I went off to Claire the next morning and made my offer. I did not quibble, agreed what was asked, even though Pierrot and Simone and Madame Titin, who ran La Colombe, looked shocked that I did not bargain, and was accepted.

When I returned from my mission, dizzy with delight, amazed at my audacity, overcome to think that I was in train to be the owner of a chunk of this glorious land, Pierrot poured me a drink and said, in a low voice, that his Maman considered the deal to be very advisable. I'd live in the house longer than she would live. Daunting, but in some way satisfying. As it happened, she was right. And Pierrot was to die before I had to leave. I often wonder if she ever knew *that*. Probably not. And just as well perhaps.

However, I was really quite relieved, after I had made my offer, to know that Maman's prognosis, or whatever you care to call it, was favourable. I would always have had a slightly uneasy feeling if her silver-fanged son had looked solemn and hissed mournfully that the signs were occluded in his usual, uncomfortable, manner of relaying unfavourable information. Although technically the house was mine, the deal having been signed, witnessed and sealed with a glass of red wine, I was, for various odd reasons, unable to take possession of my property until the following April.

However, I did manage to get into the house once or twice with my good architect Leon, who was straining at the leash to rip down walls, doors, and tear up cracked tiles and broken bricks. But that had to wait; all we could do at that stage was plan and arrange and measure. And wander about the neglected land with a suddenly doubting Simone. She was all in favour of the place, but could not really come to terms with the fact that I had voluntarily left my own country to come and live in France and, after years in the business of theatre and cinema, could give it all up and turn instead into a peasant. And, what really worried her, good Communist that she was, a very *poor* peasant. After all the years of plenty, as she imagined, would I be able to adjust to a life on the inhospitable limestone and shale of Provence? Would I really relish the splitting of logs, the mowing of the terraces, the pruning of the trees, the digging and sowing, the rough and tumble of true country life? Without very much knowledge of the French language, without newspapers, without even, at the time, a working telephone? I reckoned that I'd manage a great deal better than she and her husband, Montand, would. *They* would have been wildly out of place on my smallholding. I fitted far better.

But she loved the possibilities of the house, the plans and ideas that Forwood and I and Leon had in mind. I think too that she enjoyed our courage, as she called it, and eventually set aside her very real doubts and joined in with us joyfully.

One evening, driving her back to La Colombe, where she lived when she was not working, in preference to Paris, we stopped at her favourite bar in the square, under a great tree, at Vence. During the early days of the German Occupation she and her mother had kept discreetly out of sight here. Being half Jewish she knew it was prudent to fade into the backcloth of life. The hotel-bar gave them a small room. She worked the tables and washed dishes and glasses and survived.

We sat out on the terrace and ordered a Ricard each; they arrived with a jug of water and just one little flask of water which the elderly waiter set before her.

'*Voilà!* Madame Montand,' he said, 'do you recall these little things? They are nearly all broken now. You served enough of them in your time!' – a small flask, holding just enough water for one measure of pastis, a laughing, winking waiter engraved on its side. She gave it to me. To remind me of the evening and her first visit to the house proper, but also as the first gift for the house. A welcoming present. I have no need to be reminded of that signal event. The flask is still with me, a faded moss-rose stuck in its throat. The two of us are the only survivors of that April evening on the bar terrace in Vence. Seeing it gives me infinite comfort.

When I said that memory comes to me, now, in snatches, it is depressingly true. I chucked all my diaries and papers some time ago, so there is no possibility of being able to sit down and, say, open a diary of 1972 and look up the first Sunday in March or July, or whenever. There is no jerk, no jog, of remembrance there. I can't refer back to anything. So I suppose it is rather foolish to try and fill a book with memories brought back by small things like Simone's pastis flask, or a snatch of song, a drifting scent, a forgotten envelope with half-forgotten handwriting.

However, I do remember many, many things – vividly. I am just not always quite certain of exactly when they occurred. I don't really think it matters much? As long as one remembers a moment, a face, a situation, a planting of trees, a thread of music, the fabric of one's life is still intact, even though the pattern or the dyes are faded. But odd *things* trigger memory. A plastic bag, just now, swinging on the handle behind the door in this small London kitchen. I don't know what is in it, truthfully, it's just a plastic bag with modest bulges; probably the pickling onions. But instantly I am off down the path to Madame Meil with the goat-bag, another plastic bag which always hung on the handle of the kitchen door in a different house, a different country. But I remember it with pin-point clarity. I should, after all, because it was my usual chore almost every evening after having fed the dogs. For some reason, which I now no longer recall, the dogs got fed at five o'clock in the afternoon, not earlier. Perhaps a vet gave that advice? Perhaps it was simply because of the time I gave shelter to the ruin of an abandoned puppy, starving, with shattered leg, ribs like barrel hoops, festooned with worms (literally) and bemedalled with pussy sores. In my kitchen outside Rome one late afternoon, about five o'clock, I, most unwisely as it turned out, gave in to animal supplication and fed him. I say unwisely merely because from that instant on Labo remained. And stayed beside me for fourteen years. It was a brutal struggle between us for survival at first. However, that was dogs' feeding-hour, and it remained so from then on. While they snuffled bowls round the kennels, I took a plastic bag stuffed with all the edible kitchen refuse: green stuff, cold spaghetti, stale bread, plate scrapings, gone-bad peaches, bruised apples, fish heads – whatever a goat would eat a goat got. And as far as I was aware, the only things that a goat did not eat were barbed wire, broken glass or ten-inch nails. Everything else went down easily.

Anyway, that's what Madame Meil always said. She and her husband, Emile, lived in a farm down the lane from me on the de Beauvallon border. It had been an attractive-looking little place: outhouses, haystacks, tin baths hanging, a huge cart, a rusty tractor, scabby mongrel dogs yapping – all clustered round the main house, unremarkable but shaded by two gigantic olive trees, five or six hundred years old, which towered over the whole collection from their position on a high bank on the road just above. You really couldn't see very much for the deep silver-green leaves and the gnarled branches. A flash of tile, a pink wall, the privy roof cushioned with house-leeks, the kennel, a pitchfork thrust into a straw stack. Fragments . . . rather like my memories.

The Meils farmed diligently. She had her chickens and ducks, he his goats: a splendid herd of sable-brown beasts with black faces and hoofs. Very handsome. I don't remember what they were called, but they were rare, valuable, and produced an abundance of milk for the cheeses which Madame Meil made and sold in the village on Saturdays. I was not tremendously impressed by her mahogany brown hard-worked hands. The fingernails hooped in mourning, knuckles calloused, unwashed always. It was extremely difficult to avoid the offered cheese when I took down the goat bag. I liked goat cheese – liked it greatly. I was just a bit anxious about the proximity of the privy to the shed where the cheese was made. There was the most amazing hum of insect life emanating from that privy. The door fitted well, but had a heart cut into the front at eye level. So that, I assumed, if one was occupied, one still could see anyone approaching. Quite often as I hung the bag on a small spiky branch of one of the olive trees, I would be caught by Madame emerging from the humming privy, tucking in her pinafore, and pulling up her thick grey stockings. '*Ah! Voilà! Monsieur Fauchon! Ah bon . . .*'

Fauchon is the most famous grocer in Paris, perhaps in the world, and supplies delicacies of all kinds to the rich. I was, of course, Monsieur Fauchon because I brought delicious things down to the goats: the spaghetti, bread, stale cake and so on. It was *then* that I *had* to avoid the gift of a cheese offered in hard-worked hands straight from the privy. It was ungallant of me, I know, but as Forwood always pointed out, tetanus or typhoid can kill, dysentery and meningitis aren't a whole lot of fun either, and so it was wiser to invent any lie rather than accept a gift so primed with lingering, awful death.

'But no cheese? Ah, *dommage* . . . You should have a hat!' she said. Her silver teeth catching the sun, she brushed her greyish hair from a nut-brown forehead. Green-bellied flies hummed and droned round the scaling pine door with the cut-out heart behind her.

'I know, Madame . . . I was in a hurry.'

'But in this sun, *patron*! It's strong at this time of afternoon. Five hundred metres up, we are here. Eh? Dangerous. A hat will keep your head cool and you would also be able to shade your eyes.'

I started up her dusty garden path, past a foam of cosmos, a tumble of Bourbon roses. Apart from goats, chickens and the ducks, Madame gardened wildly, and everything she stuck in flourished; she just literally pushed things in anywhere and they were instantly ablaze with bloom. Very frustrating. I never had much success with such nonchalance and trust. The little garden she had dug out of her farmyard was as vulgar, gaudy and as unlikely as a Helen Allingham print.

'Your roses this year! Madame! Fantastic . . .'

'The goats eat them. Goats are idiots. My man has just put up an electric fence on the lower pasture. You didn't see him?'

I assured her that I had not, but I had seen the goats, huddled together in a far corner of the field. She looked a little concerned, wiped her nose with the back of her hand.

'You did not see my man? Doing the fence?'

'No. Just the goats. In the corner. Watching me. There was

a sticker with a little yellow triangle, with a red zig-zag on it.'

She nodded happily. '*Ah! Bon! Exact.* He has done it. That is to show the fence is now electric! To keep the goats from my roses and from wandering into the road. Madame de Beauvallon drives like a maniac. If you are worried about my goats and the cheese I make, ask Dr Santori . . . he is the vet from town. He inoculates my goats. He knows them well, they are a pedigree herd. You mustn't be afraid of tuberculosis! No one gets it now, from goat cheese. You should speak with Dr Santori. You have your dogs, and one day soon you will have sheep' – a decision not a suggestion – 'Your land *always* carried sheep. Three hundred. You have to have sheep to keep the land clean, in case of fire.'

I turned again by the pink and white cosmos to try and get on home. 'I have two dogs, Madame, therefore sheep are out of the question.'

She came after me, tying the strings of her black pinafore round her waist. 'Why? Two dogs? So?'

'Ticks,' I said.

'*Ah si.* Now Monsieur Labiche is a good friend of ours. He needs the grazing; he has a strong flock, three hundred head and some goats. I'll tell him that you don't need your grazing because you have dogs and because of ticks. He will be happy to oblige you, to save you the trouble of mowing and cleaning your land . . . and he needs the grazing so badly. He is a good man, from Feyance . . . I will have a word with my man when he comes in. Labiche is a good man, it is a fine herd. He will be very happy: and so will we. The risk of fire will be less if your land is grazed clean.'

'*Ticks*, Madame. Three hundred head of sheep and some goats! How many ticks?'

'Ah! You must lock your dogs up in a kennel while the sheep are here. We can arrange the time exactly when he brings them to you.' French logic.

'I don't want them! We are cleaning the land very well with our German machines.'

She looked sad. She murmured something about Labiche and how honest he was and he would pay a reasonable amount, but I just went on up the path and closed myself out of her little garden. I waved.

Then, 'Honey!' she called. 'I have good, pure honey? It is from the broom and acacias! It is better for you than sugar. Take it in your coffee . . . for cooking . . . Tomorrow, when you come with the bag, I will give you a comb. My man has it every winter, with lemon, in hot water. He never has *la grippe*. Never.'

I called my thanks and picked my way – I was barefoot often in the summer – across the lane and up into my land, turned, waved a farewell.

'Your garden is very pretty from here,' I called. 'The olives are beautiful, they are laden . . .'

'*Ah, si* . . . but tomorrow they go. Commençon is coming from Nice to take the wood.' She stood shading her eyes from the westering sun.

I stood frozen. To take the wood? 'Why will they do that? *Take* the trees?'

'My man has sold them. For the wood. Tomorrow you will hear the saws. It will be a lot of work but a lot of money . . .' She moved away, flapping at the dogs, calling, '*A demain!*'

And the next morning the roar and whine of the saws filled the valley and the two giant trees which had overshadowed her house for centuries were brutally felled. For the wood. Probably to make disgusting little pepper mills, bread boards, or mustard spoons and salad bowls. For tourists. Hundreds of years were destroyed in moments. For peasant gain.

The valley never looked quite the same again. And when I went down with the bag the next evening I walked, barefoot, through deep drifts of fragrant, moist, pink sawdust, past the two agonized stumps sticking out of the high bank. Country life.

However much one may desire to be quite self-sufficient, it really is not possible if you are running a smallholding, abandoned for years, and especially if you are a learner, which I most certainly was. By the time the terraces were cut, raked and stacked, the trees pruned (four hundred took rather a long time, and it is a specialist's job – which set me back financially at £10 a tree), logs split, dogs fed, fires laid, brambles hacked, invasive bamboo uprooted, a pond excavated and clay dug for 'puddling', there was not much time left for cooking. One had to eat.

Forwood was good at cauliflower cheese and scrambled eggs. And that was his limit. I couldn't boil water but did manage to cut up kilos of cow's cheek to feed the dogs. This was easy. Mix with biscuits and a bit of boiled cauliflower stalk and they were contented. Which was more than I was after about six months of cauliflower cheese with an apple now and again. This was not thrift, you must know, exhaustion merely: there simply wasn't enough energy left to deal with cooking. Help was essential, and was sought from Florette Ranchett, who as usual knew just 'the couple you seek. Charming, in service for years, *select* and very discreet. They worked for the King of Sweden for many years, and latterly for Lady Brancraig down on Cap Ferrat.'

'They are people you know, Madame Ranchett?'

'No. *Pas du tout.* They were in here yesterday, asking for directions to a house beyond Le Foux . . . they were being interviewed for a situation.'

'But . . .?'

'Ah. The people are Belgian! *Quite* impossible! They are almost as bad as the Arabs. They are frugal and mean. It was unsuitable for them. I told them. I *know* the family at that house.' She shuddered. 'They owe me three months' money . . . Why do I give credit! Why! For the village, of course. For rich Belgians, madness . . .'

Henri and Marie arrived for an interview with me three days later and stayed for five years. After which they retired but were still available to 'house-sit' in an emergency.

They were, it must be confessed, a great deal older than they had claimed to be. Marie must have been in her early seventies but hacked off ten years, and wore a geranium-red lipstick and thick white powder to hide her wrinkles, making her look rather like a dried fig. Henri was probably older, and had dyed his hair a sort of sherbert yellow. I suppose, at one time, it had been fair.

However, they were clearly all that Madame Ranchett had said, and we all liked each other right away. Marie cooked extremely well but would do nothing else, except buttons and darning. Henri, on the other hand, was the house-man and would drive the car to get the marketing, and polish the floors and make the beds. Except that after a short, agonizing trial run with Forwood in the Simca Brake he was never allowed near any machine again unless it was connected to a plug. Like the floor-polisher. He was quite incapable of driving anything. Except a hard bargain when it came to his 'leave' every year.

But we all managed very well, and when, eventually, the time came for them to retire to their small flat down below in the valley, I went to Madame Ranchett again and sought her help. The only problem, and it honestly was not a real problem, was that with Henri and Marie we lost any chance of guest accommodation. Which didn't matter right at the start, but got a bit irritating as the years went on, and we had to farm chums out in the village in one of the not very attractive little hotels.

So this time it was decided that a daily lady was all we needed. Two hours a day, and we would cope with the rest.

Well, we got her. She was discovered by Florette Ranchett wandering round the shop one day, a small child on one hip, looking bewildered. She was Spanish, could speak scraps of French, but with signs and a certain amount of shrieking at each other it was established that she had just moved into the area (a small, neglected house by a junk yard) with a husband who had got a job at the local golf course, mowing the greens. She had no money, or very little, and that day wanted some broken biscuits or stale bread. She could, and did, pay for some milk.

Madame Ranchett called me to alert me and a few days later Soleidad arrived up the track on a sputtering mobilette, with her awful child strapped into a chair on the back, head lolling, dummy sprouting from dribbly lips. She came round the house with me doing a full tour. I showed her the fridge, the sink, the baths, the beds, the linen cupboard, the china and all the rest. She was silent, feeling a piece of linen between thumb and forefinger here, weighing a glass there, studying a saucepan intently, opening and closing the fridge door time and again, apparently delighting in the light which sprang up each time she did so. I thought her to be one of nature's originals.

And she was. A gypsy from Granada with exceptionally bandy legs and a voice that could splinter granite. She nodded agreeably at everything I said in complete and total incomprehension, but when I said, 'Okay?', she shrugged and nodded casually, and I wrote down the figure 9 and then 12, meaning the hours she might work. And she, taking my pencil in filthy fingers, laboriously wrote 8½ and 11½ and then made a sign by rubbing her finger and thumb together. I counted out what I felt I could afford in franc notes (Madame Ranchett had advised me), which she accepted with a cackle and a nod. Then she hitched the child on to her hip and wandered down the stairs singing lightly. At the front door she called out in her rasping voice: '*Mañana! Eh!*' And the deal was made.

She stayed with me faithfully and devotedly, for fifteen years, until the time came for me to leave. By then she spoke fairly reasonable French with a disastrous accent, and ran the house with a rod of iron, washed and cleaned and polished, kicked the dogs, and screamed and laughed and worked like a fiend. And grew, deservedly, rich. Her husband, Manolo, came up at weekends, a pleasant man with a hideous scarred face (carved up in a bar room brawl by broken glass) and a fearful squint so that one spoke to the good eye only, the one on the right. He was a good, kind fellow, useful at the olive harvest, changing plugs, pruning the cypress trees every season, and making himself generally useful. She was always called just 'Lady'. Le Pigeonnier functioned smoothly from their arrival onwards.

However, Lady did not cook. And on one occasion when she brought a dish of some wretched famished chicken smothered in rice and saffron as a gift, one was rather relieved. Everything she did was fine – except the cooking.

So, back to square one. An agreement was made: I would be the scullion, that is to say I would wash up, scour saucepans, lay tables, prepare vegetables, empty dustbins and so on, and leave Forwood to do the cooking. In time he moved uneasily, but successfully, far from cauliflower cheese and deep into pilaffs, risottos, soupe au pistou, ratatouille and all manner of other Provençal delights. Pots and pans were bought, knives of astonishing sharpness, mixing-machines, mincing-machines – an entire *batterie de cuisine* formed and I did the washing-up. It took me a very considerable time for the simple reason, as he patiently explained, that cooking was not easy, and that he was what is called a 'messy cook'. That was true. After a simple gigot, flageolet, salad and cheese, it seemed to me that I had to wash up an ironmonger's. I could never understand really, why? If I made a mild protest it was quietly suggested that I take over. So I shut up . . . and we managed. But I know, I have always known, that I got the worst part of the bargain. And I had to trail off to the market every morning, sharp at seven, winter and summer, to be sure that only the best was bought for this Escoffier of the hillside. I also had to feed the dogs, but as I have said, this was not difficult, and they got better fed now that there was more variety in the green vegetables, not just bits of old cauliflower bunged in with the biscuits. In time, sadly, cheek became prohibitively expensive, and tinned muck came on the market. Easier, cheaper, and somehow the dogs seemed less aggressive to strangers now that they were no longer fed raw flesh. Like bromide in the soldiers' tea, it seemed that tinned food rather took the fizz out of things.

Emigrating to France does not mean that one hurls about the place looking for a suitable house, buys it, moves in, and lives there happily ever after. There is rather more to it than that. You have to get permission to stay there. At least, you did in my time. France is not just 'any old place', it's not somewhere that you can just dump your belongings and say, 'Here I am.' To begin with, they are not all that anxious to have you. Unless, that is, you intend to return to the land you occupy something from which you have taken, like love, care and attention. I was prepared to offer all that, and more.

But I had chosen to live in a particularly sensitive area, the Alpes Maritimes, bordered with Italy, not far from Switzerland, close to Spain, too close to North Africa. Security was tight. The great hoards of unemployed Arabs from Tunisia and Morocco, the abject poor from Calabria, the drug-pushers, the smugglers of every kind of commodity you can name, would easily swamp the A.M. if not severely curtailed. The ritzy-glitzy crowd who swarmed to Nice and Cannes, played the tables in Monte Carlo, and rented, or bought, hideous villas in the hills were watched carefully, but they never stayed very long and fled at the first signs of inclement weather. Meteorological or political. The people who came to live, that is to live for good, were considered with caution and suspicion.

So, first of all, you had to get your *carte grise*, which permitted you to live in the area for three months. It was a form of identification – your ID card, if you like – and as such, at an accident, a bank or any monetary transaction, always proved extremely useful. At least you knew who you were, so did they, and that in itself was a comfort. In Britain it would be, and it is, considered a breach of privacy. I can't think why. All you have to state is name, birth date, address and, I seem to remember, your mother's name and date of birth. Since *she* was always uncertain and, I feel sure, fibbed about that anyway, it was nothing I took very seriously. But I was pleased to be 'on record'. There was a feeling of security. Don't ask me why.

So, every three months I made the climb up my cliff and through the oakwood at the back of the house to Saint-Cyprien to see the deputy mayor. This had to be done between the hours of five and eight in the evenings. On a fixed date. If you missed it for some reason, you could always try to catch him in the bar he ran in Le Pré. But by that time he really couldn't have signed his name with an X.

So one got to the *mairie* early, sat on a rush-bottomed chair with the other emigrants, the 'legal' Arabs, the Spanish, the Italians. The anteroom was small, whitewashed, red-tiled, spartan, a poster on one wall with a map of France indicating, by a big black dot, the latest advance of rabies, on the other a notice saying when the blood donor caravan would be arriving in the village for the monthly blood donation.

The next stage, after your *carte grise*, literally a bit of grey paper covered with a riot of violet stamps and the deputy's incomprehensible signature, was your *carte de séjour*. This was orange, a proper card, and was a permit to live in, work in and inhabit the Alpes Maritimes. It was a heady moment when that was put in one's wallet. It took for ever to get, and countless journeys, queues and passionate discussions in a vast building in the heart of Nice, where it was always impossible to park a car. However, getting the beastly thing was worth the misery.

Finally – and it took longer than the others, because one's request had to go to Paris, then through officialdom in Nice, and then back to the *mairie* – and finally, one amazing day, you got your blue *carte de résidence*. Not only were you permitted to live in your house, but you had become, apart from voting and joining the army, a French resident. *Taxes compris*. This lasted you for ten years and there were four pages already for the stamp ahead. It felt really very good indeed. Because the land had been cared for, because the olives were harvested, the hay cut and sold, because, at first anyway, the sheep grazed, I was classified as an agricultural property and an agricultural proprietor. Which made an enormous difference to my taxes and in the grants made available for the house and restoration. It felt very secure. Objective gained. With no loss of passport.

Vaguely, at one time, I had thought about taking out French nationality: it was a perplexing idea, but it got pretty swiftly set aside when one realized that it was not impossible that one day, perhaps - perhaps - one could be called upon to fight one's true countrymen. And that, however remote it might have been, was *quite* unthinkable. So one quickly smothered the little spark that had glimmered and concentrated, very hard indeed, on being a good resident.

As the years progressed, the yearly return to England, to see my parents or the family, became slightly depressing. I was starting to feel more and more foreign, I did not quite behave as an Englishman – shaking hands with everyone, calling people 'Madame' or 'Monsieur' (which always caused embarrassment) – generally feeling out of place. Familiar places faded rather. I even forgot the English words for things, and the changes, between 1966 and 1976, for example, became bewildering to me: the behaviour of people; the clothes they wore; the rubbish and filth everywhere; the lack of cafés and brasseries, of reliable trains, mail or general transport to which I had so easily become accustomed – really quite trivial things, I know. But there were other, more alarming things, like the growing envy and spite of the cheap press, hitting at standards which we once had held dear. Perhaps I was out of touch stuck up on my hill in the sun of Provence? Was I spoiled? Had I got it wrong? But I did feel that the quality of life itself was altering, an apathy was growing, with a resentment against anything 'foreign' and therefore unacceptable, cheap, cheating and incomprehensible. I felt, with great reluctance, that we had started to fall back from the race, while on the continent the race was roaring ahead and ready to be won. We seemed to be jellied quite comfortably in aspic. Dunkirk, Vera Lynn, our finest hour and the Blitz! Tourist heaven – but not for today. Surely that was fifty years ago? We were marking time on one spot. Sinking slowly. It was a terribly sad, dusty, uneasy feeling. Driving out to the airport after one of those yearly trips, to catch the early flight home, I drove through the bunting and glory of a full October in the Park: the tumbling leaves, beds of scarlet dahlias, sparkle of the Household Cavalry exercising in the Row, swans on the Serpentine, two youths jogging, their breath drifting like veils in the sharp morning, just-off-frost. Familiar, cherished, but suddenly strange, distant. A complex feeling. Like looking at a sepia photograph of time past, bleached of colour and fine detail, leaving only outline. And then I knew, in one regretful moment, that I now no longer belonged. I was just a visitor in a foreign land.

The 'home stretch' is always the best part of a return. The crunch and scatter of gravel in the lane, rasp and crack of twig, bramble and broom against the bodywork of the car. The spiralling leaves of the big fig, yellow leaflets to announce the end of the season. The overgrown lane winds and dips down past the Meils' farm, she in straw hat, looking up, waving, Emile doffing his beret, leaning on his goat-crook. And then, right ahead, the big stone column built from jagged boulders long since by Fraj, decorated with bits of red glass from a forgotten accident on the corner, the bent chrome letters 'FIAT' crowning its top. His statement.

Winding then slowly up through the still olives, the tended terraces, late sun throwing orange flares from the windows, dogs squealing, barking, racing ahead to the top to greet one. Past the pond, yellowing rushes bending in a late *souffle* of wind, pattering on the water. Henri carrying logs in his arms, waving, his yellow hair spiked and flustered by the breeze, apron flapping, laughing at the dogs. Outside the kitchen, Marie leaning over the balcony rail, vegetable knife in one hand, a head of celery in the other, geranium-red lips bared in a gleaming porcelain smile. Skittering, fighting, snarling from the dogs. Marie laughing, scolding, waving the celery. *'Arrête! Arrête! Tais-toi!'*

'All well, Marie?'

'All well, Monsieur: a perfect week. So warm. And London?'

We unpacked luggage. Plastic bags: Harrods, Marks and

Spencer, Goode's. Henri bustling up, wiping his hands on his apron, laughing: 'Welcome! Welcome, messieurs.' Lugging suitcases and hand-grips from the boot. Marie calling down, '*Oh là!* So much! Did you remember my tea?' Carrying the stuff up the steps on to the balcony, into the kitchen, the smell of simmering lentil soup. 'I remembered your tea. *And* the Cooper's Oxford. Have they been good? The dogs?' And bending towards the Roman ruin, sitting upright with amber eyes: 'Have *you* behaved? I have brought you a big yellow ball! From Kensington!' A furiously thumping tail, a scream of jealousy from the other dog who might have been forgotten. Marie crying, 'Poor Daisy! Nothing for Daisy?' Balls were chucked scudding, rumps went bouncing, and belting, into the dusk. Marie, picking up the beech chopping-block left to sweeten in the afternoon sun.

'No one telephoned, not a soul. As the grave here. The mail is in the Long Room.'

'I bought you a present.'

'*Tiens* . . .'

'Bendicks Bitter Mints!'

'*Mon Dieu!* My figure . . . my teeth! *Oh là!*'

Forwood, setting the kettle on the chopping-block, plugging it in, looking for a cup and saucer. We were home.

I have the vegetable knife. Still have the chopping-board. I use them both every day, wondering, sometimes, if all the scratches, cuts and scores, the cross-hatching, the random criss-crossing of long-forgotten knives, this kitchen trigonometry, is all that is tangible now of a lost lifetime? A worn peeling-knife, a beech chopping-block? Tangible perhaps, yes. Ephemeral, no: there is much more to it all than that.

Chapter 5

Titty-Brown Hill was the highest point on my land. A flat-topped, grassy knoll, scarred with clumps of alien corn, it was an easy walk up from the terrace along what was, many, many years before, a cart and cattle track to Saint-Sulpice. On the top it was all absolutely secluded, no one could possibly see a thing; so female guests got into the habit of wandering off up through the sapling oaks and tumbled walls (this area had been rather more neglected than anywhere else) to strip off, happy in their security. The only possible observers of their behaviour would have been the little owl, a chatter of magpies or perhaps an ambling tortoise.

It wasn't very long before the grassy knoll was baptized, and became Titty-Brown Hill. I seemed to have a wish to name parts of the land, or the trees on the land: something to do with knowing, in shorthand language, exactly where one was working, or where work had to be done. For example, if one said, 'I've done all the scything among the five sisters,' it was understood that the two lower terraces beside the path down through the five cypress trees had been cleared. The density of the trees prevented the mowers from raging about, thus causing me to break my back with the scythe but saving the lives of countless lizards, praying mantises, grasshoppers and crickets. Tragically the super-efficient German giants chumbled up the slow-moving insects in vast quantities. A slender stick-insect, even a dashing mantis, simply hadn't a hope in hell of escaping the roaring red machines which whirled them into chaff in a split second.

All the trees which I bought from the nursery in the plain to give my domain instant 'timelessness' were given names so that one would know exactly where one was. 'Charlie' was the tallest, and oldest, and stood hard by the front door, towering over the corrugated pink-tiled roof; 'Rosie' stood like an exclamation mark at the top of the drive; 'Brock' (a nephew) and 'Kimbo' (his wife) shaded the pond. 'Antonia and Eduardo', called after my faithful Spanish staff who had come from England with me to help me get settled down in France, stood beyond the hangar garage and under the kitchen windows. To remind me, if I ever needed reminding, of their loyalty and the sense of loss which they engendered when they, in time, left to go back to Valencia and start up a family, something we had agreed when I left England for abroad. Out of the dozen or so vastly costly trees, only one, called 'Bella', actually slowly died off. Her roots struck a giant rock buried deep under the earth and that settled that.

Thus there were Titty-Brown Hill, Fig Meadow, Long Walk, Pond Lawn, Bamboo Fields, Crescent Lawn, Bonfire Field and so on. They were instantly identifiable if one spoke of them after work in the evenings. 'I've done all round Charlie, and raked up round Brock and Kimbo' meant that the front of the house and the flowerbeds by the terrace had been weeded and the Pond Lawn had been cleared. Simple. And equally it brought into use the names of much-loved friends or members of the family.

Some of the trees, latterly, were named for the people who had given them as gifts – much more useful and enduring than anything else – and if I was ever asked by some generous guest what to offer as a token of thanks it was always a rose bush, a plant or a sapling tree which proved the most acceptable.

From Titty-Brown you could look out over a giant patchwork of vines, carnations, jasmine, roses, and acres and acres of olive trees. Olive groves, I should perhaps say. Our area was known to produce a particularly excellent fruit, and my land, L'Aire Pigeonnier, was noted for the best olives of all. For years, well, ever since the war, the trees had been neglected badly. The land had flooded from time to time, the trees were saturated and had grown lavishly, producing no fruit. Within about three years (olives fruit only every two years or so) I had once again a good harvest.

At first there were only two of us, Forwood and myself, to do the picking. Crawling about on hands and knees in an anorak and boots, with fingers blue from cold, sodden knees and an aching back, collecting the fallen berries in the frosted grass and wide-spread nets was not at all what I had imagined the olive harvest to be. Fortunately, in time, Monsieur Rémy and Madame Bruna, plus their children, came into the act: they took what they could pick and kept the oil, which provided them with enough virgin-pressing from the mill for a year at least. Our crops were prodigious, and the trip down to the mill in Saint-Sulpice was always one of the splendours of the endeavour.

At dusk, about four o'clock (the harvest started in mid-December and lasted until mid-March), we carted the sacks and buckets down to the village, queued up to get them weighed, took the *fiche* which stated the quantity (to the last gram) we were due, and then tipped the sacks into the great churning mess being crushed and pulped by the giant granite wheel. The scent of the virgin oil, the heavy sweet odour of the brown pulp, with a thread of paraffin wafting from the lamps hung high on the rough stone walls and, above all, the smoke of rough Gitane cigarettes drifting through it, a binding scent for the others, were pungent and immensely comforting. The physical result of hours of back-breaking labour, it was altogether most satisfying.

But quite apart from the vineyards, the roses, carnations, jasmine fields and dense olive groves below Titty-Brown, by far the most exciting, and to some extent worrying, thing was the glorious view over all this land far down to the sea and Africa beyond. Sometimes (fortunately rarely) the great bank of clouds on the distant horizon of the sea would lift for half an hour and the jagged peaks of Corsica, soft pink in the early morning sun, would thrust shimmering high into the pale aching winter sky. I use the words 'worrying' and 'fortunately' here because I had been told often enough by Monsieur Danté that if you could see the mountains on Corsica, then a terrible mistral would shortly arrive. It was time to batten down the hatches, secure the doors and shutters, and huddle in the depths of the huge fireplace under the chimney. Safest place in a really bad mistral or forest fire. Should this occur, then Monsieur Rémy, Danté and Plum-Bum called to each other in concern like chickens, and with a deal of head shaking they would rattle off in the battered truck before the end of the working-day to get their own places ready. You used mostly to see the mountains in the very early morning for some reason. And seldom in summer. When you caught the awesome sight, the mountains were washed by the rising sun glinting on the snows. Corsica has pretty high mountains. Anyway, to see them was not good news, and it always proved to be the case.

Sometimes the mistral would blow for days, and life became extremely miserable: even the dogs crept about wincing, their eyes half closed against the stinging dust, tails curled between their legs, ears flat. The pond turned into a raging sea, waves leapt and bounced, spilling into the rushes, roaring away down the rutted track to the gates in a furious cataract of stones, fish and foaming water. The rain pelted steel arrows, olives writhed and tossed in agony, cypress trees waved, bent and whipped like pheasant plumes. The noise was as savage as a bombardment of rockets. My main anxiety was for the oaks up the rocky hill behind the house: the wind roared and tore among their dense branches with such brutal force that one could only communicate by screaming to each other in short bursts. But, as they'd stood there for many centuries, one prayed they'd hang on a bit longer. And they did, save for a limb or two and bushels of leaves. But they stood stolid and solid. There *were* occasions when the mistral caught us all on the hop, so to speak – then we had to dive for shelter before decapitation from flying roof tiles.

Once we all huddled in the woodshed. Monsieur Danté, Fraj, Plum-Bum and Monsieur Rémy started to scratch at the wall with a piece of twig. The old whitewash, not yet restored, flaked away. '*Voyez?* A name?' he said. 'Many names here, *regardez*.' What I had thought was just a haze of dust and spiders' webs on the cracked wall were, in fact, tiny gestures of defiance. Human determination in pencil scribbles; a pattern of anguish from a lost time. Name after name was criss-crossed on the crumbling plaster. Esthers, Daniels, Rivkas and Jacobs. All Jewish, all stating, after their names, the date and the town whence they had come. And their morale. 'Felix Levant. Avignon. Mai 2 '43. In good heart. Age 13½.' Across the wall these whispers spread behind the stacked logs, hanging saws, scythes and coiled hose pipe, the rakes and *pioches*. Monsieur Rémy pushed his cap to the back of his head, a habit which he had when concentrating, a spent match between his gold teeth (in even a moderate mistral like the present one a cigarette was madness). 'Children. Jewish children. They were collected all over the region. A brave woman from Paillas. She was a singer before the war, very noble, proud. She collected the Jewish children, brought them here, to this house. It was very isolated, the Germans didn't ever come so far into the valley. When she had a few together we moved them down to the coast, to La Napoule . . . some to Théoule . . . Oh! *Malheur!* It was dangerous! We hid them under the harvest corn, melons, olives, in carts. From the coast they went by fishing-boat to the Spanish coast. At night. Not easy, *mon Dieu*, not easy. We didn't lose *one*! No one gave them away. We stay silent in Provence.'

Apparently the house itself had been empty for years. Only the land was vaguely tended, and during the early days of 1939 and 1940 a French cavalry regiment had been billeted there with their mounts. After June, and the fall of France, they withdrew and the house mouldered into dust and silence, buried in tall grass, rampant myrtle and ruined olive trees. The village youths, and their girls, were the only people who ever came down the track through the oaks to linger and embrace in the silent rooms.

That was how, and where, he had met Madame Mandelli, staying on a visit from Cremona. Apart from the Jewish children, and these self-exploring adolescents hiding from the eyes of parents and occupiers, Le Pigeonnier was deserted on its tumbled terraces and olives. Monsieur Rémy spat on a finger, drew it through a name. 'Nellie Kaplan. Draguignan.

I am well . . .' The rest he wiped away in spittle. 'Long ago. Long ago . . . Perhaps today she has her own children. Eh?'

They all left shortly after, but I told him to leave a part of the wall unpainted when he came to redecorate, as a memorial. He thought I was idiotic. But he thought that of me anyway. But generously. Humour the lunatic. So, anyway, he left a strip untouched. I suppose he was right? It was pretty silly. But they remained. The scribbled defiances and courage.

My father was being evasive. I knew the signs very well. Every time I suggested that we walk down to the little house which I had every intention of securing as a retirement place for him and my mother, if they agreed, he managed to be doing something greatly preoccupying and which he could not leave. 'I'm just getting into the swing of things: I've got the right "mix" for the sky, I always have difficulty with skies, as you know . . . you run along.' Or else he had decided to walk up to the village to buy some cigarettes, or open a beer in the shade, anything as an excuse not to come down through the orchard to the little shuttered house. However, eventually, towards the end of their first visit, I forced the issue and he grudgingly agreed to come with me. 'It's fearfully hot for walking, dear boy. I'm getting on, you know.'

'Nonsense. We'll be in the shade under the trees, and it's all level down to the house. It's a ruin, you realize, but it's full of possibilities and it's mine for £18,000 plus *all* the land. But I *have* to decide by the end of the year.'

'Gun at your head. Wretched business,' said my father.

'No gun at all. Very reasonable. I've had a year to make my decision – it's just over to you really. It's a snip at £18,000, plus a vineyard and three hundred olive trees.'

'I really do prefer a bottle of Worthington, you know. What would we do, your mother and I, with three hundred olive trees? At our age . . . do be reasonable.'

And so we bickered on down the track, ducking under overgrown apple trees, easing through rampant bamboo and tussocky grass, being whipped by heavy blossomed broom. The house, when we reached it, stood like a small stone box.

Facing south, unadorned, a tiled roof, a front door, two floors, a wide dusty track set before it where carts had once turned, with a giant elm of great age shading it from the burning sun. It had almost the same view as that from my house, just slightly tilted to the west, but ahead lay the same valley, the plain, the ridge of the mountains and the silver glitter of the distant sea. I was constantly ravished, my father far less impressed. His pessimism increased as we opened the front door with a big key and trod into the damp-scented dark of the shuttered house.

'It smells like a tunnel! Good God, boy, the place is sodden!'

'It's been empty for years. And I'm told it's surrounded by springs . . . it just needs airing.'

'Needs a charge of dynamite. Rotten with woodworm, I shouldn't wonder. Or damp rot. You can smell it. Wonderful place for mushrooms. You'll make a fortune!'

'Jean-Claude keeps all his work materials here. It can't be *that* damp. He also stores his apples, olives, wine here.'

'That I can smell. Sour stink. Really awful.'

In the narrow hall, tiled floor, staircase ahead, long cracks in the walls, my father stood quite still. 'I think you might open a shutter? Get some light, unless you think they'd fall off?'

They didn't. But the light seemed to compound the scent

of decay with the sight of tumbled crates of glass (Jean-Claude was an artist of some kind and made stained-glass windows set in rough concrete), hammers, chisels, buckets and plastic bags from Galleries Lafayette and Casino, filled with hinges, bolts, brackets and yards of rusting chain.

In a corner of one room (there were only two anyway on the ground floor, left and right of the front door), half a dozen wine barrels were ranged along the side of a rough wooden manger. The cracked tile floor was strewn with trodden straw and old, withered, apples. I thought it was quite a pleasant smell: fruit, wine, straw. Pa thought otherwise but conceded that he could make a very good little sketch of the still-life before him and started feeling about his pockets for the stub of pencil which he always carried on him, only I got him to come up the stairs and look about. We finally went all over the house. It didn't take three minutes.

Four minute bedrooms, no bathroom, but a staggering view from all the windows. Pa was determinedly unimpressed. 'I do see what you mean. It *has* possibilities. But after securing it for £18,000 you'd have to spend double that on improving it. Damp courses – I bet it's built on a marsh from the stink – bathrooms, new floors and what about drains? And *lavs*? You'll have to instal lavs . . . can't go off into the garden! Not at your mother's age and mine. Good Lord! What a thought!'

'We'd do all that. Of course. It would be a tremendous investment. All this land, peace and quiet . . . off the main road. I really think you'd be very comfortable here. I'd be next door . . .'

Pa walked carefully down the, admittedly, sagging tile staircase holding on anxiously to the thin iron banister. 'You know what your mother would say, don't you? She'd say that she would go mad here in a week. And so she would.'

'Quite mad, darling,' she said at lunch under the vine. 'You are being marvellously dear thinking of Pa and me, but, frankly, at our ages it just wouldn't work. I'd go *quite* mad. What would we do? Stuck up here in the dark? No one to talk to, just sheep. Nowhere to go . . . miles for shopping and your father can't speak French very well.'

'I do, Margaret. I do not badly,' my father protested mildly.

'It's the stuff you learned in that war of yours. It's quite old fashioned and out of date now . . . No, we simply couldn't manage.'

Pa helped himself to mustard, tapping it briskly on the edge of his plate, concealing impatience. 'Well, I warned you. Your mother is gregarious. Loves people. *Lots* of people. All the time. Amazing really.'

'Oh I do! *I do!* I have to make up for all the years I lost when your father wouldn't let me go back to the theatre. I *need* an audience!'

Pa sighed, reached for his beer. 'I told you . . . it would be impossible.'

'Well, there is nothing to *do* up here,' she said. 'Nothing! I don't know how you and Tote' – Forwood's name in the family – 'can stick it. Perhaps you won't, for long? But for me, just sitting about reading, or sewing or darning. I'd go potty. Anyway, I don't read now . . .'

'Why not? You used to *eat* books.'

'I keep on losing my glasses. Daddy reads to me. Trollope. I ask you . . .'

'Wilkie Collins. You enjoy Wilkie Collins,' said Pa wearily, starting on his *jambon persillé*.

Ma raised her glass and held it up to the sunlight. 'So pretty! Golden. I was bored *witless* by *The Woman in White* . . . no good pretending. And up here, with bare tiles on the floor and no telephone that really works . . . No, darling, not *us*.'

'I'd rather miss the pub, you know?' said Pa. 'And we have been in Fletching a long time now, got lots of friends there . . . it'd be a wrench to leave. We're very settled in our ways, and that little house down there will always be damp. Built on a marsh, as I said. Interesting idea. But we'll just count this as a splendid holiday, eh?'

My mother usually got her own way, although Pa was pretty stubborn too, so between them I realized that I had lost the chance of the little house and the privacy that the extra acres, adjoining my present land, would give me. But I did see their point. They were nodding at seventy, too late now to alter, and Ma would miss the grandchildren which my brother and sister had provided. So . . . The dream faded, and at the end of the year I had to confront Jean-Claude and regretfully decline the option to buy: he was quite relieved, and said that he really didn't want to sell the last bit of his family's property, after five hundred years, and would use the place as a studio and a store room for his 'work'. He arrived at the house at the hour which we had arranged, on a huge, new, glittering Honda, his long fingernails painted red, his hair, henna'd as brilliantly as Bruna Mandelli's, falling in long, thin straggles over the shoulders of his expensive leather jacket. Obviously the £75,000 I had paid him for my share of his land had been put to good use. His family, the Marxist wife and a scatter of children, were out of sight somewhere behind the SNCF goods-yard in Nice. A successful man, Jean-Claude. Heaving himself off his bike and attempting to pull it up on to its stand, both he and it fell over.

Forwood muttered something about not slipping a disc and we left him to get to his feet on his own. He was a tall man, angular, with long fingers and longer legs. Petrol poured from the bike, seeping into the dusty path outside the damp house. He struggled for a bit, pulling the bike up, blowing through yellow teeth, brushing his leather jacket, tossing his hair, unsteadily, over his shoulders. There was a pungent smell of pot and petrol; he smiled nonchalantly, and asked me for a front door key, which he dropped, giggling. I picked it up and he shrugged. '*Gentil*,' he said. '*Félicitations!*' And took it with a mock bow.

In the damp-smelling room with the manger and barrels, he admitted that the place was too damp for anyone to live in; it was, as my father had suggested, built on a marsh. There were many springs in the area, so water would never be our problem even in the intense heat of summer, and that would be very useful if, and when, he would decide to sell up finally, in *years* to come, because he had a secret dream to take his family to a remote place in India and join an ashram, where they would be close to 'life' and 'Krishna'. I asked, unease scratching like a pin in a new shirt, when that might possibly be. He *had* wanted to hold on to the family land? Now he was cheerfully talking about ashrams and India and Krishna and peace and love in a warm climate! He waved a scarlet-tipped hand vaguely, stumbled up the sagging tile staircase and called down, over his shoulder, that he had had the land surveyed in the last few months and that it was quite possible to turn the whole area into an 'up-market *lotissement*'. That is to say, a building-site. They could drain the land, channel the springs and build seven to eight 'high-class villas' on the land my father had so carelessly discarded in favour of his pub in Fletching.

The terrible threat of a *lotissement* and seven or eight 'high-class villas' cast a fearful blight on events for some time to come, but for the moment we were, I thought, safe. Very occasionally the Honda would roar down into the dusty track outside the damp house; there would be a hammering and banging for a time, turquoise sparks flew from some high-powered welding torch, but nothing much else happened. I almost settled down to my usual complacency. Jean-Claude would *never* go to India, they'd never give permission, in this glorious place, for a *lotissement*. And then, one day, some peripheral friends, that is to say people I knew but had never entertained, and by whom I had never been entertained in England, arrived on the coast with their two girls to look 'for somewhere to buy for a holiday home'. The wife, a cheerful, pretty woman, said it would be lovely if we could all meet and perhaps we could give them some advice? About finding a holiday home, I supposed. And I thought of the damp house down the track. Instantly. After all, a pleasant middle-class family with two young girls would be a great deal more attractive than a housing estate of seven or eight villas plus swimming pools. They came up the hill, saw the house, fell instantly in rapturous love with it. Words like 'possibilities', 'peace', 'fantastic views', 'extensions' and so on flew about the place like bats at sundown. They were hooked – I was uncertain, not convinced that I had done quite the right thing. After all, it did mean neighbours, even if it was only for a few weeks in the year when the girls were on holiday from school. And what would Jean-Claude say? He was furious. At first. There was the usual breast-beating about 'family heritage and five hundred years', and then, when I said that the people who wanted the place were a very good family, careful and loving, who would lavish care and taste on the house and restore the olives and the vineyard because money seemed not to be a problem, he became a little more interested and said that he hoped I had not mentioned the price he had offered the property to me for? I assured him that I had not. And I had not. I wasn't such an idiot as that. *I* had the special price for the simple reason that I had been given the year's option on the property before Jean-Claude had come to realize that money could buy him Hondas and henna, or an Indian ashram.

Anyway, after long and contentious telephone calls from London the pleasant family I hardly knew succumbed to Jean-Claude and his lawyers and paid him a sum *far* in excess of the original £18,000 I had been asked for, and possibly in excess of the price I had had to pay for Le Pigeonnier. Jean-Claude really didn't want to sell. He was perfectly happy as things were, but when he heard that the head of the jolly little English family was quite determined to own the damp house and, added to which, would never countenance the word 'No' under any circumstances, he gave in and for this, frankly, bloated amount sold the house on the marsh.

Thus I was saved from a huge building-site and got neighbours instead. It worked out pretty well eventually, although I had terrible feelings of guilt and doubt when the drainage diggers started 'next door', and received a shattering blow when they began to prune the three hundred olives.

The hillside beyond my apple trees resembled a John Nash painting or, more explicitly, Passchendaele. It was to look like this for at least two years. And, what was perhaps sadder, was the fact that one morning, on my usual promenade about my land with the dogs, sorting out the jobs to be done in the day, I saw, to my consternation, a vivid crimson slash of paint on a big stone. Bright as a huge gout of blood, the vicious strokes of crimson marked every stone on every terrace from the top road right down the length of my land to the bottom road. Jean-Claude had, quite properly I suppose, marked out the boundary. I found that it was also marked with equal ferocity on the boundary between the de Beauvallons' land on the east. So now we knew where we all belonged.

In time Monsieur Rémy, at my urgent request, erected a long chestnut paling fence down the length of the west boundary, cutting me off from the damp house. It was less intrusive than chain link, and one day, talking with Madame de Beauvallon over sherry in the Long Room, I learned that her son-in-law was about to build a house on her land adjoining mine. Nothing I could do.

They had owned the place, like Jean-Claude, for centuries, it was theirs to do with as they wished. Madame de Beauvallon, because she spoke such good English, was sent to break the unwelcome news. The house, she said, would be very sympathetic, we were above the site so we would never see it, and they would place it so that all the windows faced away from Le Pigeonnier in any case, to take advantage of the view. She was sure we would all get on very well together, and they would plant a great many trees to shelter my privacy. It was all extremely generous and understanding. Only Titty-Brown Hill would suffer. It would be isolated no longer. 'Outside' was closing in.

I always used to prune the big fig tree down by the gates on the morning of Christmas Eve. I can't think at this moment exactly why. Had mournful Monsieur Danté told me, perhaps? He was, when he chose to speak at all, well informed about local agricultural tips. Or perhaps I simply did it out of ignorance? I had never had a fig tree in my life before, until I came to Le Pigeonnier, so it is quite possible that sheer enthusiastic ignorance guided my cutters to the bare branches. The tree was enormous, and hung over the track scratching the paint-work off cars and knocking the postman, on one memorable occasion, off his yellow Mobylette. Christmas time was usually golden and warm. We ate out on the terrace sometimes, always drank our kir royale outside, admired the early marigolds and anemones, rejoiced at the sharp green thrusts of the wild daffodils in the sere grass under the pomegranate, and knew that they were the warning signs alerting us to the fact that the sap was rising and would be surging through the trunks of the big vines on the metal cage above one's head which sheltered the terrace. But that chore, the pruning of the vine down to the last three buds on each branch, had to be done on a certain day at the beginning of February, before the sap had fully risen. It was a brutal business as, armed with monstrously sharp clippers and secateurs, one staggered about dragging ladders and steps, cutting out the prodigal growth of the past year.

The bonfires raged, in a controlled state because of the fire risk, for days. They had to be doused every evening at the end of work with endless cans of water from the well. You can say that it was a remarkable, and exhausting, keep fit class which exercised every muscle you ever had and a good number you didn't know you possessed. It also sweated off pounds in weight. Healthy you would be, exhausted you would be, but proud you would be when the first grey buds blushed pink, burst, and opened tiny green hands to welcome the early spring sunlight. Not an excess length in sight, trim, tied in, perfect; ready to cover the terrace once again and hang its clusters of plump muscat grapes, palest green, translucent as polished jade. They, of course, would bring the vicious *frolon* (hornet) and the lithe, big-eared, yellow-breasted vine rat, which went scampering across the dense growth of leaves and branches, scattering guests in anxious disarray. They were careless creatures and defecated, or urinated, gleefully at will. Hence people's understandable confusion, although, really, few ever received a direct hit. However, that was all to come later, long after Christmas and the cruellest part of the year up on the hill, the vicious January and February. Christmas in France is very unlike the five to six day glut which we seem to endure in England. It only really lasts for a day and a half: Christmas Eve and Christmas Day (even on Christmas Day the bars and bakers are still open). That desperate feeling of having to hoard enough food and drink for almost a week of siege never takes place. Trains run, buses move about. It is merely the celebration of the birth of Christ, and that is celebrated lavishly on Christmas Eve at Midnight Mass.

When they were retired and living in a little flat in the valley, I usually had a tea-party for Marie and Henri, up on the hill, after the fig-pruning. They had no family and no living relatives. Marie would dress up in her best, usually a blue angora or cashmere sweater from Marks and Sparks, thick stockings concealing elastic ones, good white shoes and handbag, and the furious red slash of lipstick. She had her hair 'done': tight, white curls, gently tinted palest lavender. Henri was stuffed, not always comfortably, into a tweed jacket and heavy brogues and sweated. We had Jackson's tea, toast, Gentleman's Relish, Dundee cake, Fox's Ascot biscuits and, if I could make the effort after burning the fig cuttings and laying up the table, cucumber sandwiches. It had to be, at Marie's insistence, a real English tea. There was no point in making the journey up the hill otherwise.

After tea, round the fire, we exchanged presents with little cries of surprise and pleasure, as if we had none of us expected to receive any. The dogs were lavished with love, chewed up the wrapping-paper and string, and everything ended, rather thankfully, with a glass of port. Considered to be correct, heart-warming, rather dashing *and* festive.

Those were the quiet Christmases. Some were busier and, frankly, more fun, especially if the family arrived from England. A bigger adventure, a larger deal for which to cater. But we never had turkey and plum pudding and that stuff. Never saw a cracker or, even worse, a Christmas tree or decorations, which seemed always inappropriate in the sun. Ice clinking in long glasses, melting in the champagne bucket. Bees zooming into the orange and lemon trees heavy with almost sickly scent. Lunch, traditionally, was *boudin blanc*, mashed potato, Brussels sprouts, a giant trifle and a cheese board with fresh fruit. With copious libations of wine. Supper came after Midnight Mass (if one went), with a snack of smoked salmon and hot toast or Brittany oysters before making the journey through the dark, twisting lanes to town and the twelfth-century cathedral.

The bells summonsed us over the hills and little valleys, across the groves and fields. Turning the last corner before climbing up to the town, the cathedral suddenly burst upon the astonished eye lit all over, glowing amber and gold, standing high on the ramparts like an enormous galleon, except galleons don't have towers and belfries; but it *had* a sailing splendour about it. Inside the great doors, the huge stone pillars soared into the shadowy vault of the roof with a faded coat of arms painted on to the planked ceiling. The scent of incense, of hundreds of years of incense, loitered and meandered about, mixing with the fatty smell of melting tallow, as a thousand candles guttered and glittered in the draught, throwing dancing shadows across the rough stone walls, all gold and silver. Honey-light on the limestone pillars, cracked and gouged here and there from a distant, devastating fire which had almost once destroyed the cathedral.

The place was animated by excited chatter, the clatter and scrape of wooden chairs and pews, the patter and clacking of feet, the smothered laughter of sniggering choir boys, the sonorous organ, the flushed expectant faces, the new suits and best coats, the smart hats with little veils, the modest handkerchiefs over modest hair, the dark clothes of the peasants, the sparkier ones of the shop-keepers, the nodding lilies, tuberoses and carnations on the high altar, the soaring Christ, arms outspread, the tall candles, the great oil paintings in elaborate frames, all gilt and curly stucco, glowing from the side walls and the distant little private chapels. There was altogether a jolly, festive air, a feeling of 'coming together', of joining. Some people had journeyed for miles through the hills, and families greeted each other with low calls of pleasure and recognition, bobbing and smiling, the children smothered in nylon net and giant white plastic lace bows, the boys in bow ties and oiled hair. All one's friends were there; discreet little nods and waves across the wooden pews identified us:

Madame Bruna and Monsieur Rémy, Madame Pasquini, Florette Ranchett and her disagreeable husband in a sharp grey suit, the Meils flashing silver smiles, the de Beauvallon family in the large family pew, boxed in as befitted the ancient gentry, the bakers, the vet, Dr Santori, the girls from the check-out at Monoprix, the manager of Casino with his sparkling wife a-glitter, rhinestones and faux pearls at wrist and neck, and the very old with sticks, crutches and medals, bent backs and shaking heads. All life was present to celebrate the birth of the Christ child and to worship at his giant crèche, ablaze with fairy lights and worshipping angels, by the great doors.

I enjoyed Christmas Mass very much. The sheer theatricality of it all gave me enormous pleasure. There was absolutely no sense of religion about it as far as I was concerned: the war had put paid to the last embers I might have concealed somewhere deep within. Picking bombing-targets, being responsible for the death of, sometimes, hundreds of people (people just like these at the crèche and before the high altar), blundering into the unspeakable agony of Belsen, watching bulldozers shovel bloodied carnage into open graves, all that and more put paid to religion for me. I went to enjoy the lights, scents and music, in much the same way that I would have attended a village fair: for the excitement, the lights, the fun.

Forwood, from a staunchly Protestant family background, had faint interest in any part of the proceedings (dismissed amusedly as 'popery'), but came along because he could drive and I could not and it would be impolite to the guests who had come for a 'real French Christmas' not to. So they got it, and driving home through the frosted lanes, the stars bright in the southern sky, the hoar heavy in the hollows, embalming grasses and the few remaining leaves on the brambles in white velvet, the crackle of ice on the puddles and the thought of the big iron stove in the Long Room glowing with embers and a big olive log (from the pruning), sighing and flickering across the rough stone walls kept everyone in a joyous mood; to the extent that everyone sang what they could remember of 'Silent Night' in various keys and banished, for a time, its banality. This is how it *should* have sounded. Not as it usually did, droning out as muzak in Monoprix.

Supper at the long walnut table: a giant golden *feuilleté de jambon*, hot from the oven; bowls of salads – tomato, potato, early lettuce, spring onions; cheeses in quantity, if only to prove to the disbelieving British that not *all* French cheeses were Camembert simply because they were round; baguettes crisp, cracked and packed with Normandy butter; wine in brimming goblets. Candles flaring and cries of delight at the arrival of the *bûche de Noël*, a huge 'log' of chocolate, coffee, sugar and sponge-cake, spiked with a robin or two and filled with promises of good luck.

It was all enormous pleasure. The house was bathed in laughter, music and the chink and scraping of plates as Lady and Madame Bruna cleared, set, and chattered and beamed away into the kitchen. By the time we had all finished and the last car had wavered a little uncertainly down the track into the starry, frosty night, one sort of Christmas was finally over, but the ancient house had been alive again with life and happiness. However, it is really true to say, remembering it as now I do, that the best Christmases were really those when the day was just an ordinary day . . . not *quite* ordinary. I remember I always put on a clean shirt, changed my jeans, and there were rather more flowers than I usually allowed myself to buy, anemones in big rough pots, perhaps an azalea from someone, an old Spode footbath planted, ages before, with paper whites and hyacinths. I would bring in the logs at dusk, just as the day faded to night above the mountains, and lights sprang up in the valley and the wind rose. But *ordinary*. That's really what happened every winter evening for a great many years. No one came to feast or for Mass, the dogs slumped snoring before the blazing Godin stove, wide open in vermilion light, Forwood in his chair reading or working at his journal, which he kept faithfully every day. I'd be in my chair scratching away at a drawing for a new book or, more often, correcting and redrafting the work I had done that day in the olive-store office, or studio. Faint on the wind, thin and tinny, the church at Saint-Sulpice clanging the halves and the hour.

It was perhaps pretty dull, although it never occurred to me that it was. I was far too happy to have renounced the cinema, discovered that perhaps I could write a little, which at least paid for some of the bounty with which I was surrounded. It was a very good feeling and even the surprise telephone call, perhaps from some friend in a distant land (I remember Kathleen Tynan once calling from Ontario to send messages of love and bridge the distances) or the family in Sussex, made the day less 'ordinary', but then it is so easy to take security and peace for granted: to accept them, because they have become quite familiar, as just normal. Expected, usual.

I would know, sitting there with my pen, exactly what the remaining hours of that evening would bring: a supper of a sort, a few amber whiskies, shoving the reluctant dogs out for their final pee before bed, and then stoking the stove for the morning, laying up the tea trays, closing the last of the shutters, turning keys, winding up the old wall-clock . . . perfectly normal, routine behaviour stemming from security and contentment.

It never even remotely occurred to me then that all this could be transient, and that as with Bella the cypress tree I had planted with such care and lost years before, this existence was planted above a giant rock buried deep below, and that the 'roots' would one day strike the rock and that the withering would commence. Never once did I really think of that.

I do now.

Chapter 6

After about eight years or so I got bored with all the chairs and fat sofas in the Long Room and wondered, idly at first and then with growing interest, if I should try to have them re-covered. They were fitted and comfortable in coarse blue linen which I once had considered to be suitable for a white-washed room in a seventeenth-century converted shepherd's house. But after eight years the cornflower blue seemed to fade to a kind of drab blotting-paper haze and looked depressing. Previously the chairs and things had been assembled together in this one long room, all of fifty-six feet long, from many different rooms in the house in England. Thus there were bits of Colefax and Fowler chintz, stripes from somewhere else, and things in tight buttoned velvets. All hideously unsuitable and reminiscent of a furniture display at the Old Times Furnishing Company. And shabby. So into the blue they were buttoned, stitched and frilled, at great cost. Now, I felt, they had to be discarded. The Long Room must be lighter, integrated.

Sitting hunched in the empty fireplace, a glass of beer in my hand, a cigarette hanging from earth-stained fingers, I pondered the ungainly clutter before me. Forwood came down from somewhere above with a clatter and panting of dogs at his heels, went down to the bar cupboard to mix his Bloody Mary. It was, I realized, noon exactly. I was uncertain of the day or the date. They seemed to melt into timelessness on the hill, unless a dentist, lawyer, bank, barber beckoned.

'What's up? Is this the *last* tin of tomato juice, for God's sake?'

'More in the cellar. I got it yesterday.'

'What are you doing?'

'I'm just thinking.'

'You are the only person in the world I know who can imbue the word "thinking" with chilling terror.'

'Well, the chairs and settees. They really are tatty now. Shabby. Tired . . . And it'll soon be summer and the guests will be upon us . . .'

'So?'

'We ought to have everything recovered. In white.'

'*White!* With two dogs and wellingtons and mud everywhere!'

'I suppose it would cost the earth to do?'

'The earth.'

He came slowly up through the middle room holding his glass with care. 'I knew I should be alarmed when you said "thinking". Where do you suppose the money is coming from? And white . . . Six armchairs and one, two, *three* sofas. Christ!'

'Well, sell one of the pictures. We never see them, sitting wrapped up in the vaults at Lloyds in Cannes. Now do we? Too valuable to have on the walls, so there they lie, in brown paper and Sellotape. They cost money to store too . . . Better to have something to look at for the price I pay in storage.'

'The pictures are supposed to be your "insurance" against disaster.'

'Well, it *is* a sort of disaster. Living in this awful room. Drab, used, mucky.'

Forwood sat in one of the offending chairs, sipped his drink. 'How will you go about selling them? Any idea?'

When confronted by difficult questions I rather try to gain

thinking-time. So I wandered down to the bar, opened up another beer. 'Monte Carlo. That's what I'll do . . .'

'Monte Carlo what?'

'Sotheby's, Christie's. Lots of important dealers down there. Good market; they all have representatives in that hideous little place. All vastly rich, catering for *vastly* rich people.' I joined the small tableau of Forwood flanked by his dogs.

'What do you have in mind to sell? The Ben Nicholson? Or the Egon Schiele? You'd be mad if you did. They are neither of them "fashionable" at the moment. Wait a little longer. You bought them as an investment, so wait until the time is right. Advice offered. Do as you see fit. Not my pictures.'

'I'd try for the Schiele, I think. I don't like it much. I think it might sell pretty well down here. The Nicholson is very English; they don't even know who he is in France. Not popular at any rate. And I feel it might be wiser to sit on that for a while. It cost enough; it should be an investment. But the Egon Schiele could go. I think it might make enough to cover all these . . .'

'I have doubts,' Forwood said. 'Your Schiele is about the only "respectable" one he ever drew; painted, whatever. Monte Carlo would far prefer the erotic open-legged ones. Not enough sexuality in yours. No gaunt depravity . . .'

'I think it very beautiful. *Reclining Woman.* It came from the Marlborough Galleries: they don't make mistakes.'

'*You* may be. Selling too soon. Anyway, please yourself. You usually do. But take my advice about the Nicholson. One day it'll be worth a lot. Keep it.' He got up and went out on to the terrace, stood in the brilliant spring sunlight. 'The cherry trees are pink with bud. I'll have to get down to the ants soon.'

He had an obsession about the little *fourmis d'Argentine*, millions of which swarmed up and down and over the vine, the cherries, the citrus trees in undulating black ropes, and which (it was said by Monsieur Rémy) had arrived in the area at the beginning of the century in the luggage of some idiot Brazilian. (French logic again.) They had, within a very few years, spread up from the coast at Nice and almost destroyed the entire orange and lemon crops, the vineyards and the fruit in the area. The olives, for some reason, had been more or less spared. Forwood's battle against the insects was harsh, unending and passionate.

But I, once I had an idea in my mind, would not be deflected – an all white Long Room: chairs, sofas trim and clean on the highly polished tile and brick floors on which Lady spent hours with her electric buffer and which presently shone conker-brown in the early sunlight. White it should be. Occupied with my overwhelming picture of glittering perfection to come, I paid scant attention to the *fourmis d'Argentine*. A pity, as it turned out.

Various establishments were contacted in Monte Carlo; some even in Geneva. It all took some time and a lot of telephoning, which, by now, had become a little easier. No longer did one have to spell the exchanges phonetically: amazingly we were on automatic by this time and simply dialled numbers.

Eventually three gentlemen were summonsed from three hugely respectable firms and arrived at Le Pigeonnier for the, *apparent*, purpose of valuing its entire contents. For insurance. This way, I reckoned, they'd all get a look at the Schiele and the Nicholson without undue pressure and would give me an idea of their worth. Forwood viewed the whole thing with lurking suspicion: he didn't reckon that the contents of the whole house amounted to much more than a few thousand, most of it, if not all, having been gathered together from auctions, junk shops and modest antique shops in the Home Counties area. I had an eclectic collection of what he called 'bogus old masters', some quite good modern works and one or two, like the ones I was presently considering flogging off for yards of heavy white cotton, bought mainly as safe investments. But there really was nothing there to excite any smooth young gentleman from long-established houses. I'd be ridiculed he felt. Wisely.

The first gentleman to arrive bounced slowly and unhappily up the rough track in a white Mercedes, terror-stricken that his springs would bust. They didn't, and he drew up at the *porte d'entrée* in a frantically apprehensive state, only considering his journey back *down* the track.

'My God! How did you find this place? By helicopter? It has taken me nearly *two hours*! I took the wrong turning after the *autoroute* . . .' He calmed down with a glass of sherry (he refused anything stronger until he had done his survey) and, armed with a biro and a pad, went off alone, as he wished, and combed the house. I showed him where to go and told him to holler if he needed explanations. He didn't bother.

After about two hours he came down on to the terrace, greeted effusively by the dogs, which clearly alarmed him – rabies and the fear that they might soil his elegant Féraud suit. Forwood, strapped into the vast cylinder of ant poison, straw hat on his head, spray-gun in hand, called 'Good morning' and I offered a glass of chilled champagne, left over from Christmas or something. He declined but accepted a Perrier and sat, gingerly, in a chair with his pad and biro.

He wore one of those smug, half smiling expressions which indicated clearly that only he knew that he farted honey. I disliked him instantly, for I knew that his pad contained nothing of any interest to him or, for that matter, myself. He had obviously been quietly amused by my English presumption that I was Randolph Hearst or even a minor Paul Getty. However, he retained basic good manners, and instead of just suggesting that I dynamite the house and contents instantly and claim some form of modest compensation, he spoke kindly of a 'pleasing' Georgian table in the top little bedroom, an 'attractive', but 'heavily restored' Carolean chair, a not 'important' but 'amusing' buffet and so on and so on. I was wearying of the safe platitudes which accompany rejection. I asked boldly about my two investments and he dismissed the Schiele as 'interesting but unfashionable' and the Ben Nicholson as 'unknown English, twentieth century. Abstract, but rather naive.' I was absolutely delighted watching him wince his Mercedes down the track to the coast, irritated greatly by Forwood's quiet smile pumping up the ant-cylinder, and angered by my own stupidity in asking him.

However, he was only one of the three, and over the next weeks they arrived. One behaved precisely in the same manner, drank only a large vodka-tonic, dismissed both paintings with a sad smile and drove away in a BMW; and the third (and last) was a plump, pink young man with impeccable English and slightly exaggerated English suiting, weskits and a nipped-in hacking jacket and brogues, who dismissed the contents of the house as 'very pleasant things to live with' and of no intrinsic value, but flipped, in a very controlled manner, for the Schiele. Like the others he was fairly dismissive of the Ben Nicholson but did admit that he *had* heard of him. He had worked for two years in London with a major auction house. I liked him instantly. The champagne was reoffered and this time accepted and even Forwood joined us with his Bloody Mary and oil-stained overalls, wreathed in a heavy odour of ant poison.

Having lived in England for two years, Theo (his name) was accustomed to eccentricity. He had also seen me in some movies and was as silly as all the others who were suddenly confronted by a familiar figure of normal height instead of one in Cinemascope or Panavision. We talked easily and comfortably. Schiele, he knew, was unfashionable at the moment, but his time was coming and he knew 'a gentleman in Geneva' who could be very interested. He asked permission to take it away with him when he left? To 'offer it up', so to speak?

I agreed. Forwood looked acutely alarmed but said nothing – after all it was *my* picture – and Theo eventually bounced cheerfully down the track in his shooting brake, the Schiele repacked in its brown paper and Sellotape, and, for this important voyage, wrapped up in a good linen sheet. He promised to write, or call, as soon as he had any news. Forwood pointed out, pleasantly enough, that he thought this was most unlikely. 'You have just let the chap cart the thing away. You don't really know if he is who he says he is. If he works for whom he says . . . Total, idiot trust! Sometimes I do wonder for your sanity. After over thirty years of your company I begin to seriously consider you to be barmy.' The ant poison was strapped on and he strode off with his spray-gun held high, the dogs at his heels.

But some months later, when we sat surrounded by splendid white chairs and sofas tightly covered in expensive

Cogolin cotton, he nodded wisely and almost claimed it all as his idea. Anyway, he conceded, it *was* better to look at the splendour of the sparkling Long Room than at Egon Schiele's *Reclining Woman* wrapped up in a vault. Theo had managed to get me a glorious five-figure sum from his contact in Geneva, and in spite of his own commission and the French tax (less venal by far than the British), I still had enough to spend as I had never done since arriving in France. I even agreed, albeit reluctantly, to a tiny Sony TV set, which was hidden on the lower shelf of one of the bookcases so that Forwood could watch Yvonne Printemps, Josephine Baker, Jean Gabin, Mistinguette and others in the old black and white films which flickered about on Sunday. It was only about ten inches by eight, so it didn't really show, and I never watched it anyway. Beds were bought for the guest room, new chintzes brought roses-and-lilac-on-trellis to the lives of the *invités*, a new oven and rotisserie arrived, and more cypress trees were stuck across the land, and, at some expense, Next Door were completely hidden from sight by a long line of flourishing golden bamboo which marched down the length of the boundary fence and caused faint, but protesting, whimpers that it was 'unsuitable' for the landscape and cut off their view of something or other. But it, and I, prevailed. And in time (a couple of years) a veritable jungle, ready to hide lurking tigers, raced down the chestnut paling fence under the apple trees. I was secured in my acres.

A pretty fatuous thing to observe: no one, and nothing, is ever secure.

By secure, in this instance, I of course really mean 'safe and for ever', which is what I have, like the rest of mankind, believed from my earliest days to be perfectly possible. Even expected. *And in the end they lived happily ever after.*

So I was taught. And what does 'ever after' mean? Anyway, this childish notion was really soundly abused each and every time it dared to thread its way into my young, and tumultuous, thoughts. I learned very early on in my life that nothing was for ever; so I should have been aware of disillusion in early middle age. But, somehow, we try to obliterate early warnings and go cantering along hopefully, idiotically.

I can remember, so vividly, brilliant summer mornings when we went down to the beach at Deauville or Trouville. The beaches there always seemed to be so much wider than the beaches in England. The sea lay like a glittering silver sheet far, far away across the hard rippled sand. The sky arched above transparently blue, with lazy chalk marks scrawling little clouds so that they could drift gently across the sun. I remember bare feet splashing through the little pools of left-over sea among the ridged sand, the salt smell of the long strands of bladderwrack drifted in from a rockier part of the coast and curled now like bits of brown bobble-edged ribbons; remember scrabbling in the heavy damp sand with a little red spade to start the foundations of what would be the fort. Moats were dug, walls patted into shape, towers and turrets built, cemented with water carried from the distant sea in a red and blue pail, the water slopping down the bucket sides and bare brown legs. The sea, frilled all along the immense length of the beach, flapped softly in the sunlight, sparkling, sighing, winking in the high morning light. Shells were sought along its crystal edge: razor shells, tiny pink ones, like a baby's fingernails, shards of blue mussel and, most prized of all, limpet shells with their conical tops – these were to cap the turrets, so four, at least, were essential. They crowned the huge efforts of the morning. A morning obliterated completely by achievement or the desire for achievement.

The building of the fort occupied one so completely that even food and drink were taken in one sand-encrusted hand while the other shaped the crenellations and loopholes of the battlements, working against time. The turning of the tide. Sitting back on one's heels, surveying the work accomplished, the moat, the drawbridge, the limpet-capped towers, the arches and ramps drying hard in the midday sun, one relished work well done and quite forgot its impermanence until, suddenly looking up, the tiny little seabirds which had seemed to look like sparrows bobbing and teetering along the sea rim miles away, were no longer sparrows and no longer miles away. They were at arm's length and they were gulls. Black, gold and bold of eye, hooked of beak, orange legs striding arrogantly, plumage taut and silky. They were the unwelcome heralds of coming destruction. The limpid edge of the sea was starting to nudge, run, trickle, dribble and spill over one's feet, into the moat, swirling in lacy wavelets round the shell-decked walls, sparkling and glinting as it seeped beneath the towers, crumbled the ramp to the arched drawbridge. Sighs of despair from children's throats, the deadly call from the grown-ups! '*The tide has turned! Be sharp now. Come along, come along . . .*'

Then the hopeless droop of shoulder, the shrug of helplessness, sanded hands hanging limp with despair while the moat filled with swirling water, turrets began to dribble down, sag and spill, limpet shells tumbling, walls bulging, flopping with whispering splashes into the deepening water hurrying away the brown-bobbled ribbons into the dancing distance. The fort slowly dissolved before one's eyes. The inevitable was mutely accepted. The 'work done' was obliterated in the scream and wheel of gulls.

Remembering that instance, how odd it is that one is not prepared for the 'dissolving of the fort' one has constructed with such care in later life. But we do not learn. We always believe that it'll be all right for us. That *our* fort will stand, the tide will never turn. But, of course, it does.

The years on the hill were partially measured for me by the growing-up of Monsieur Rémy's children. Marie-Thérèse, in the early days of the washing machine, was a plump mewling creature in a push-chair, draped with broderie anglaise frills. Her brother, Christian, was a bit older and sometimes came with his father to throw stones at the goldfish in the pond, a gleeful, curly-haired child. One day Marie-Thérèse was five, then ten, then twenty and then in love and then married, and Madame Bruna was, to her hysterical delight, a grandmother.

Christian, ahead of his sister by a couple of years, first caught tadpoles, then beat the olives, then drove the battered truck, was apprenticed to a nursery gardener, and smoked shag-filled cigarettes which he rolled himself. His presence in the house lingered in every nook and cranny, even in the upholstery of the white chairs and sofas, for days. But he was a splendid worker so that had to be set aside . . . Anyway, he was 'family'.

Marie-Thérèse married Gilles, a football fanatic from Aix who drove long-distance trucks, the Paris–Nice–Brussels route. The wedding was in the village church on a brilliant Saturday afternoon in March. Marie-Thérèse was radiant in a gigantic crinoline, tiara and floating veil, clutching a bouquet, tottering in high-heeled silver shoes; Madame Bruna tearful in rustly grey nylon taffeta, a feathered confection sitting high on her bright henna'd hair, lace gloves on hard-worked hands; Monsieur Rémy bulging in a too-tight suit, collar and an alarming geometric tie, a giant spray of carnation and fern on his chest. Dr Poteau was there with his one-armed, pretty wife. Florette Ranchett, Madame Pasquini, even Monsieur Danté had come, stooped in a crumpled blue suit and waistcoat, white carnation and drooping white moustache. Christian was Gilles's best man and supporter. Truck driver or not, he was sweating with terror beside his laughing, sparkling bride. The family sat together in a close huddle, heads bowed; we, the *invités*, sat discreetly at the back. Children ran around playing tag, a small dog ran in, looked around, ran out again. An organ soared and a full girls' choir rang lightly and cheerfully from a tape, hired for the occasion, crackling and reverberating through a pair of speakers rigged high above the altar by Christian.

Afterwards there were kisses all round in the car park, and everyone clambered into cars and trucks and drove off to the wedding breakfast at the Lion d'Or in town.

'When you go away to England next time,' said Marie-Thérèse, '*I* can come and look after your house. We'll need the money. I'm going to have a baby.'

Leaving the house for any length of time was always something to be dreaded. Usually it was for a film, in order to make some money, or, latterly, to promote a book, as I now had started to write seriously rather than act. Every year, while my parents were still alive, I went back to England for family reunions, which were fun and usually of short duration.

Duties done, touching base with friends again, buying books for the long winter haul on the hill (English books were hard to get outside Paris: Cannes and Nice had bookshops but they usually sold only paperback thrillers or guide books), stocking up with Marmite, face flannels (unknown in France) and pudding bowls (equally unknown) and the hard rubber balls for the dogs, the return journey was made on the earliest flight out. With relief.

Someone who lived in a nearby village once told me that, when he and his wife had to leave for the UK, he would be in such distress the night before his departure that he would go weeping among his olive trees and embrace them passionately, promising to return as quickly as possible. I didn't quite go to those lengths, but I fully understood his feelings. He was Irish, of course, which made him more emotional and volatile, but I could well imagine behaving in that manner. If pushed. Instead, I quietly touched a tree here and there, murmuring that I wouldn't be away for long, wasn't deserting them again as they had been before, and that I'd be back. Potty, I suppose. But that was how things were. Mind you, I did have four hundred trees to my local friend's dozen, so it would have posed quite a problem to salute each and every one. Some, in any case, were vast in girth, unembraceable. One, indeed, was so old and so huge that it had split into five separate trees. It was reckoned to be well over eight hundred years old and was always counted as a single tree because the five 'splits' all grew from the same enormous root which was buried deep in the tussocky grass when it wasn't sneaking down in arm-thick roots through the big stones of the terrace wall above which it stood. I remember Glenda Jackson standing in among the five 'trees' struck silent by the majesty of something so old and still living. 'It was here before Elizabeth! Before Columbus! Perhaps before the *Conqueror* . . .'

And, indeed, if carbon dating is true, so it was. There was one near Menton which was considered to be over a thousand years old. I never saw it, but there were lots of postcards to prove it was a very aged thing. Olive trees, I reckon, are lucky.

Making a film usually meant a three-month absence and then my sister Elizabeth and her family came out to take over. Her husband, George, was a tree surgeon and landscape gardener, so he was in his element on the hill and the trees were cherished. So that was all right. For shorter absences, like book promotions, which only took about a week or ten days, Marie-Thérèse and Gilles and their abominably spoiled baby came instead. The house was rapidly filled with plastic toys, trucks and stuffed dolls, boxes of baby food, plates and dishes covered in bunnies and badgers, piles of disposable nappies and ropes of coloured plastic beads and baubles. The air was filled with the odour of cheap talcum powder, regurgitated milk and mashed carrot. Gilles also smoked shag and that drifted about and caught in the throat. The dogs slunk through the fug, choking, with half-closed eyes of resentment; but Marie-Thérèse loved them dearly (after all, she had grown up with them), and only hit them savagely when they attacked her wretched child. Which was not often, but did, on occasion, occur in a gentle sort of way: a 'snap' rather than a 'rending'. Anyway, departure from them all was hastened. Even the airport seemed less frantic. Certainly less smelly.

This is how it was for some time, at least until Marie-Thérèse's child could stagger about on its own and chuck the Picasso ashtrays into the fireplace. It was very gradual, the change, when it came. Almost imperceptible.

Forwood had a slight ache one day in his foot. Nothing much: just an ache and slightly irritating. It went on for a week or two.

'You tripped up again today. In the market. Is your foot playing up?' We were unloading the car in the garage behind the house.

'A bit. Nothing really, I must have wrenched it. Can you cope with the Codec bag? I'll open the kitchen door.'

I dumped the stuff in the kitchen and went up to my office, back to the typewriter, to round off a paragraph which was working out pretty well. I'd sorted out a finishing line driving into town.

But it wasn't 'nothing really'. Poteau, who had by this time retired but kept a 'friendly and caring eye' on us, said that it was 'just a touch of Parkinson's. There is a pill which will control it.'

Well, there is no such thing as 'just a *touch* of Parkinson's'. Even I knew that. But I kept silent. However, a signal light had gone on in my mind. Red for Alert. Life just moved on as if nothing had slipped in to change things. Although I knew, and I suppose Forwood knew, that something had. The tide had changed far across the sands: I don't know which of us really realized this at the time. We neither of us discussed the situation.

What we did discuss, however, was the arrival of the new Socialist government in France, who, among many other changes, made it illegal to employ unregistered aliens. No more 'moonlighting', no more Plum-Bum and Fraj; Monsieur Rémy was reduced to picking up only registered workers when and where he needed them and only for specific jobs. No longer did I have a more or less permanent gang to help on the land. It was possible to engage those refugees from Sousse, Tunis and other lost colonies only if they had their 'papers'. So that was that.

We were now left with the terraces and the mowing, the harvest and the stone-walling, all to do on our own. I was sixty-one, Forwood five years older and slowly finding that 'a touch of Parkinson's' was exhausting. He was not able to do as much on the land as he had before. This irritated him greatly. Helplessly he would sit on the terrace and watch the ants race up and down the vines which he had once so savagely sprayed, no longer able now to carry the weighty cylinder of the poison on his back, nor to stride, as once he had done, up and down the steep terraces with the German giants. He had to content himself with quietly raking up the tall grasses which I had had to cut, inexpertly: I was not as good with the heavy machines as he had been. Gradually, very gradually, terraces were regretfully abandoned. I concentrated on the ones immediately round the house, and he cut long, elegant, green pathways through the rest. It was a bitter compromise, but all life had quietly become a series of compromises.

For the time being driving the car was no great problem – he still had perfect control of that – but one day, sitting beside him on the way back from market, I noticed, with that dull stab of fear, that a slim trickle of saliva had run down his chin. He felt it later, brushed it off, but it was to remain part of his life from now on. A part of 'just a touch'.

Florette Ranchett one day called me into the store-room behind the Mini Market, and, among crates of mineral water, beer, stacked tins of beans, peas, pineapple, and great avalanches of kitchen paper and washing powders, told me that a new young doctor had arrived in the village. She was certain I would be glad to know that. Didn't say why, but we both understood exactly what was implied.

'He's taken rooms, for his *bureau*, just up the hill. The tall house with the blue shutters. It's been empty for years, but Monsieur the Maire, my husband, is having it restored. We *need* a doctor in the village. It is developing so quickly.'

Patrick was young, very bright (it would appear), spoke excellent English, and was married to a very pretty wife, Solange. Certainly Forwood had a mild form of Parkinson's, and a hernia which was caused by wrenching about with the big mowers, but apart from those things all was well. For a time anyway. And we all settled down as friends as well as doctor and patients, for I joined in too: with no Poteau now to ease the tensions of life, one was in need of a sympathetic ear.

Patrick was mad about jazz, and pop, and knew and followed all the groups with the passion of a 'groupie'. Together he and Solange raced off to any of the huge pop concerts which exploded all along the coast during the summer; so getting ill had to be rather 'arranged', although he did hold his morning surgery in the new *bureau* in the village.

For a while no one went near him. He was new, young, a stranger from the north. The older people were afraid of him, the younger men didn't want their wives examined by a young, and handsome, doctor, the women didn't trust him with their children because, as Madame Pasquini said, he 'is a child himself! Hardly out of school! He has no experience of life! How can he be a *doctor*?'

So life was pretty dull at first, and the pop concerts were a great relief to him and filled in his time. However, after two terrible traffic accidents at the crossroads in the village, which he attended, and at which he was seen to be extremely capable and tough, there was a slight easing of tension, and when Florette Ranchett's aged mother was suddenly taken desperately ill with a twisted hernia, after lugging sacks of potatoes about, she summonsed Patrick. The only other doctor was six kilometres away, her mother was in agony, so Patrick it was. And that gesture of Florette Ranchett saved both her mother and Patrick. He coped perfectly, the old lady made an exemplary recovery. He had been efficient, impressive, knew all the top surgeons at the Clinique des Magnolias in town, and there was no longer any doubt in the village that he was, in fact, '*un vrai!*' A real doctor. He was almost swamped with patients from then on; bought a bright red car and raced about the countryside bringing relief to numbers of ailing farmers and their families, scattering prescriptions about like confetti, a normal occurrence in France where six bottles of different pills, or suppositories, are usually recommended for tennis elbow. It is all very comforting. And the Government pays for it anyway. So . . .

My office up in the olive store became a sort of refuge: now that I was writing seriously, or anyway seriously for myself, I was faced with the anxiety of deadlines and a slightly impatient publisher who wanted everything as 'soon as can be managed'. Also, I became greatly involved with my characters, which was right and proper – after all, I had invented them – and spent hours staring, apparently, into space but in fact trying to work out the twists and turns of ever more complicated plots and patterns of construction. Time spent like this melted away, but I could hear, at all times, the muted roar of the mower (the lighter one) while Forwood was cutting his elegant swathes through the high grass of the terraces. I knew that as long as I could hear that sound all was well, I could continue work in my womb-like little room. If it stopped then I too stopped, hands raised above the typewriter, frozen, listening, alert like a frightened hare.

Sometimes the stopping indicated only that a terrace had been finished, or a blade had hit a stone, a plug had got furred up with chaff. Sometimes it only meant a rest period. But at all times I was aware, never at ease, and if the pause continued I went, with extremely controlled casualness, down to seek the cause. If questioned I would simply say that I had got stuck. I had to clear my head for a minute. This was accepted, and as soon as I had checked to my satisfaction that the stopping was of no import, I'd go back and settle down to work. With one ear alert for the next stop.

And one day it *was* longer than usual. I heard Forwood crunching heavily across the pebbles under the lime tree beneath my window. He went into the house. I heard the door opened, heard him clinking and rummaging about in the bar-cupboard. I gave it ten minutes, so that I did not appear to be anxious. It was almost, by my watch, noon anyway. Time for the morning's Bloody Mary. He was sitting in one of the big white sofas, the tall scarlet glass in his hand. He looked up when I came in, stirring his drink with a plastic swizzle-stick we'd pinched in a bunch years ago from the Plaza, in New York.

'Finished? Or stuck again?' he said.

I poured a beer. 'Finished. Well, a paragraph. I'll take a break, it's no use forcing things.' I sat down on the stool by the telephone. 'Have you finished? It's about time. It's getting hot now. Don't overdo things.'

He set the swizzle-stick in an ashtray. 'I can't,' he said. 'Can't overdo things now. I'm too feeble.'

I lit a cigarette. 'Nonsense. Feeble! You have a hernia . . . mild . . . that'll pull you down. It is tiring anyway, pushing that Wolf about.'

'It's no good pretending. I'm bloody feeble. I've noticed it happening. I just feel flat, not up to par.'

'It's the weather. Humid. I feel drained today. That's why I've packed it in.'

Bendo, his prize boxer, whose father was champion of Austria, came crashing into the room, tongue hanging, saliva dripping, heaving for breath. He huffed about, then slumped with a crash and a sickening shudder in the middle of the rush matting of the cockpit, a sunken area at the far end of the Long Room where we were sitting.

'Where has he been? Did you leave the gates open?'

'No. There's a cat in the oak wood. He's determined to get it.'

We sat in silence for a moment; silent apart from Bendo's gasping and sudden bursts of panting.

'It's a bugger frankly.'

I reached up for an ashtray. 'What's a bugger? The cat . . .?'

'No. Falling apart like this . . .'

'Don't be daft.'

'I never meant to get old.'

'You aren't old! Balls to that. But you are over sixty. Can't expect to do all the things we did when we came here first. I'm over sixty, too, for Pete's sake . . .'

'I'm losing weight.'

'I can't see it.'

'I can. The scales in my bathroom are accurate. I weigh myself every day.'

'It's the heat! Honestly . . . and we don't eat all that much in the heat . . . you don't put on weight eating salads and fruit . . .'

'I'm losing it. And too quickly. I know. Not a fool.'

'Well, Patrick is coming in this morning. He's got a tape he wants us to hear.'

'Oh God, not one of his *own*? Strumming his guitar?'

'Afraid it is. Plus his own English lyrics. But ask him to have a look at you? If you are worried?' Playing the casual bit was pretty difficult sometimes. But it was far wiser to appear perfectly normal and calm because I knew that he was feeling anything but calm. He always gave one the impression of enormous ease and confidence, but underneath that very cool English exterior anxiety lay shallow.

Patrick, when he arrived, was brisk, practical. Two days later, thanks to his influence with the top surgeons at the Clinique des Magnolias, we got an early appointment, followed by barium meals, followed a day later by X-rays, and then a bit more waiting. Waiting was something that became familiar from then on. Patience and a calm heart became essential parts of learning courage.

I saw the little red car come racing up the track one morning. Patrick jumped out, slammed his door, grinning. 'What do you feel about my tape? I'm worried about my English grammar. I only pick it up from the radio and the Beatles or Elton John. He's terrific, yes?'

'Terrific, yes. I haven't really listened to your *own* tape.

Not yet. I will as soon as I can. Have you got the X-rays? From the clinic?'

He had arrived unexpectedly. Forwood was walking with Bendo high up by the oak wood looking, I supposed, for the cat. He had seen the red car and was on his way down. I heard him calling to the dog. Patrick accepted a vodka and tonic, stretched long legs. 'No problem! Just some *matière*, some, what do you call it? Matter? Maybe a little polyp . . . they can just nick it out. Easy.' He raised his glass in salute just as Forwood came in, slightly behind an eager, gasping, shouldering, snuffling boxer.

'It's a polyp, maybe. Or just some *matière*. So be calm! But you have a *double* hernia now! Too much work . . . I did tell you to stop.'

Forwood lost years in seconds, poured a Bloody Mary, mixed in the Worcestershire sauce, stirred it too rapidly. 'That all? Really? Nothing worse, Patrick?'

We sat about for a while, agreeing that it was perhaps wiser to go to London to get the polyp, if that was what it was, 'nicked out'. It was easier to deal with in English. Forwood had said that he was pretty good at coping with the inside of a washing-machine, a television set, record-player or even, at a pinch, a car in French, but that the medical terms in French of his own guts completely eluded him. 'I'd rather be ill in my own language.'

He went upstairs to get Patrick his fee. One had to pay, or it was better to pay, in cash and at the time. Especially as Patrick and Solange were pretty hard up and she had discovered a week before, to her delight, that she was pregnant.

'You are certain, about a polyp?'

Patrick set his empty glass down, gathered the X-rays up

in a bundle, shuffled them into an envelope. Shot a quick look at the staircase.

'I think so. They do occur quite frequently, after a certain age. But get him to London, he'll be more comfortable there. I know he hated the clinic.'

'How long have I got? To get him there, make arrangements?'

'This week? It might be a good idea . . . no use in letting things wait . . .' He patted the dog affectionately. 'Good fellow! *What* a hot dog! It's only Monday today . . .'

'Could it be anything else, Patrick?'

He was rubbing his hand over Bendo's head and neck, smoothing it along his muscular back. He didn't look directly at me when he said: 'It could be cancer. They'll check in London. I can't do it . . . and the clinic say it is just a polyp.'

'But it *could* be cancer?'

He looked at me directly. Bendo loped off out into the garden.

'It's possible. Yes. But look, this is important. When you go to London, will you try to get this album for me? It's quite new, impossible to get it here, they have never heard of them. They're terrific, amazing, quite, quite amazing! Will you try? I have written down all the information here, serial number . . .' He gave me one of his visiting-cards with something scribbled on the back.

'Try for me? Please? They are *amazing*. It's a new group, called the Cure.'

Chapter 7

It's so easy, writing like this, without any firm reference book, diary, journal at hand to set one on one's path (I burned all my stuff just before I left) to forget to round up all one's sheep.

My first publisher, and editor, Norah Smallwood, always used that phrase when I had submitted a few chapters to her for her tough criticism. 'Round up all your stray sheep. It drives the reader mad if you don't and you'll get into a *ghastly* mess yourself.' Right of course. She almost always was: I am still enormously influenced by her – always will be. So I'd better chivvy in some stray sheep. Like a dog . . . And dogs are what immediately come to mind.

There were dogs all through my life. I am not, oddly enough, a dog person, nor yet a cat person. I swoon at the sight of neither and am pleased to avoid both when possible. I don't, frankly, need them. I think one 'needs' animals for comfort, as a sort of surrogate companion, lover, child, what you will. That's about all. But I will perfectly cheerfully have one if the situation demands their presence in my life.

And thus it was with dogs. I lived a country life from my earliest childhood; impossible *not* to have a dog under those circumstances: fields, woods, long dusty lanes, wild moorland, curving, swelling Downs, all demanded, as it were, the presence of a dog. A childhood without an animal is unthinkable, and extremely bad for the future man or woman. Through an animal one is taught responsibility, comfort, trust, authority, duty, care and, to a great degree, love. So you have a dog. It seems reasonable. There have been masses of dogs in my existence. All sorts, kinds, conditions. Some wonderful, some awful, a few mad, most just perfectly pleasant 'dogs'. There were a Rogan, Chug, Chug 2, Chug 3, Sheba, Carla, Candida, Bogey and so on: they provided part of the calm, secure, background to ordinary country life. To life, actually. But, frankly, I gave most, if not all, my *childish* affection to grass snakes, toads, mice, tree frogs, rats and any other small rodent, mammal, reptile or fish available to me.

Fish and reptiles were, I suppose, my favourites. I spent hours building aquariums, or vivariums, and stuffed them with ferns and weeds, rocks and pebbles, and did my best to create a fragment for myself of living rock-pools or damp and steamy tropical marshes. The theory was always much better than the practice. But there lay my love. Dogs were very secondary to these scaly, warted, tailed, finned creatures.

Leaving England for abroad (I was at first uncertain where exactly I would settle: Italy, France or even, at one time, Austria, an aberration quickly excised from my whirling mind by one crashingly severe winter in Vienna – cold is not fun) was made poignant for me by the dumping, as it were, of two dogs – a large English mastiff (Candida) and an ageing corgi (Bogey) – a Siamese cat and a flutter of tropical finches in a bamboo cage, plus, and this was the most painful part of all, the abandoning of my beloved parrot, Annie, a perfectly ordinary Brazilian green, who was detested by everyone and reciprocated happily by loathing (with red-eyed hatred) everyone in sight: *except* me. I loved her with unbridled passion. We kissed, whispered and muttered together in a most nauseating manner, and if she flew away it was never very far, just to the top of a local wild cherry. She sat up there all day, screaming and laughing like a mad woman, until dusk fell, and then she would condescend to descend, slowly, clambering branch by branch from her perch to my arm. But only if I verbally flattered her, cajoled her softly, and whistled the first few bars of 'As Long As He Needs Me' from *Oliver*. It was an act we built up together. Most impressive to ourselves, viewed with hostility or alarm by others. However, when I left the UK, she had to go. Just as the dogs and the cats and finches were forced to find alternative accommodation, so, alas, was she.

Elizabeth took the dogs, the cat; the gardener took the finches; and Annie was given to a fearfully grand private zoo not far away where she spent the rest of her days screaming 'Dirk!' at the top of her voice and hysterically laying eggs from time to time. I don't know if there was any message there? She lasted for years anyway, and as I had had her for many years before, it seemed a reasonable time of loving for us both. But leaving her caused me far more grief than leaving the dogs. There has to be something pretty squint there.

However, when I got to Le Pigeonnier, I was quite determined that there would be no more painful separations, no responsibilities to helpless animals, no fuss, heartbreak and bother. Never again. Blithely forgetting that I already had a dog of a sort, Labo, which I had been hauling across Europe, from Rome to Paris, Munich, Trieste, etc. I would just build the pond of my dreams, stock it with carp and orfe, impersonal things, and that would be that. I reckoned without Forwood, who was as 'doggy' as I was 'un-doggy': 'I *know* that it is your house and that you are, as you always have been, Little Master, even at your advanced age, but *I* can't live up here on this hillside, surrounded by acres and acres of rock and brush, rabbits, pheasant, partridge and even foxes and a badger without a bloody dog . . . So put up with it.'

One day, after finishing marketing at Marché Forville in Cannes, he saw a small boxer puppy tumbling about in a too small cage with some other dogs in a chic pet shop near the Croisette and, against all my earnest and gentle protests, bought it. Never, under any circumstances, buy a dog from a chic pet shop. Especially such an establishment in, of all places, Cannes. Those fiendish people, the breeders, usually destroy the runts of the litters and puppies which are surplus to their needs, or, on the other hand, sell them off to pet shops with extremely vague pedigrees (usually 'mislaid' at the cash register). 'Daisy' (this is what she got called, after Forwood's grandmother, Daisy Lockton) was such a creature. Her stump was bleeding from poor docking, but her ears were unclipped. That is to say, they were not bandaged or in points, which is why he bought her. Cutting, pricking, the ears he rightly considered to be barbaric. So hers just flopped. And I of course, a year or so before, had been adopted by the stray hill dog in Rome during the time that I was deciding just where to put down my roots. This was Labo. So I really couldn't, in all fairness, sulk about Daisy. Thus she came to the hill, and we had – hey presto! – 'instant country household'.

Irritating but inevitable. As she grew older, Daisy became rather evil, for she sensed, as all animals do, that Labo was disabled in that he had been savagely beaten at some time – his leg broken in three places – and he limped. So she got him into corners from time to time and tried to tear out his throat. This was not too bad in open country, but very tiresome in a dining-room full of eating guests. Blood flew in spattering arcs across whitewashed walls, women screamed, glasses crashed, bottles fell, Labo shrieked and howled and, after furious separation, Daisy beamed brightly around the room wagging her stump, while Labo dragged himself to hide upstairs, under my bed. It was all 'delightfully real and rural', and everyone rather enjoyed it. It was part and parcel of the *vie de bohème en France*.

Daisy died eventually; she got some ugly disease. We spent days over in town sitting with a mixed clutter of ailing cats, dogs, budgerigars, rabbits and gerbils, hunched sickly in wicker cages, for hours until Dr Santori could see us. Plump, kind, careful, wise and vastly expensive, he failed to save cancerous Daisy and she had to be put down. A glorious, easy, dignified way of death if ever I saw one. Forwood, stubborn and untrusting, refused to leave her body with Dr Santori for fear of vivisection, and she was carried, head lolling, in the car boot, back to a private burial up in the *potager*, where the soil was more or less friable and holes were easier to dig, a boulder to mark the place.

Forwood was broody for some weeks, Labo radiant, I relieved to have only one meal a day to prepare. But the brooding gave way to beaming smiles when Dr Santori was summonsed to a 'quite wonderful litter of boxers with *astounding* pedigrees'. The sire was champion of all Austria. They were five weeks old, in three weeks they'd be ready for collection. Bendo joined us on the hill. Ears unpricked, he therefore never made the Kennel Club in Europe. However, he was a splendid animal and, being a dog, got on pretty well with Labo, who took him off on secret journeys and taught him the facts of life. Forwood was forever trailing round local farms and smallholdings where there was a bitch on heat. Tiresome, perfectly natural, but smelly often and the cause of severe, and bloody, battles between the village dogs and the team from Le Pigeonnier. However, one was assured, that was life and perfectly all right.

Labo died after about fifteen years of companionship, or thereabouts. It was difficult to age him exactly, for when he arrived in my life, broken and starving, he was about a year or even two. Anyhow, one day, washing up and in a hurry, unthinkingly I chucked a small lamb bone across the kitchen. Too late heard him snap frantically at it, too late saw him gulp it down. Too late all round. He died, a day after, haemorrhaging copiously, in my guilty arms. He was carried up to the *potager*, buried in a deepish hole under a pear tree, his grave marked by another large boulder. End of a chapter. Or series of chapters.

Thus it was only Bendo who was left for Marie-Thérèse to care for when we eventually left for London after Patrick's cautious warning about cancer and his desperate imploring that I should find him a recording of the Cure. The trip was pretty unpleasant. Marie-Thérèse and Gilles, with his hand-rolled shag, and their disgusting baby had to hang on for some weeks while Forwood recovered from a five-hour operation at Edward VII for cancer of the colon. No polyp here – a savage growth. Patrick had been right, and on one of those desolate afternoons wedged anxiously between hospital visits I managed to find his wretched album in a shop in Marylebone High Street. Mission accomplished.

We returned to the hill just as the late-March daffodils nodded and bowed in the coarse grass round the pond, where toads cavorted obscenely in their mating waltz and long tassels fell with golden splashes from the tall willow I had planted as a wand years before. Spring had arrived: Forwood became stronger, and it seemed more and more unlikely that it would ever come to leaving that beloved patch. We'd surely join the dogs one day, under boulders in the *potager*. Wouldn't we?

We wouldn't.

Every three months we had to make the trip to London to be sure that all was well. I became adept at packing swiftly, neatly, and only cabin baggage. The scent of shag seeped into the Cogolin cotton covers, and the disgusting child grew old enough to throttle at the sight of yet another piece of ineptly mended china lying in the slowly accumulating pile on my desk in the office.

'Oh dear! Marie-Thérèse . . . *ma belle* . . . this *was* a piece of Chelsea . . .'

'That's a place, eh?' Wiping the crumb-and-spittled chin of her child.

'Yes. Some china comes from there. Lovely things. I think, next time, I'd better put everything away, don't you? Gabriella is starting to move about pretty well now.'

'Ah! You don't *trust* me? I try to stop her! But I can't be here and there all the time, and with the tiled floors! *Voilà*, what do you expect? Poor Gabriella! She didn't mean any harm. Did you, *ma chérie?* I am sure *you* were as naughty when you were her age? Silly china! Naughty china! It could have cut my poor little Gabriella! Eh?'

Cut her throat would have been more to the point and very acceptable. I tactfully removed everything breakable to a height of five feet or more, carried some Staffordshire bits up to my office, and hid some Meissen birds behind boxes in the wardrobes. Marie-Thérèse looked sullen and vexed, but I would only smile agreeably: I'd need her and her family again in three months. Every visit to London very gradually increased hope, encouraged strength. Nothing had 'spread'. Only the Parkinson's increased; not violently, just cruelly, so that a cup of tea had now to be in a mug – a tea-cup resembled a mid-Atlantic storm too easily. But we managed: sharing out the jobs, employing outside help for the really tough mowing and pruning, and reassuring ourselves, to ourselves (for we still did not discuss things at this stage), that we would sweat things out.

One day in the market in town, weighing something or other, I found Poteau at my side. He had his string bag and was buying leeks for the evening soup. We talked amiably, discussed our mutual problems: he had been hit by a car while on a ladder trimming his hedge and had suffered various breaks and contusions. 'The Parkinson's?' he asked. I said not too good. Increasing rather. 'It will . . .' he sighed. 'It will. It is so sad for very active men. He was a *serious* gardener, eh?' I corrected him – he was an *active* one, to be sure – and admitted that he had worked from dawn until dusk, but that he was now desperately distressed at his incapacity to cut, rake, mow, burn and spray. The ants had beaten him, finally; he could no longer carry the poison cylinder: too heavy.

I remember, now, Poteau reaching across the stall for a bunch of red and white radish. 'He *did* use his mask?' he said, and dropped the radish in with the leeks and carrots, handed his tin over to the stallkeeper.

'Not all the time. No. Frankly never. He hated wearing the mask. Couldn't breathe, he said.'

Poteau looked up at me with astonishment through his spectacles. They were speckled with leaf shade from the trees above. 'He breathed all right,' he said. 'Deadly poison. *Voilà* – toxic, *so* toxic . . .'

I can still see the bright scarlet and white bunch lying in his weighing-tin as he shook his little leather purse looking for small change. 'Do you mean that the poison, the ant-stuff, could be responsible for the Parkinson's?'

He sorted out his money, handed it over, shrugged gently. 'Ah! Difficult to be *certain*. But you know there are very clear instructions on the bottles? Even a skull and cross-bones. It is *folly* to inhale that stuff. How long has he been using it?' He emptied his tin into his string bag.

'Years, I'm afraid. We gave up using the little arsenic envelopes years ago.'

Poteau grunted in agreement. 'Useless! They only have power to protect a single tree . . . no use at all. The Co-operative in Saint-Jennet has the stuff.'

I walked with him through the bustle and noise of the market. 'That's where this stuff came from, the Co-operative. They have allowed us to go there now that I am officially an agriculturalist.'

He stopped at the street leading down the hill to the *parking*. '*Voilà!* It is possible, I'm afraid. You may be told it is not so, in England . . . but here it is different. We *know* that poison, there are many cases like that. He should have used his mask. At all times . . . *Alors* . . .'

We shook hands and I wandered back up to the market stalls miserably. Resolved never to say what might possibly have brought such disaster to a strong, gentle giant of a man. Too late for recriminations, for 'if onlys' . . . the damage had been done and would never be mended. Set that all aside and continue with the performance.

Life had simply changed gear, I told myself, nothing very much more. The engine was still running, the car was perfectly serviceable, one just had to take things a little more carefully, coast down hills when possible, avoid curves, and try to ease the load going uphill. It was all perfectly manageable: just a question of sensible compromise and careful improvising. It was wiser to take each day just as it came and not to think ahead. Thinking ahead was a pretty silly thing to do now; there was the constant pricking of fright, like a buried thorn in the thumb, about the result of every three-monthly trip to Harley Street, the concealed look when a glass was lifted, a plate set down, a saucepan filled, a page turned, and handwriting grew smaller. Trivial things became, very slightly, hazardous. But I tried to batter along and find things to do which would be convincing proof that everything was, in fact, perfectly normal. I even made an appearance in a gigantic TV series for the Japanese about the glories and treasures of the Louvre, with Charlotte Rampling. We did the commentary on Ancient Rome and the wonders of Flemish art. I knew as much about both as I know about taxidermy. Less, frankly. But we mugged it all up from guide books and the rather dire script provided. I never saw a foot of the two-week epic – I rather think that the Japanese had the same good fortune – but I was paid a whacking great fee which covered the fares on Air France and the bills at the Connaught when the London visits arrived. I even accepted, because it was apparently an honour, and it was not very far away, to be the President of the Cannes Film Festival, which

I enjoyed about as much as being squeezed into the Iron Maiden. However, I did it with passionate seriousness, thereby making quite certain that I'd never be invited to be President again, or even, I reckoned, invited to the Festival.

This time Marie-Thérèse and Gilles would not be at the house: while I stayed in modest luxury in the Hotel Majestic (it was impossible to try and commute daily), Forwood stayed on the hill and Elizabeth and George came out to take charge. A lovely little break for them after the rigours and grey light of an English winter. Except that it was the wettest Festival on record and the hill was, at all times, in deep cloud, the rains tore across the land, swamped the pond, broke terraces, trundled boulders everywhere and wrenched branches from the trees. The fire burned brightly night and day and so did the electric lights. It was a sodden group of four who finally, when the cinema stint was over, all went back to London for the May check-up. Forwood now had to use a wheelchair, which he accepted with enormous good humour, and Air France saw to it that the British press never knew, and that he had a seat right beside the door at all times. This was something that 'The World's Favourite Airline' found it quite impossible to arrange. So Air France gained handsomely every time: it was the only possible way to travel.

This particular trip was rather a problem. No cancer but an enlarged prostate. So. Back to Edward VII. And a few more weeks of convalescence at the ever-welcoming Connaught, which had really now, over the years, become my London home – anyway since 1951, when I first dined there with Kay Kendall and Lilian Craig, when Kate, as her friends called her, had a tiny maid's room in the roof for eighteen shillings a week with the bathroom at the end of the corridor, and King Farouk had the table at which I now sit when I am there. Things have altered rather with the years. Apart, that is, from the familiarity, warmth, affection and absolute perfection.

Eventually back to the hill in fairly good nick, to the peace again, to the office and typewriter, and to listening, once more, for the song of the mower, which, alas, was now becoming more irregular and slower. But still nothing was ever said: we were both anxious, I suppose, not to put the truth into actual words, hard, clear, fearsome words. Somehow one feels that by not admitting something aloud, unpleasantness will fade away, will never quite become fact. The thing that was most feared was the overt admission that it was time to 'go back': the dreaded phrase, used in those days by elderly ex-patriots, was '*the big E*'. Retired people had suddenly to face the return to England: often because of finances, more often because of illness or the break-up of a marriage. But one tried desperately not to consider that, hung on with hope for as long as possible; but the unthinkable *was* drifting lazily in the mind, like wood smoke, faint, bitter, reminding, meandering. Privately.

We had been back from the prostate trip about two weeks when Forwood came to my room at three in the morning with a mustard glass full of blood.

'What's that? What's wrong?'

'Blood. I'm haemorrhaging. There are four more of these in my bathroom.'

'Full? Why?'

'I don't know. Call Patrick . . . It's stopped now, but call him . . .'

Patrick arrived half an hour later, unshaven, rumpled,

asked me the blood group, got me to help dress a fragile, frightened patient, half carried, half dragged him down the stairs to his car. 'I'll take him over right away. Clinique des Magnolias. *He can't wait!* Get his blood group and get to the clinic quickly.'

I watched the car race down the track, bouncing and lurching, Forwood's head rolling helplessly against the seat. Unconscious. Desperately I searched papers, medical reports, everything I could find in the file. No blood group. Called Edward VII and got, I assume, night staff – it was still not dawn – and also (most wonderful hospital) the blood group. And then rang Monsieur Antoine, who had a taxi and a bar in Le Pré. He blearily, and silently, drove me into town, where we sat and waited in the *parking*, watching the sun rise brilliantly, flooding the world with light, turning the sky from indigo to palest blue. In a small room where he had been hurriedly placed as an emergency, on a too-short bed, to join two other haggard men surrounded by their entire families, Forwood lay with a wan smile and a dead white face. Patrick was on his usual ebullient form.

'Just in time! I got him here just in time! If we had waited another ten minutes his bladder would have burst! I got Monsieur Alvaro, the best surgeon we have, he's my friend – He operated before we even got his jacket off! Pulled off his trousers, on to the table, and *voilà! c'était fait!* We did not waste a moment. He's lost litres of blood! *Mon Dieu!* –'

The room was crammed with people – the beds had been hurriedly pushed back against the walls. There was one blank window looking out into a dark well. People sat on the edge of the beds or leant against the walls wretchedly, just watching their ailing relatives. The smell of old bodies and stale ether was overpowering, but I tried to enjoy, as best I could, Patrick's enormous pride in his job well done. Forwood was only capable, at that moment, of a pale smile which faded into apprehension at the sudden brisk and explosive intrusion of an exhausted-looking nurse. She pushed past roughly, thrust a thermometer at him, shouted, in disastrous English, 'Shove this up your arse!' and crashed out again. Patrick assisted Forwood, looked apologetically at me. 'Is the *best* I could find, the nurse. She speaks English because she worked for a year in Sydney, Australia. Maybe her speech is a little rough?' I nodded helplessly, and Patrick assured me that she had a very good heart and would be back immediately; he'd wait with his patient and why didn't I go home? I left, giving Forwood a look which I hoped might appear encouraging, and wandered out into the corridors and downstairs into the reception area. People in white coats, in plaster, people with crutches, some in bandages, some weeping, all drifting about. It was 8.30 a.m.

In the *parking*, no sign of Monsieur Antoine – he'd cleared off to open up his bar, I supposed, so I waited until Patrick, after a time, came hurrying down and, surprised to see me still there, drove me back to the hill. He drove fast, too fast for me, but I sat tautly in my seat trying to listen calmly, and to understand, his exhausting tirade of abuse about the clinic and its staff, and then, in more detail, a full medical report, in French, on Forwood and what had happened. He chuntered on in a high babble of enthusiasm with a great deal of violent handwaving, apparently avoiding collisions every four seconds. I just hung on desperately. In the same way that he could not understand medical terms in English, so I was absolutely incapable of understanding them in French. The

Achilles' heel of living in France. I gradually managed to put together the pieces he scattered so liberally in my direction.

Since the London operation a small blood vessel, or something like that, had, over the weeks of convalescence, engorged and finally, as I had all too clearly seen, it had ruptured. It was amazing, he assured me, that Monsieur Ricardo Alvaro was on duty at les Magnolias that night, otherwise the journey we were presently taking would have been very different. I had met Monsieur Alvaro and liked him very much, a jovial man, a cigarette hanging from his lower lip, peeling off his bloody overalls, looking as much like a butcher as a surgeon possibly could. He offered me an elbow to shake as his hands were covered in grease from his rubber gloves. All would now be well, he assured me; it was a simple, if frightening, little 'hiccup'. Rest for a while, but he should leave the clinic that night: they were terribly overcrowded and he'd be far better off in his own bed.

At Le Pigeonnier, Patrick dropped me at the gates and then raced off to shave and prepare for his morning surgery. I let a frantic Bendo out of his kennel and clambered wearily up the stairs to the kitchen to find Lady (whom I had forgotten about) crouched on a chair in the dining-room sobbing in helpless anguish. Seeing me, she suddenly screamed very loudly, crossed herself twice, and hurled gabbled prayers to a number of saints she knew, and the Virgin Mary, rocking backwards and forwards, eyes closed in horror, moaning. The ruin, it seemed, of Forwood's room, together with assorted mustard glasses slopping over with old blood and blood smears scattered round the bathroom and corridor, had done for her. The shock, she kept crying, would kill her; she could *never* recover! She had thought, naturally enough, that with an open house, dog locked in kennel, blood everywhere, murder and pillage had taken place. It took half an hour to get her to come to terms with what had actually happened. This was difficult to do because every time I moved to take her hands she shrieked loudly, drew back, hissed at me, spat and buried her face in her woolly jacket, convinced that I was the murderer.

Eventually, after a slug of cognac, and my repeated assurances that Forwood was alive and well, the sobs faded gradually to sniffs and strangled sobs, until she agreed uneasily to come and clear up the sullied rooms. She finally did it all with great composure once she had been thoroughly convinced by my presence, and I even heard her singing '*Volare*' after a time, while she busied herself tearing off bloody sheets, banging about, running taps and flushing lavatories. It had been a *very* stiff cognac which had gone straight to her head. I took charge of the bloody glasses, chucked them into the dustbins. Reassured that Forwood was not yet dead, that I was not a murderer, and that life would be returning to normal as soon as I went into town to collect him that evening, she polished and vacuumed and hurled the towels and pillowcases about with abandon and, finally, wobbled off down the track on her Mobylette, waving cheerfully, her helmet unstrapped, bouncing about on her head. '*Volare!* Ho! Ho! *Cantarè*, oh ho, ho, ho! . . . *Volare!* Into the blue . . .'

I took a handful of olives, a piece of cheese, a can of beer, and sat under the vine on the terrace. A solitary lunch. I seem to remember it was the first time. Always there were two, sometimes six or eight, on occasion fifty. There had been parties. Had been. Time lost: time past. The writing was now on the wall: scrawled in thin letters, but there to read. The

Beginning the *porte d'entrée*, 1973

Finished. Autumn 1973

November 1968

September 1977

The first time I saw the house after the conversion, July 1968

The Long Room, 1985

The chimneyplace, 1968

The chimneyplace, 1985

Starting the kitchen extension. Self, Monsieur Danté, Monsieur Rémy. 1974

Finished. May 1980

Le Pigeonnier, August 1979

The start of the Big Fire, August 1986

The moon country. Crête de Ferrier, Provence. Winter

The first Christmas, 1969

The terrace, 1986

Last photo of the terrace, 1986

unthinkable had to be at last considered. So, after I'd done the clinic run, got the patient back and into his bed, we'd just have to rest up a little and then face the ugliness. If you cut out any form of sentiment whatever, it wouldn't be difficult. Really.

Bendo chose that exact moment, I can now see and hear, to lumber up the steps and crash out in the shade, puffing, gasping, fly-snapping. Not a good moment to arrive. It would all be pretty bloody when the actual time arrived.

I sold the house, on a Wednesday morning, quietly, privately. No one knew. Took it back again the following week (to the consternation of the couple to whom I'd offered it) and decided to try and sweat it out for another year. Apart from health, money was the problem. I had long chucked the cinema – in a way I think it had started to chuck me, but no matter. I left it before the axe fell. A disastrously unhappy experience in a war film which I had been jollied into making as a sprat to catch a mackerel (I was told) put paid, for ever, to any desire I might have had to continue to work in the cinema. It had everything about it that was most detestable and unpleasant in the business, and as a sprat I got stuck right until the final awful day of shooting. We, Larry Olivier, Liv Ullman, Edward Fox, myself and other European players were the sprats needed to catch the American stars who would, of course, guarantee a box-office success worldwide for a thoroughly British disaster. I can't remember, nor do I wish to know, what happened to the piece finally. I only know that the few sprats caught a boatload of mackerel at obscene expense, and that cheap bait was something I no longer wished to be. I did, a little later, attempt a final trip into the Magic Lantern Land and although this was a remarkable German product, from a director of genius, with some degree of intellect and a serious attempt to honour the writer, Nabokov, by Tom Stoppard, it got hacked about in the cutting-room and I finally pulled up my drawbridge for good.

Now writing had to support me, and the olive store was never so occupied. Working from home, as they say, meant that I was there to look out for the shaking hands and head, to arrange the London trips, succour a steadily weakening patient, be steady at the often anguished results of lavatorial examination, be encouraging when the car appeared difficult to steer, ready to carry a cup, button a cuff, pour from a bottle, joke lightly at frailty and *never* let the patient suspect, for one moment, that any future there might be was less than certain.

Refusing cinema work did, for a little time, cause him alarm. Was it, he wondered miserably, *because* of him? I was able, I think, to assure him that after the war epic I had turned my back on the cinema and never wished to return. He appeared satisfied with this. Up to a point. But when one time I was asked to accept an extremely attractive, indeed mammoth, role in a film which seemed to have everything going for it except perhaps its location in Colombia, it was difficult to lie convincingly – especially as the doctors in London had, unwisely I couldn't help feeling, given their permission for me to go, provided the proper injections against all manner of ailments and insects had been administered. So I prevaricated and whined away about my fear of flying, and who would look after the house for so long, and so on. I convinced him really only when I reminded him of the long journey, the heat and disease, and the distance from medical help if it were needed suddenly; and what, I said, about the three-monthly check-ups? They couldn't be left in abeyance. And, anyway, I had renounced the movies.

He was, more or less, reassured. We never discussed it again after that, and I never even read the script. But I was rather relieved to hear that the player who finally did the film spent a great deal of his time climbing gigantic waterfalls, cliff faces, gasping through dense jungle or wandering about in priestly raiment drenched by spume and torrential rain. It seemed that even though I might be the right age for the role I was the wrong age for so much agonizing activity, blundering around piously in South America. I stayed in the olive store and wrote my books.

Norah Smallwood had, by this time, died. Wretchedly, miserably, frail and bedraggled, in a public ward in Westminster Hospital. An era had ended. I was accepted by a powerful and attractive literary agent, Pat Kavanagh, and as my old publishers made no effort to keep me, she got my new book auctioned and I found myself with a brand new publisher, and a new beginning. In a world as uncertain and shifting as the one into which I now found myself entering, it was vastly important to me to have security, some feeling of constancy and encouragement . . . and I received this to a very comforting degree. There was now nothing to challenge my work at the hardboard desk on the pair of trestles from Galleries Lafayette. I spent all my time and effort (when not on the land) at a typewriter, or thumbing through the *Concise Oxford Dictionary*, *Larousse* and *Fowler*.

One day over at La Colombe in Saint-Paul, where we had driven (a confidence test run, really) for lunch, I learned of a brilliant professor at the Institut Pasteur in Nice who specialized in Parkinson's. My informant suffered herself from the disease, but Professor Martin had helped her 'amazingly' and she was convinced that he could cure her – or at the very least bring the hideous symptoms to a manageable degree. She generously agreed to speak to the Professor and arrange an appointment. His 'book', she said, was 'closed', he could cope with only a very limited number of patients. He agreed to see Forwood.

At that time I had been offered a Graham Greene short story to adapt for TV. Since this fell into my writing life, I accepted. And when it was suggested that I also *play* in the piece, I accepted that, for one simple reason: it was all to be shot in the South of France over a period of six weeks. In Nice. And six weeks was exactly the amount of time that Professor Martin needed to assess the needs of his patient. If there were no improvements after six weeks the case was possibly too far advanced for treatment. I accepted both jobs, and the house was left to Marie-Thérèse and Gilles once again, while rooms were taken at the Hotel Negresco. Martin's treatments usually took place in the early mornings, and the waiting about could be for hours, for he treated every one of his patients with extreme care and personal attention. So you never knew how long you might have to hang about the weary waiting-room of the Pasteur. Wiser therefore to be stationed in Nice. After six weeks, indeed after only three, the treatment seemed to be working: the Professor himself became cautiously encouraging, hope glimmered for a time, but it was a false dawn. However, it was a tremendous morale booster.

The Professor's office was a perfect illustration of what all absent-minded professors' offices should look like: a shabby room, peeling walls, grimy windows, a cluttered desk set in the centre of a sea of pamphlets and tumbled books looking like the aftermath of a hurricane. On the desk, prominently placed between him and his patient, a human brain, sliced, dissected and pickled in some brackish liquid. It very much resembled yellow bully beef and put me off that for years to come. But the man was full of kindness and encouragement, gentleness and confidence. He pointed out very fairly that it was all 'experiment'. As a willing guinea-pig this had to be, and was, fully accepted. In any case, it was better to be at the Pasteur with *hope* than to be isolated on the hill with only apprehension.

The television film and the treatment finished almost together, and it was back to Le Pigeonnier and the routine of summer once more. Spring had arrived for its extremely short duration and summer had exploded, as it always did on the hill, in abundance and acres of lush green grass. There never was that gentle distance between the fading daffodil or narcissus, the primrose and the bluebell, and the wanton whoring of the gloire de Dijon or Grandemère Jenny, or the prodigal spillings of alyssum, eschscholtzia and dianthus. It was all, quite suddenly, a splendour of scents and colours. The things I had managed to grow in beds hacked from the limestone shale and filled with good loam and compost which arrived up the track in great trucks were simple cottage plants that I had known as a child in Sussex and knew how to handle: larkspur, delphiniums, Canterbury bells, petunias, antirrhinums, pelargoniums and so on. I never went in for anything exotic: just the ordinary old seed packet favourites.

And there was nothing much wrong in that. They flowered

far more extravagantly than they ever did in the cool of England; the blooms were larger, more brilliant, in the clear, dazzling light of the hill, and seemed to be more strongly scented. However, the bounty was excessive: the grass on the terraces was hip-high, the broom bushes tumbled uncontrolled, valerian exploded from the terrace walls, roses became smothered in every kind of aphid and grub and, of course, the spraying, now that it had taken its human toll, was banished. However, the vine flourished in green profusion, the de-bunching business (a back-breaking process which had to take place every May and June as one stripped the too-many bunches away and carted them down in barrow-loads to the compost heap) had gone on, as had all the other garden jobs which were now 'manageable' for one pair of hands and another pair less certain but eager and determined to assist. Everything that could be done as before was done. More or less.

Life, for the last summer on the hill, went along much as it had done for twenty years. There was no way that a change of pace should, or could, be introduced. The house had very tactfully been sold, to friends of the original people who had so wanted it, but it was agreed that everything would go on as usual. Until October. Then, and then only, would I hand over the keys, close the shutters for the last time, and quit. Parkinson's, the vague threat always present of something untoward happening to the lymph glands, the general unease now when driving in the car to the market and the one overwhelmingly disastrous fault of mine, the fact that *I* was unable to drive, sealed the fate of life at Le Pigeonnier. It was a matter of now saving what one could and abandoning ship. A door had slammed, the corridor had crashed into darkness.

I told very few people: my friends in the village, Florette Ranchett, Madame Pasquini, the Mandellis of course and those others who were particularly close, somehow knew or guessed and had to know. I tried, in some futile way, never to put it into words, hating to state the fact brutally. Marie, a widow now, living alone in her cramped little flat, arrived for tea one day, well aware that all was not well and that I would be bound to give her information she would prefer not to hear: when I did, as gently as I could, she wept silently, hopelessly, her head in her hands, and all I could hear were her smothered words of grief. Now she was quite alone in the world: Le Pigeonnier had been her only family. I never told the Meils, I never told anyone in the market or in the villages. I never even told the de Beauvallons, my neighbours in their splendid new house under Titty-Brown Hill. I had it in mind that, when the time came, I would just go away as silently and as unannounced as I had arrived that hot summer day so long ago. Every farewell would be a deep laceration, a wounding which I knew Forwood in his condition would not be able to sustain and which I must not myself endure, for I had to be the strong one now. It was all on my shoulders. I hoped very much they'd not weakened after the years of happiness and peace. So the final summer went as planned. People came to stay, Lady (who, of course, I did tell and who immediately asked if I was taking all the furniture because if I was selling anything she'd like first offer – she had, after all, polished and cared for everything, and she had had her eye for years on the Magi-Mix) – anyway, Lady whipped sheets off beds, changed pillowcases, and we went on, it might appear to a stranger, pretty much as always. Only very close friends like Rosalind and Nicholas Bowlby, who came out to help me through a difficult four-day shoot for a TV documentary, Pat Kavanagh and my new editor, Fanny Blake, knew the full facts. Elizabeth and my brother Gareth were told, for I would desperately need their help when the final shutters were closed. They were both ready. 'That's what families are for,' said Gareth. 'We'll be there, don't worry.'

It would not, I knew, be a question of a severance, but of an amputation.

In September, when the last of the guests had departed and the bathing-towels had long since been washed and folded away by Lady, Forwood and I sat under the vine and watched the sun slide in an apricot glow behind the mountain above the town. The air was soft and cool in the shade. A cicada was singing on the lime tree. Bendo lay sprawled exhaustedly under a big pot of white petunias.

'And him?' said Forwood.

'I'll deal with all that. In good time.'

'Thank you. I'm very grateful,' he said.

Chapter 8

Occupied, as I was in the last chapter, in rounding up metaphorical sheep, I now realize that I quite forgot to round up the real ones: the ones on the hoof. They did, in fact, inhabit the land for a while.

Madame Meil got her way in the end, and I got her old friend the shepherd Labiche from Feyance. Plus flock. No longer young, he was a tall, stooped man, in a ragged overcoat, a frayed tweed cap, heavy, cracked calloused hands clasped over his blackthorn crook, polished and shining as a liquorice stick. His flock amounted to about 250 beasts: I never managed to count them truthfully, but they were pretty mouldy looking, and when I first set eyes on their scrawny bodies skittering about beneath my lovingly tended olives I confess that I was mildly alarmed. I suppose that I was thinking of the fat roly-poly sheep with which I had become familiar in childhood on the South Downs: fat, complacent, trim and woolly. Not a whit like these wretched mountain creatures, lean to the point of famine, long of knobbly leg, wild of yellow-orbed eye, feeding frantically on my lush spring grass, then starred all about with wild anemones and crocuses.

The land, as Madame Meil said, had always carried sheep in the old days, and now she had seen to it that it was carrying sheep once again. It was obvious really that it should: it was well watered and grew an abundant crop of excellent green fodder, the best on the hill, and for a time I was persuaded that the scraggy flock saved me an immense amount of toil. They cropped close to the root. Every fragment of moss or lichen went down, each stunted myrtle, broom or box-bush was cropped to the very stumps. The entire area looked as if a great blanket of green baize, undulating over the bumps and humps, had been thrown for approval before my apprehensive eyes. So far, so good. Clean the land they did and all was perfectly acceptable – if you didn't count the outraged screams and howls coming from the dogs locked in their kennels and the massive quantity of ticks they released liberally over the entire area. Not to mention the fact that the only things permitted actually to grow were the olives: and as they were as old as the land itself, and as tough, they remained. Lesser vegetation went swiftly.

But sometimes, I confess, it gave me intense pleasure to sit and watch this biblical scene being played before me on my own fragment of France. Olive trees of great age, silence, green terraces, lambs gambolling, or whatever the things do, the pleasing wrenching sound of grass and herb being devoured by gentle creatures, skinny but none the less charming to look at, with only the tonkle-tonkle of their bells to break the serenity.

However, there were some alarming problems connected with all this serenity. The dogs worked themselves into hysterical frenzies from which I sometimes thought that they would never recover. So great was their hatred for the old Labiche sheepdog, and the entire flock of invading stilt-legged creatures, that they literally foamed at the mouth, eyes rolling in their heads, bulging, gleaming like hard-boiled eggs. It was unnerving and not at all restful; it quite frankly ruined the peaceful contemplation of my biblical scene. The terrace walls suffered greatly as well: so carefully repaired, and with such precision and elegance, by Fraj, they had the hell bashed out of them by capering animals intent on leaping to the next patch of tempting green. Fraj watched, impassively, as huge corner stones spun like empty cigarette packets among the trees, and showers of smaller pebbles and limestone shards rattled down on to the lower fields jamming the mowers and bending the blades. (Mowing, incidentally, still went on even with the sheep to assist us.) Fraj stoically shrugged, wiped his nose on his sleeve, and began all over again, relaying stones constantly. Calm, unruffled. I was far less equable. I had to pay for his labour every time, and it didn't really come cheap on a limited budget.

I suppose, though, that the ticks were the final disastrous problem, and were most certainly the reason that Next Door and, indeed, the de Beauvallons, firmly refused to have Labiche and his troupe on their land. Both families were extremely urban and would honestly have been far better off in Gerrards Cross or Neuilly respectively, for they shuddered at the sight of a toad, shrieked if a lizard got jammed in a shutter, even winced in polite frenzy if they were approached by a welcoming dog. They were not country people at all. However, I rather saw their point about the ticks. Labiche did not: he was furious, because the estates all joined and, together, would have provided him, as they had in the past, with enough grazing until he marched his leggy creatures up to the high hills for the summer.

However, he made do with my piece, paying me, as the law insisted, grazing-rights yearly. This I established as one single franc, and this he gave me wrapped in a piece of paper among the glittering foil-wrapped bonbons contained in the belly of a chocolate fish every 1st of April: *le poisson d'Avril*, a French custom like our April Fools' Day. Sometimes I did wonder if I was being had, but on two early occasions he most generously added to the *poisson* one newborn lamb, headless, skinned, gutted, bloody, ready for the spit. My anguished face may have suggested to him that I was either mad or vegetarian, or both. Either way the gift was abandoned and so indeed were the grazing-rights eventually.

After a few years it really did become a burden rather than a pleasure: what with frenzied dogs, falling walls, a total lack of wild flowers and a plethora of ticks, I had to call it, very regretfully, a day. Labiche was pretty cross and Madame Meil shook a finger at me from time to time, scowling. But in the end it all faded away.

One of the main problems turned out to be the sheep-droppings, which were precisely the same size, shape and colour as the olives which spilled so abundantly across my land from December until March. Monsieur Rémy always insisted that they added body to the oil. I have no doubt that he was right. I only know that my *bidons*, brought heavy from the mill and filled with the golden treasure so painfully gathered at every harvest, did indeed have a particularly 'fruity' flavour. I didn't admit to enthusiastic gourmets, who praised it lavishly, the possible reason for their delight. Well, consider things: numb fingers in frost-spiked grass, back and knees aching, eyes watering from the bitter wind blowing down from the mountain. It was not impossible that one had reached out for a scatter of doubtful fruits. One little black sphere, under those conditions, did look very much like another. Anyway, no one died. As far as I am aware.

So. That was the herd of sheep, part of the lyrical life I led. The olives, the mowing, the grazing and the whole glory of, at last, being an accredited agriculturalist and, what was much more important, being taxed as such. I could, and did, claim grants for restoration of the neglected property, the State profited from my oil and, one supposed, the excellence of Labiche's sheep – and, incidentally, from Madame Meil's ewe's-milk cheese, which I am assured was delicious. In spite of her fingernails and the noisy privy.

But apart from rounding up sheep, I have almost forgotten that I also nearly mislaid a dynasty. Forwood, divorced rather unhappily after the war, had a son, Gareth, who became a permanent part of his regular life from about the age of seven and continued to be so for a long time to come. At university in Aix he met an enchanting French girl, Véronique, married her, and had a son, Thomas. Thus Forwood became, to his intense pride and overwhelming joy, a grandfather. Thomas first arrived on the hill when he was less than one year old, but at three he sat on his grandfather's knee and 'drove' the Peugeot up the track.

The Forwood dynasty was secure, and the doting grandfather smothered the walls of his little office with photographs of his grandson: an hour old, in arms, aged twelve months, in a bath with a yellow plastic duck, taking first steps with his aged *great*-grandfather, as a cowboy, standing under a Christmas tree, riding his first tricycle, wearing a paper hat, kicking a football, lugging a satchel to school. Gradually the baby gave way to the child, the child to a boy, the boy to a tall youth. All recorded on the office walls until the time came for them to be unpinned and packed away. Thomas's parents divorced very early in his life. Véronique remarried and he then had a new 'father' and, in time, two stepbrothers, plus his doting grandfather, who kept a cautious, but continual, eye on his progress: a progress which brought him up the hill, for the last time, when he was thirteen. He came with his 'new' parents, as usual, and as usual no one spoke at all about the tiny warning cracks which had first started with a very slight ache in one foot. Least said, one thought, soonest mended.

Every year Lady and Manolo, plus their two children (a small boy had been born almost on the kitchen floor one morning, but she managed to hang on to him until she reached her own kitchen and had him on the floor there), drove off in a battered Renault to Granada and their cave-haunting families. That they should go on a well-deserved holiday no one could possibly dispute; what one did dispute was the kindness of her heart and the taste which produced such perfectly awful presents. And what, and how, to do anything about them once they had been so proudly offered and warmly accepted? It was quite impossible to ever be rid of the things which accrued through the years, for she dusted and adjusted each and every one every day of her life, preening with pleasure that they were so prominently displayed even though, she did once admit, she had not meant them for the bedrooms or the offices, but rather for the Long Room or, at a pinch, the dining-room.

There is a limit, one would imagine, to dancing ladies in frilly and spotted flamenco skirts, to long-legged gentlemen twisted into agonizing shapes on their high heels, to castanets with 'GRANADA' painted on them in gold or, worse, glittering in pink sequins. A limit to the 'antique' worm-holed wood plaques holding one thermometer and two key-rings, to ashtrays with bulls and matadors on them, to lampshades covered in wine labels. But there was no limit. There were enough souvenirs of sunny Spain gathered together under the roof of Le Pigeonnier to fill a funfair, and there was absolutely no way that I could dispose of them by, say, any artful fall, sudden gust of vicious wind, or just having one of the dogs savage a frilly lady. They stayed and endured, grim reminders of a loving heart.

But the worst gift of all, perhaps, was the one which had cost her the most thought and pesetas. It was to be the last she ever did bring back from her holidays and it was brought, on her lap, all the way from the mountains behind Granada or Alicante or wherever she had found it, to remind me of all the years of devotion she had given the house and its owners. Wherever we went, she said, we would be reminded of her. And how . . .

So delicate was this gift that it could not even be wrapped for fear of damage to the exquisite elegance of its shape and form (the same thing, but that's what she said). For two whole days and one long night (they slept in the car in a lay-by) it was proudly carried in her hands so that nothing could possibly disturb the elegance and sleek perfection of her possession. A fat red-legged partridge. Stuffed. Alert, head to one side listening for the hunter, it stared glassily into space, speckled, plump, firmly wired through vermilion legs to a chunk of plaster rock glued here and there with viridian green moss. Unbreakable, unspeakable, destined, as she pointed out as I held it in stunned hands, for the stone bracket high in the dining-room where the 'imitation' bird stood: my Picasso owl. That was merely 'old pot', she said, whereas this was the real thing, and as I collected birds she knew that I would be overwhelmed. Well, I was. In a manner of speaking.

While she dusted all my Meissen birds with infinite care, as long as I was present, she assured me that she would never have to dust the partridge. A flick with a feather duster was all it needed, but never actually got, because, after I had glumly placed it on the bracket, it proved to be far too high for her. So there it stood for ages, feathers, feet, folded wings and tilted head, commanding the room. Plumes riffling in any draught, eyes growing gradually filmier with dust. I know that it gave her infinite pleasure each time she passed it; it reminded her, she said, of the long journey home and I almost expected her to genuflect as she went up to the top floor with the polisher and the can of beeswax, for she venerated the bird as she would have venerated a fragment of the True Cross or the Turin Shroud. When the time came to begin to pack up the house she anxiously suggested that the removal men accord the bird a separate large box. With, she thought, sawdust to protect it. I promised her that when the time came the partridge would be greatly cared for and the very last thing to go.

It was.

There was a final check-up in London before the packing began. Just to be quite clear about things and where we stood generally. No real sign of anything untoward, but the three-monthly check-ups could not be abandoned. Sudden changes could occur swiftly. One could *never* be absolutely certain. The patient was not told this – I was; but the three-monthly business was made clear to him. To continue to try and do this from the South was impossible: exhausting, and far too costly. The taxi to the airport was not a gift, air fares were expensive, the hotel situation, although pleasant, was simply not affordable with, anyway, Marie-Thérèse and her family living happily up on the hill.

This latest London check-up coincided comfortably with the publication of my book *Backcloth*, so the hotel, the cars, the fares even, were paid for – but I was not capable of publishing a book every three months. So a new idea began to formulate in my mind. Neither Forwood nor I wanted to leave France. I had spent more than a third of my life there, had grown to love and respect its people and the quality of its life. I had come to terms not only with the language but also the logic. I was an agriculturalist and a resident, and I had been honoured by my adopted country with the ribbon of the Commandeur des Arts et des Lettres, a singular honour for a foreigner. To leave after so long, with roots so strongly planted, would be unthinkable, but to move up to Paris and find a pleasant flat was not. Near to London for emergency, but still in France. The fear of sudden illness (the prostate panic was ever in mind) and costly taxi journeys down to Nice, where the best hospitals and clinics were, settled things. A flat in Paris could be a perfectly splendid way of restarting an interrupted life.

The London doctors had given me my train set. Tunnels, crossings, signals and even the stations. The lines had been laid, the engine set firmly on the track, now all that I had to do was insert the key and wind it all up. That done, the tender, the trucks and the carriages would all follow along behind. Somehow or other. The hardest job I had to face was the inserting of the key and making the first twist. It started, of course, with Bendo.

Forwood was quietly, perfectly, calmly, distraught.

'He's not going to be put down because *he's* ill. But because *I* am.'

'And because, if it's a flat in Paris, he'll go spare after all these acres and never having to wear a collar or be on a leash, and if it's England, as it could be – we have to face that – he'll die anyway with six months in quarantine.'

'Perhaps the Mandellis or Marie-Thérèse would take him . . .?'

'He's only ever belonged to one master since he was eight weeks old. Yourself. Even sleeps up in your room. He'd never come to terms with the children and a three-roomed flat in town.'

'You could visit him in quarantine . . . every week . . .'

'I *could*, and it would distress him desperately. It always does. And, in any event, the RSPCA people at Dover would put him down anyway because of his foot problem, the infection he's picked up from the stubble and the sheep.'

We talked and worried at this subject for far too long. In the end the kindest and wisest possible thing to do was done one hot, still afternoon when Dr Santori, with a very heavy heart, sent Bendo on his way, radiantly happy, all unaware, lying on his back on his favourite part of the floor in the cock-pit, legs apart like a milking-stool, stump wagging joyously, yellow ball clamped in his mouth. His 'present' to his doctor whom he knew and trusted. A bitter thought. Forwood, holding one paw, only said, in a tired voice, how much he wished that he could go as peacefully and as happily.

I wrapped him in his old bed blanket, and Monsieur Rémy carried him down to the hole he had previously dug, and we buried him with his food bowl, the yellow ball from Kensington, and set a giant boulder on top, so that wandering foxes or badgers would not disturb him. He had a big white oleander to shade him.

So that was done. '*Malheur,*' said Monsieur Rémy. '*C'est tellement triste ça . . .*'

'The infection in his pads was the real problem. He had to have them dressed *every* night, and I was the only person he'd ever let do it, not even Monsieur Forwood . . . they were terribly painful.'

We walked together back to the tool shed carrying the big spade and the choke-chain.

'*Comme même, c'est triste.* It is *all* sad, *all* sad, Madame and I, Madame Bruna, will be losing our *true* friends . . .'

To my surprise, and to my grief, I saw that his eyes were rimmed with tears and he made it clear with a brusque movement of a hand that he had no wish to speak any more. I stood on the terrace and watched *my* true friend bump slowly down the track. I confess that my vision of his departure was not perfectly clear.

The hot still day on which Bendo died, 'the vile day', as Forwood called it, was the signal for further disaster. The following day, after a still, blistering night, sinister in its utter silence and breathlessness, a moderate mistral began to blow. Nothing much, as far as violence was concerned, no pots were smashed and hurled about, no limbs torn from the trees, no tiles sent scudding into the grass. Just a steady, blistering, parching wind. An oven, belching fire. And that is precisely what it did: about three in the afternoon.

Forwood, who had been sorting out papers up in his office, called down to say that there was smoke, a lot of smoke, across the valley up on the Tanneron range. We stood and watched in sudden horror as the plume became a massive cloud, then a gigantic mushroom, tumbling, towering, bellying, forking sheets of distant flame into the shattering blue of the sky. It was to be the worst, and most catastrophic, mistral we had ever known. It blew for three days. The fires raged unabated, uncontrollable, in spite of a massive onslaught made by the Canadair pilots who dumped thousands and thousands of gallons of sea water, scooped up from the bay, over the blazing forests.

Before nightfall of the first day, the wind had veered, grown in fury, and thundered into us up on the hill, howling, raging, slamming shutters, wrenching at doors, ripping the vine about like tangled knitting, scorching the plants, tearing, whipping at the cypress trees, flattening the arum lilies round the pond and surging the once placid water into towering waves which crashed over the banks, shouldering boulders and rocks aside, spewing fish and water-weed churned into balls of mud and silt. We huddled, shutters clamped, doors locked, under the big chimney in the Long Room in the dark. The only light came from the ghastly rosy glare of the fires through cracks in the woodwork of the door and the wind-split shutters. Later I lit an oil lamp, standing it with great care *inside* the empty stove against any possible accident. We were too scared to light the gas to boil some soup.

Forwood had managed to back the cars (we had two, a shopping car and a travelling car) out of the garage as far away from the house as he could get them for fear that the petrol tanks might explode. I had to crawl on my belly to drag him back across the field behind the house. It took us quite a time: even though he had lost a great deal of weight, he was still a heavy man. We lay in a heap at the foot of the stairs up to the kitchen terrace, breathless, exhausted, old and, frankly, fearful. Around us the night was crimson, yellow, orange and, wavering right above our heads, rosy pink filled with a hideous black confetti of ash, spiralling and spinning, in the belching eddies of hot air. It was altogether a disagreeable business and it took a bit of time to drag my companion up the stairs and get the kitchen door opened. We did this on hands and knees, rather wobbly, in the flickering palette of vicious light from the fires. However, the kitchen was relatively calm; we sat on the steps down to the dining-room and tried to sleep, heads against the wall. It didn't work, of course, and eventually we lay flat and, in spite of the roar of the wind, did sleep.

After three days it blew itself out and trailed away to sea. We were pummelled, bearded and weak. The damage before me, in the first light of the first windless day, was daunting. Far over the Tanneron range the smoke still drifted for over sixty square miles, a slow meandering veil which now and again would rend apart to throw out a sudden burst of carmine flame or the intense blue of the sky. The land was overwhelmed with fallen boughs, clumps of branch and leaf, bits of fencing from somewhere, a tatter of blowing plastic sheeting from some old sack and shattered tiles.

Monsieur Rémy arrived one morning, after he had coped with the damage at his own house, and brought with him Monsieur Danté and, of all people, Plum-Bum. I was astonished to see him after so many years. Hardly recognizable now, a paunch, grizzled hair, a stippled beard, the splendid teeth long since removed, replaced with a chatter of what looked like Chiclets. We shook hands warmly, nodded and smiled, the Chiclets gleamed. Four children now, and he had managed to secure himself a *carte de résidence*, or whatever he needed to make him legal. His father had served with the French Army in Benghazi or somewhere. It didn't matter much, we just got down to work trying to clear up the wreckage. But the very sight of him served to remind me, if I had even remotely forgotten, just how long a time it was that I had been the 'proprietor' of my acres.

Here he was, from radiant glossy youth to sagging gut-heavy, middle-aged Arab. With false teeth. How we change! I wondered how much I had altered in the years and put the fleeting thought behind me. There was enough work ahead to cope with. Without vanity.

The telephone was pretty busy with friends calling from all over to know if we had been spared. The news had obviously spread to Paris, London, New York, even insular Los Angeles. The house had faced worse days and nights, I supposed, since its walls had been raised, foundationless, on its little plateau in 1641. But the friends and the family who called were all those who, at one time or another, had sat out under the vine and watched the fireflies sparking away across the grass under the olives in the soft velvet hush of evenings, and heard the frogs fiddle and agree far down in the valley while the nightingales sang joyously in the willow by the pond. But we were safe. For the time being. Not, however, secure.

Forwood grew more and more frail, Patrick more concerned, and there was yet another trip down to Nice, not to the Pasteur this time, but to a clinic where two more polyps were removed and X-rays were done. A new taxi this time, a big fat American number, a good driver, Monsieur Jacques, who was patient, understanding and silent. I hung on to him. The problem with Monsieur Antoine at the bar in Le Pré was that the bar came first and his taxi a poor second: willing though he was, and kindly, reliability could not possibly be his first, or even fourth, name. So Monsieur Jacques from

Nice stayed with me on call and did the Institut Pasteur runs to Professor Martin until the day that Patrick arrived on the terrace with the X-rays. A shadow on the liver.

I think that we had had so many ugly moments that this one seemed almost easy to accept. It made leaving now imperative. A few days later, in my dark suit, white shirt and London shoes, I was standing in the *notaire*'s office in his village ready to sign the house away. It was the same *notaire*, and the same office, as when, so long ago, Jean-Claude's ageing father, as head of his family, had renounced, as was then required by law, all rights to his house and land in perpetuity to me. The land had been in his family for many centuries; he can only have felt a little sadder than I as I did exactly the same for Alain and his wife, Christine.

They drove me back to the hill in complete silence after we had signed and shuffled papers and shaken hands all round and bobbed and bowed ourselves away from the offices. Silence because I had a bit of a lump in my throat and had nothing to say, and because their tact was as graceful and elegant as their appearance.

In the dining-room I poured tea, and we discussed what they would purchase by way of furniture. Alain said, with a shrug, that he'd be happy if I just took my suits and left everything, but realistically we came to terms with the ugliness of profit and loss and cost generally. But all of us were flummoxed by the value of the things. Finally, they indicated what items they felt would be essential to them and we were left to fix our own prices. How big a flat would it be in Paris? What would I be able to afford? I had been forced to sell the house at the maximum price under the strict Socialist government rules as an agricultural property. It was absurdly little, the wealth tax bit deep. So the flat would have to be, to begin with anyway, modest.

All the big stuff, the contents of the Long Room for example, would never fit into a modest flat, and the long walnut table, erected from a wreckage of legs, planks and stretchers in the dining-room, could never be taken out again unless it was, once more, reduced to kindling. So that would have to stay, plus the eight chairs, and the big pine dresser, and on and on it went, right down to all the terrace furniture and the garden pots and urns, for who could possibly find room for all those in a Paris apartment? Some things, garden statues, would go into storage against such time as they were perhaps, one day, needed, but everything which had given Le Pigeonnier its 'air' should, as far as possible, be retained. This seemed only fair, and Alain and his wife wanted nothing whatever changed. They were, later, to copy or reproduce almost everything which I removed.

It is said that it takes four months to clear the Baie des Anges, that blue arc of glittering sea between Nice and Cannes, of the film of oil left by the holidaymakers of summer. Much of it is oil from motor boats and cabin cruisers, *most* of it, astonishingly, is sun-tan lotion. Ambre Solaire and all the rest. It spreads an iridescent membrane of rainbow colours over the water, and four months of winter weather is how long it takes to drift it away. It took four *days* to clear Le Pigeonnier after two decades of life there.

Elizabeth, Gareth and one of his sons, Rupert, arrived to help pack up. The Mandelli family pitched in as well. Monsieur Rémy's truck carted away mowing-machines, garden tools, the sawing-horse, clothes props and the entire contents of the woodshed and workshop, which I begged him to strip. He did. So thoroughly that he made a new discovery, in a dark corner which we had never really explored and in which spare shutters, poles, lengths of wood and reclaimed ancient oak beams were stacked. He discovered, on the plaster, yet more scribbled names of Jewish children to be added to those we had preserved.

'I guard these? Or not?' he said, cap at the back of his head, Gitane drooping from his lip.

'No. Don't keep them. I think the new owners will probably turn this into a flat for their guardian. With my office studio above.'

He shrugged and dragged away an old door (moved from the original kitchen), and ripped off half the plaster and all the timid scribbles of hope and defiance. I was too weary to be saddened and, after all, it was all a long time ago now.

One evening, while Gareth was unravelling yards of tangled flex from the many picture lights and Rupert was loading his battered car with the sewing-machine, blankets and various iron casseroles and things which he and his wife, Jacquie, would need in their new house near Perpignan, Elizabeth and I went down to the pond with a couple of watering-cans. Forwood was in his room looking out his clothes. I had burned all my papers from my office in careful piles, right by the pond, watering-cans at the ready to douse any possible spark (which is why we were there: it was a useful reservoir). The evening was soft and still; we had that day just eased into October and the sun had lost some of its heat.

'What have you burned? Everything? Not *everything*, surely?' She dunked her can.

'Stuff I really can't cart around. Letters, postcards, diaries, journals, all the press cuttings I ever saved, that sort of stuff . . .'

'What about your American friend, whatever her name was? She wrote every day . . .'

'And those. Hundreds of them. What's the use of keeping them? I'll never use them. I started to work on an edited bundle of my letters to her, but no one was interested. So that's gone too, all kinds of bits and pieces. There's too much to cope with now. I think I'll have about fourteen suitcases to cart around, plus typewriters and walking-sticks.'

I remember there was suddenly a little riffle of a breeze and a sharp leap of flame from the smouldering piles by the cane-break. We were both alert instantly, lugging the cans of water, dousing everything to steaming, sodden, black ash.

'Your books? You haven't burnt *those* here, have you? You can't have done that!'

I was more worried about starting another fire than my books.

'No. The manuscripts and some personal letters, important ones, from Olivier, Gielgud, Garland, that sort of stuff, my school reports, first poems, you know? I've kept them. Boston University want them. So I'll ship them out.'

'Why Boston? In America?'

'No one else wanted them.'

'All the letters you sent Daddy, during the war? He saved them all for you.'

'Burned those too . . .'

She stood watching me dribble the last of a can into the steaming embers of half a lifetime.

'I think you're quite daft,' she said.

I suppose that she was right. But at that time, without any

clear idea of a future, or where there would be one, I wanted to cut everything down to the minimum so that I would be free to travel light. It was an old trick learned, very sensibly, in the Army. Everything I had during those six years fitted neatly into one canvas bag which I could carry. I never lacked for anything, that I can remember.

Elizabeth was in charge, during the pack-up, of the kitchen stuff and the laundry and linen. She doled the three of us out with one knife, fork and spoon, a plate, a mug and a glass each. That left everything, apart from a saucepan, frying-pan, a potato-peeler plus kitchen knife and kettle, free for the removal men who were to arrive from Cannes at dawn. She would, as she had done when I left England, oversee the packing. She was very good at that, and removal men seem to take more notice of women than they ever do of their own kind. The arrival at Le Pigeonnier all that time ago had been a disaster. The packers in England had managed to break more than half the contents of their vans. To such an extent that the French customs men who attended the 'breaking of the seals', that hot morning so long ago, had shaken their heads in dismay and with sympathetic salutes drove away. They didn't examine anything at all. Not even the pictures.

I didn't want the reverse to happen this time around: that the British would shake their heads in dismay at the wreckage caused by the 'hopeless' French packers.

So Elizabeth would keep guard, although, to be fair, the people who were to move us back to the UK had been present at the arrival of my stuff from England and had had the misfortune to see for themselves the grotesque wreckage from London. They were the most renowned firm on the entire coast, so I felt a great degree of ease there. However, a bossy Englishwoman, with a beady eye, would be no hindrance. But I knew that enormous care would be taken; and so it was.

'My dear!' said Elizabeth. 'They wrap everything in yards of paper. Tissue paper, then *brown* paper, and then cardboard, and then, after all *that*, everything gets sealed with huge strips of yellow and red sticky tape. It's ghastly! The firm's name everywhere. You'll *never* get it off.'

I felt very much safer. There is a reason for this short diversion into care, packing and storage. You'll discover why later.

Walking up with the empty watering-cans from the damped-down fires, we saw Forwood leaning out of his bedroom window. We waved, he leant out wagging something in a fist.

'What is it?'

'Coat hangers. I've looked out all my stuff, ready to pack. What about coat hangers?'

'Leave them all in a neat pile on the floor, the men'll pack them tomorrow.'

'They are expensive. Coat hangers. These ones. Wood. I've got hundreds . . .'

'Just put them in a pile. Do you want a drink? There's a bottle of vodka and I've washed your glass from lunchtime.'

I remember that clearly, but I'm not so good at what followed in the next two days. It is all, as I said earlier, snatching at memories, memories of moments etched on glass, vision through space, to vision. I remember Gareth going off to the airport for his flight, remember Rupert's car sagging on its springs, overloaded with what we all called loot. Remember us watching him ease down the track, pause at the gate, wave, and turn left into the lane and Gareth saying something about him breaking down on the first hill he'd encounter; and embracing, and thanking him, his taxi humming outside the *porte d'entrée* and then Elizabeth and I quite alone. She found a rubber bone, blue, we looked at it in silence, and then she threw it into the evening.

A car came up, and it was Madame Bruna, brisk, 'surprised' eyebrows, with a large cardboard box with 'JAFFA ORANGES' on the side. She told me to put all the dirty linen and stuff into it and that Monsieur Rémy would come up to collect it before we left on the last day.

'And after that?' I said.

'After that I send it to Paris. You have somewhere in Paris where I can send it?'

'Well, not yet . . . well, yes. Hotel Lancaster. Rue de Berri. Eighth. They'll accept it. We'll be there for a little while. Thank you, Madame . . . It'll be sheets from five beds, and pillowcases . . . towels . . . napkins, five . . . I can't think how many . . . face cloths . . .' I was trying, automatically, to do our 'clean' and 'dirty' list, but she cut me short with a hand wave, got back into her car.

'You are *impertinent*, Monsieur. Eh? Madame?' She was half smiling. 'Your brother? *A demain* . . .' and she reversed and drove very quickly down the track.

I don't have the least recollection of the rest of that evening. I suppose we ate something? I think I checked the dead bonfires, I know I fixed Forwood a few decent vodkas and we washed up and set out the mugs for breakfast and filled the kettle. The teabags were in a half-used packet. I remember that clearly. And there was a brown teapot. And the one spoon we had to share, and Elizabeth taking a bunch of wilting flowers (some yellow anthemis daisies) and stuffing them into a dustbin sack and then all of us going up to bed in the echoing house.

Forwood called down to her about having something to read? And she called back that she was too tired, but she'd have a look at the Virginia Woolf she hadn't packed yet. And then it was the next day, last day but one, and the vans arrived and we just loaded things. That's all. When they had driven away, about six in the evening, the house seemed to be holding its breath with the shock, indignation and distress of being raped. The rooms were still; pillaged. The green plants stood patiently in a huddle in the Long Room waiting for Marie-Thérèse, to whom they had been promised, and a powder blue car came racing up the drive, bumping and battering, and pulled into the curve outside the *porte d'entrée* with a scatter of gravel. It was Florette Ranchett. She mouthed a muffled greeting, wound down a window, looked apprehensively about the *parking*.

'There is no dog,' I said. She nodded, reached to the seat beside her, handed me a *bidon*.

'*Potage*. My Mama's special. With my compliments. For your supper.'

I can remember very clearly how she deliberately avoided my eye, and how she handed me three soup plates and said, briskly, 'Don't bother about them. For the *poubelle* (dustbin) tomorrow, they are only from Monoprix. It'll save Madame cooking, or washing up . . .' She wound up the window, reversed, drove rapidly away. I never saw her again. I still have one plate.

Vivienne (the widow of the man who embraced his olive

trees) arrived a bit later with a bottle of Bollinger cradled in an ice bucket in a plastic bag from Monoprix. So we sat out on the terrace, under the vine, for the very last time, and it really didn't hurt. So much. Elizabeth was extremely irritated by the arrival of Marie-Thérèse and her ebullient child, Gabriella, when they came to collect the plants from the Long Room.

'Clambering in and out the bloody window all the time! I could *brain* them. Honestly! Simply no sense of occasion. No feelings . . .' They went away after a time, all my cherished plants crammed into the small car and its bulging boot. We waved. What else?

Wandering about the empty house, mugs in our hands, Vivienne suddenly said, 'I see a stuffed partridge. Unpacked. Are you having a *problem*?'

'Yes. Frankly. A huge problem.'

She reached up and took it from its dusty perch. 'You aren't any longer,' she said, and shoved it under her arm.

We went down on to the terrace, she dropped the bird into the Monoprix bag, and I poured the last of the champagne. It seemed fitting, somehow. I had not lied to Lady when I said it would be the last thing to go. Apart from ourselves, it was.

I have only the vaguest memories of the last day. A man in the kitchen packing all the knives and forks. Someone whistling 'La Petite Tonkinoise'. Watching my bed being taken round the deep bend in the staircase. Stubbing a cigarette carefully in a saucer of water on the terrace. Dead-heading a fuchsia by the door. Looking to see if the vine had started to turn. Nothing. Futile incidents. Moments. Sounds.

And then watching the cheerful, gaudy vans swaying

slowly down the track, hesitantly turning left like great yellow elephants. A majestic, stately, lumbering pair, moving carefully down the narrow winding lane to the main road. I saw the last of the sun flicker and ripple along the lengths of their roofs until they were quite lost to sight behind the fig trees up on the high bank.

On the terrace Elizabeth went over to her modest pile of luggage; checked it. I looked at Forwood, he looked at me. We smiled.

'Having your drink?'

'Sun's over the yard arm.' Banality. I'd only ever laughed at people who actually said it.

Elizabeth called, 'Here he is. Awfully late . . .'

Up at Titty-Brown Hill, Alain and Christine had seen him too. They turned and came slowly, reluctantly down towards us.

But this, I think, is where you came in?

It was Forwood's seventy-first birthday.

Chapter 9

The Hotel Lancaster is the last of the splendid *hôtels particuliers* left standing in rue de Berri. I watched all the others being demolished over the years and hideous modern buildings take their place. Now it sits rather like an ageing, still-elegant duchess at a rave-up, bewildered by the awfulness around her, steadily pretending that all is as it was before.

So discreet is the hotel that it is quite possible to walk past it and never even know it exists. Which is fine by those of us who seek its shelter. Marble floors, thick carpets, brass, light, tapestries, walls ablaze with family portraits of the thirties (it was a private house then), great urns of floral splendour; and, right in the centre, almost the hub of this lovely building, is the scarlet- and gold-lacquered lift which silently ascends to the top floor and the rooms which have terraces and views from Sacré Coeur to the Eiffel Tower, and where I normally stayed.

But that was a long time ago, before I left Le Pigeonnier. Now, a refugee, with some fourteen suitcases, an invalid, plus a bundle of walking-sticks and umbrellas, I could no longer afford the top floor: we were hotel residents now, and made do with a modest suite elsewhere, but still with a view over the secret garden in the courtyard below, and the trees and ivy of the neighbouring buildings. I mean, there was something green to look at, not just grey walls and slate roofs. The suite was small: a tiny sitting-room, a twin bedroom with, thank God, two bathrooms and two beds. This, until I could find the perfect flat in Paris, was now home. It is alarming how easily one can become institutionalized. Rather like being in a hospital, one settles down to the routine which is, in some odd way, imposed on one. I had never actually *lived* in an hotel before. Staying and living are not at all the same thing. To cope with life on the third floor – the narrowness of the little sitting-room, the unwished for intimacy of the twin-bedded room, each bathroom up a step in opposite walls so that the most private functions were no longer possible (from the sound point of view anyway) – one arranged life carefully and accordingly.

Thus, *petit déjeuner* arrived in the sitting-room, a tray for two: coffee, croissants, butter, milk, *confiture* or marmalade. A *Herald Tribune* and *The Times*. I got myself dressed and out of the way to give Forwood plenty of time for all his various activities. The outline of the day would commence after he had closed the door to the bedroom. I'd look at a paper, out the window, at the heavy silk curtains, at the ivy over the courtyard on the wall of a tall house opposite. Six storeys high. Bosky green. The roosting place for a million starlings who swept in screaming and wheeling at dusk every evening. I'd go for a walk. Perhaps to the paper stall opposite the Travellers Club, maybe down to the Place de la Concorde and back. Nothing.

At precisely eleven-thirty I'd be in my chair, a large winged thing, in the bar. It was permanently reserved, with a small table and a bucket of ice and a bottle of the house champagne. I'd talk to any member of the staff who was there or willing, skim a magazine I might have bought, accept the luncheon menu.

'Today we offer Poulet Sauté Espagnol? Or, if you order now, there are *three* delicious Loup de Mer . . . Shall I reserve one?'

And Forwood, dressed as elegantly as the English M'Lor he was always considered to be, came down in the red lacquer lift, tapping carefully with his dog's-head stick, across the marble hall.

'Did you get *Figaro*?' He eased himself into the twin of my chair, the wine poured by an attentive waiter.

So we sat. Every morning. Two elderly men in suits, sipping champagne. Reading the property column in *Figaro*.

'There is nothing *we'd* want. A mass of places in the wrong *arrondissements* . . . not much in Seven or Six . . . nothing in the Marais . . .'

By noon people were drifting in from outside, actors, lawyers, pretty girls who could have been either. There was chatter, chinking glasses and cigarette smoke. We reserved the Loup de Mer, agreed we'd go to see a flat in the Claridge building, knowing I'd hate it and could not afford it.

That was, suddenly, what life became. The trip, after leaving Le Pigeonnier, to London to check on the lurking shadow on the liver proved inconclusive, not the trip so much as the examination. No one agreed what it was. Decided that it wasn't; sent us back to Paris if not elated at least relieved. To some extent. But it wasn't much of an existence, just sitting like this. There was no room to write in the suite: the desk was meant to hold a jar of flowers, a telephone, an ashtray and the breakfast menu. That was all.

We got to the Claridge, a dark conversion job in what had been a famous old hotel. Beige walls, orange carpet, high cracked-tiled bathrooms, a view over a tarred courtyard to fifty other conversions. All shuttered. The sky somewhere above. You had to take that on trust.

'Which way does it face? North or south?'

Forwood shrugged. 'Does it matter? They want half a million. Quid. I don't see why we'd have to pay so much for an invitation to suicide.'

Or otherwise there were apartments for Rich Sheikhs – with the emphasis on the capital letters – Glittering, carpeted, gold and pale blue, miles of marble, yards of ruched pink silk. At no time, in the five months I trailed about looking at dreadful places, was there even one with a balcony, or one which looked out on to trees. Anything green. Even the sky would do.

Nothing until someone suggested a family in the Swedish or Danish embassy who had finished their tour of duty and had a 'ravishing' flat on Parc Monceau. Apart from all the nannies, and the romping children screaming up and down on swings and slides, the Parc was in the right area and fairly green – for Paris. I mean, there were trees, and shrubs, and paths to walk about on if one wanted to walk. A vaguely Proustian atmosphere. One might have seen Swann or Odette.

But the flat was hideous, the top part of an old house, facing north. No one had done anything to it, apart from smoke and eat in it, for some years. The Scandinavians are not all, as this awful place proved, house-proud or even, for that matter, very clean. Lady would have had a fit. I did.

And that, with a moment or two of delight, was the 'even tenor of our days', as they say. The moments of delight came from seeing friends, dining with or lunching with them in brasseries or restaurants. One is seldom asked to anyone's house or apartment. So one lived in suits, clean shirts, polished shoes, a good tie. All day. Every day. 'Restaurant clothes', I called them. Olga, Charlotte, Jean-Michel, Rolande, Loulou, Jane, Benedict and Dominique were all fun, all loving, all wonderfully kind. But they all of them worked, had families, kept house, marketed, telephoned, wrote and were, quite simply, occupied in living their lives. The time *they* could spare was limited, and splendid as it was to be with them, there was little that I could contribute in the way of conversation. I hardly ever went anywhere: no theatre, rarely a cinema, never a concert. Sitting for any length of time among a lot of people panicked Forwood, used, as he had been, to the silence and freedom of the hill. As, indeed, it panicked me. We walked once as far as the Left Bank and I bought some prints on the Quai Voltaire, for the new flat. Its first gift. Only we never found a flat. Nothing was considered to be possible, or else affordable.

Once, I remember, we walked in arctic crystal-clear air, under a sky the blue of a thrush's egg, beneath tall chestnut trees rusting slowly in autumn frost, and down at the Rond Point, where the gardens were massed with crimson, yellow and bronze chrysanthemums, the police held us back as Monsieur Mitterrand raced up the broad avenue, outriders roaring, huge black cars following, sirens screaming, lights flashing, heading for the Arc de Triomphe to lay his wreath on the tomb of the Unknown Soldier. It was the 11th of November. Armistice Day.

'It's Armistice Day. Did you know?' I said.

Forwood pulled the big beaver collar tight round his neck. 'Don't get chilled. Standing here. It's really bloody freezing. Let's wander back,' he said.

So we did. We drifted back up the Champs-Elysées among the crowds surging up to the Arc. Children were running, a girl was laughing, holding on to her lover's, or husband's, arm, there was the sound of distant military music, and it was just exactly twenty years to the day and hour that I had first looked through the oak trees down to Le Pigeonnier. But I didn't say anything. No point.

We turned back to rue de Berri, and the champagne bucket, as distant guns boomed out for the silence. I reckon that he knew.

I can't remember what colour the wallpaper in the little sitting-room was. God knows, I should remember it: I stared at it for long enough. Five months all told. I remember the carpet was green; the silk curtains a slate green. Can't at all remember the walls. I suppose, like so many other dreary things, I have wiped them from memory. Sometimes I saw my face in my bathroom mirror and caught it with surprise. So *that's* what anxiety looks like? Blank, no worry-lines, just flat. I've always thought anxiety, worry, made one frown. It doesn't really. If it's very serious the face just goes sort of slack. I must remember that; another clove to stick in the orange of my observing mind, to make up a rough pomander of 'visual odour'. I haven't wiped those faces from my mind. I marked them at the time for later use. I suppose all players, and writers, do that? Squirreling bits of self away. I can't remember the sitting-room walls but I can remember the curtains in the bedroom. I suppose because I got fierce bronchitis twice, and lay in coughing misery for nights. Desperate that I was keeping Forwood awake, that I would be exhausted the next day. Which I was. The curtains were yellow. Parakeets looping about with blue and red balloons and spiralling ribbons. A wide repeat. I looked at them all night through hacking, barking coughs and tears of anguish streaming. Wavering, yellow, blurry silk.

And then there was Christmas. I remember that too: but this is *all* about remembering bits and pieces, as I have told you. The first prick of horror that we were moving towards the festive season was a great jar of berried holly being set up on a pedestal. Then a tree, simpering, twinkling, wreathed in gold loops of tinsel. The first hideous poinsettia in the bar, ivy strung about, a branch of mistletoe over the telephonist in the corner. A hotel Christmas, if you are a resident anyway, isn't a great deal of fun. The menu alters a little and more seasonal fare is displayed. But young people never seem to stay in hotels. Only the old do. The young go to the mountains to ski. Anyway they do in France. There is a spurt of excitement just before Christmas Mass on Christmas Eve, and then the silence settles like dust and stays there thickly laid until the eve of New Year. That is marginally jollier.

There was a staff party, and I was made a member of the Concierges' private club, a rare honour. I was presented with the two crossed keys in gold, which was very pleasant. And Charlotte Rampling had invited us to lunch with her family and the children on 'the day' and we drove back through snow and sleet just as the starlings swung into the great wall of ivy opposite, squealing and chattering as dusk fell. We didn't fare too badly for the first Christmas away. Apart from bronchitis twice and steadily increasing Parkinson's.

Forwood had a desperate and touching belief in his professor in Nice, so we bundled off there once more and Martin looked as he always looked: unfathomable. He'd be in London, perhaps, in February. He had a paper to read at some hospital. Perhaps we could meet there? Perhaps another specialist might be approached? Perhaps. Everything was moving into perhaps-time. Unsettling.

But to London anyway for the three-monthly check and that mainly proved that getting to London from Paris was not a quick flip of half an hour or so. It was almost five hours from door to door. Exhausting for a sick man. The consultation in Harley Street was not, this time, worrying, but it was not, on the other hand, comforting. Perhaps we 'might do better to stay in London for a time?' 'How long? What is "a time"?' Polite shrugs. How could anyone possibly tell me?

The bills at the hotel, although most generously adapted to my situation, were still tremendous by the standards of life at Le Pigeonnier. The taxis and air fares, the consultants' fees, the pills and potions all added up to a frightening amount, weakening disastrously the supporting beams of my ever-optimistic structure, which began to sag now quite a lot. Added to which the drabness of an inactive life, the routine of meals, wandering off to look at hideous and unsuitable apartments, living in cramped, if elegant, quarters were desperately bad for morale.

And now that Forwood could no longer, with safety, really be allowed to go for his walk round the block unattended, it made life cruelly restricting for him. He was able to go down to the lobby on his own, provided he used the lift, and took his stick, and one morning he came back with the mail. A packet from London. From the BBC. A script for a TV film. To be shot, over seven weeks, in London starting early March. It just seemed that fate might have had a hand in things.

'What's it like? Any good? I'd be surprised . . .'

'It's not bad. It's literate. Well written. I am not being asked to play someone's grandfather or a druid.'

'Is it a decent part. Size, I mean?'

'Three main characters. Yes. I mean I'm not supporting or anything.'

He read it, as he always did every film script or play I had ever accepted, and passed his opinion. Whatever his opinions, I always made the final decision. 'I'd think it was quite a decent idea. I'd go for it, if the director is any use. Do we know him?'

Knew of, had all the details to hand: splendid Eileen Atkins had agreed, they were trying to get Lee Remick to commit. She would if I would. In that little sitting-room I suddenly knew this was a chance I'd not be offered again. The chance to get out of the welcoming, caring hotel, out of the deadening routine of a non-life, and a reason (if I really needed one) for going back to England. I now realized, fully, that I could no longer avoid the obvious. Life was shredding away rapidly. I would have to accept. Pack the fourteen cases (fifteen with a large box which had arrived one day with 'JAFFA ORANGES' on its side) and get up and move on to something with at least the chance of a future.

'I'll say yes. Okay?'

'Okay. Fine.'

'You know what it means. Actually? Brutally?'

'Back. I know that. Accept the thing. Let's start up again. There is still time.'

'Well, we can always come back. I'll rent a house somewhere. Short lease. Chelsea area. If things work out we can come right back, it'll be summer then, easier to flat-hunt here.'

'Don't pretend. We won't come back. This part is over. Call them and accept.'

★

A long time ago, outside Senequier on the port at Saint-Tropez, toying with an early drink, I saw, with a slight fall of pleasure I confess, a young actor I barely knew (I had once worked with his stepfather) preening along on this bright September day with a tall, vivid, red-headed girl wearing not very much at all, but what there was were pink and white dots, and it was a bikini. That's how long ago it was. Seeing me he waved and bounded towards my table, the bikini'd girl dragged protestingly (from shyness) behind him. His wife, it transpired, and how were we all? We were all delightfully well, thanks, and do sit down. So they did. I mean, what else?

We all shook hands, ordered drinks, laughed a good deal and were still happily together in a restaurant on the port much later eating lobsters. Maude (my name for her) and I have remained devoted friends ever since. We have been through pretty well every eventuality, good and bad, that life can chuck at one and survived intact. A friendship of that kind is for treasuring.

Her regular friends call her merely by her surname, Melford; her given name is Jill, which dates her and doesn't suit her. I call her Maude because she more resembles a Gaiety Girl than a suburban Jill. Maude Melford is very music hall and jolly. And, with some reluctance at first, she accepted the name and it has stayed thus.

A long preamble, this, but she is a fixture in my life, so it is essential to know her. She acts, she decorates, she can fix fuses and cook up a feast, gardens and plants things, can paint walls and clean floors, muck out ponds, knows every auction room in town as well as half the estate agents. She will drive you to hospital, to a funeral, a garden party. She is gay, bawdy, sentimental and joyful – in short, she is a sort of Swiss Army knife: screwdriver to scissors, corkscrew and nail file. And extremely attractive. Every man should have one. Who else to call from Paris, therefore, once I knew that I was taking the show on the road again, than Maude?

'Maudie? Hi. It's me.'

'Hi! How's "me"? Problems?'

'In one. I'm in Paris, as you know. Coming back.'

A longish pause.

'What do you need?'

'A house. Short lease. Small. Hasker Street, Markham, Bourn? One of those.'

'I see. Anything else?'

'South facing. With a garden if possible?'

'Goodness me. You *do* ask a lot of your friend.'

'Furnished, darling.'

'Guessed that. Medical reasons or work?'

'Bit of both. But work. In a month, six weeks.'

'You've been away so long you probably don't know how impossible it is to get anything like that. Unless you are very, very rich?'

'I'm not. Poor after five months here. Pennies.'

'You *are* in for a surprise. Where do I call you and when?'

I packed the fourteen suitcases in the cramped little sitting-room, gave away enough old clothing to fill a single Oxfam depot to the hotel staff, most of whom, below stairs, were from Vietnam or Algeria, and left for the airport in two enormous cars. It had been suggested that with so much luggage it would have been wise, and more comfortable for Forwood, if we took the train and the ferry. But I insisted on flying, thinking it less tiring, so we did. And that evening, as we slumped into chairs in a small suite at the Connaught, exhausted but safe, with a large drink each, we watched the news on television.

A ferry capsized in Zeebrugge – Fate obviously had some other trick in store for us. Maude had found a house, just what I had asked for, garden and all, for a very fair rent. The owner, a chum of hers, lived in the basement, I got the rest. It was an agreeable place altogether, and Maude sped about with sheets, soap, magazines and flowers, and after two or three days at the Connaught (to deal with the BBC and the television people) we moved to Chelsea. A new chapter started.

It seemed to me that the line had been traced on the map of the future and that it would be unwise to ignore the route laid down. I was now near (within walking distance of) doctors, there were friends close by, Maude took me to Safeway's and Tesco, explained the prices and money, and we walked round Peter Jones, rented a television set, bought some tea, milk, sugar and so on, and, finally, I unpacked and started to settle down until I learned, too late to weep, that the entire film was now to be made in *Cardiff*. Not London after all. I had signed a contract; we were too far in. Cardiff it had to be, and Cardiff and its alarming Holiday Inn it was. Except that I insisted on getting back to London every weekend. I got to know the motorway extremely well. So one commuted between a plastic and veneer suite five floors up in the Holiday Inn, overlooking a car park and a Private Bookshop, and I started work on my first British-made product for over twenty years.

Before work begins it is necessary to submit oneself to a medical examination for insurance; just so that, in the event of you suddenly falling dead, no one is going to be ruined in the company. It is not a very serious matter this. As long as you can haul yourself, upright, over the doctor's threshold, give a urine sample without much fuss, and sign the questionnaire without shaking, you'll be passed fit. I was – to my mild astonishment, for the bronchitis attacks in Paris had left lingering trails of wheezing and gasping and a general feeling of malaise. So I sought a medical for myself, which I deemed essential if I were now to be responsible for two people, plus a rented house, plus a very long role in a saga for TV.

All seemed well, although my legs turned to jelly at the sight of two intense black spots on the X-rays over both lungs. I was briskly assured that these were my nipples and not important. However, smoking three packs of cigarettes a day was of importance. I was strongly advised to stop. That day. I did: finished off my packet of Extra Longs, chucked it away and never smoked again. I had smoked since I was at school in Scotland, from the age of thirteen. Grabbing secret fags in the school lavatories was about as exciting and fulfilling as anything that happened to me up there. But ever since Patrick had introduced the word 'cancer' into my vocabulary that hot day down in the Long Room, I had given in to my weakness and took a cigarette as soon as the last one was finished. It was particularly intense, I found, when I was writing up in the olive store. I smoked constantly, ash piled in ugly mounds everywhere, crushed butts stank to heaven. It was astonishing to me after my examination that I had suffered as mildly as I had. A 'little touch of asthma' was all I was told. It was enough to be going on with.

I knew very well, driving down that first day to Cardiff and the saga, that I was about to play two roles. One for which I would be paid, modestly, which people would see, and the other which merited no payment at all and which no one must see. The role of carer, the dictionary states, means, among other things, 'heed, caution, charge and protection'. I did not really require a definition. I knew very well. The film work was pleasant, my companions warm and affectionate, all was pretty well. Sometimes I got an afternoon off and went down to the coast to walk along a beach, smell the salt, listen to the sea, feel the wind. One returned to the fifth floor of the ill-named Holiday Inn almost recharged.

But it was, other than work on the show, a soul-less existence. Especially for my ailing manager. He had nothing to do, apart from scribble down sums on sheets of paper and fuss about with his pocket-calculator.

'We can't *possibly* have spent that much in Paris! All I ever bought were those two bloody animal prints on Quai Voltaire, and they were for peanuts . . .'

But the figures grew more and more alarming. Paris, for five months, in a small, but charming, suite, plus air fares, taxis, doctors, not to mention the house champagne, all made a disastrous hole in my fortunes. Such as they were.

Though at least it did give him something to do, apart from the walks along the beach, which he could manage because the sands, or pebbles, were firm to walk on, and which almost broke the spell of ill health for a little. However, two days before the very end of shooting, after such a walk, he suddenly collapsed in the suite with a temperature of 103°. So cold that his teeth rattled like dice in a box.

Piling him into his bed, grabbing all my bedding from my room, covering all with our coats made no difference. I called down urgently to the ever-smiling uncaring automatons at the desk ('Welcome! I am Debbie, how can I help you have a nice day?') for a hot-water bottle. It took them by horrified surprise and an hour and a half to deliver. When it arrived I'd almost forgotten why I'd called for the thing, and the grudging elderly maid asked if I wanted it filled with hot water? I said, 'Yes. *Very* hot', and she said, '*Du!*' and that she never knew where she was! The last people in the suite had been an entire football team celebrating their victory, and she had a terrible time of it, and *Du!* the water in the bath would be hot enough. So . . .

Forwood said weakly that he was sick to death of hotel rooms and rented houses, for God's sake, and that he was certain he'd be better just as long as he could get settled down 'with my own things around me. They're still in store, in Cannes.'

Two days later I drove with him up the M4 to London. For the last time. His temperature had temporarily stabilized, the saga was finished (or my part in it anyway), and although he looked pretty frail and washed out, he appeared to get better from the moment that we paid the toll on the Severn Bridge.

'Selectivity' was one of Norah Smallwood's favourite words, which she drummed into me every time she returned a manuscript, or part of, covered with her vigorous deletions. 'Get to the point! Don't faff about, carry on with the story line. Be *selective*!'

So I'm trying to follow her instructions. There is no need to witter on about lawyers, accountants, solicitors, how I got my first cheque book, or how strangely difficult it was to find oneself a French resident in one's own land.

My arrival in London was a bit of a shock, after the familiarity of living, as I had done for so long, cosseted by the Connaught. Now, thrown suddenly into urban life, on one's own, after so many years, in someone else's house, having to cope by oneself with food, and drink, the laundry, the gas meter, the shopping (a very different matter to the market in town, and far more nerve-wracking), I confess that I found myself in an extremely disjointed state. I had to remember how to cross a road, not to call people in shops 'Monsieur' or 'Madame', as had been my habit, never to shake hands with a waiter (I do, anyway), and try to work out that there were now fifty pence to what had been, when I left, ten shillings. It was bewildering, to say the least. So I'll be selective, leave all that stuff as background, and get down to basics.

Maude and I went from one unsuitable house, or flat, to another. I grew weary of other people's grubby kitchens, tobacco-filled rooms, dingy curtains, filthy bathrooms and refrigerators full of left-overs and fish fingers, underwear hanging over baths to dry. Not all the places we saw were like this – some were staggering in their splendour, opulence and the absurdity of their prices – but in the main it was evident to me that the French could teach the British and Scandinavians a good deal about cleanliness and house-pride. However, nothing was of the least interest. Too expensive, too dark, the wrong area or a pub on the corner. Bernard Walsh, the excellent fellow who had dealt with all my house sales and purchases since the fifties, was delighted to hear from me, saddened by the reason. But, yes indeed, he'd start to look about for what I needed, took down the particulars, and launched into the attack.

The little house in Chelsea was a wonderful haven for temporary living, while breath was caught and cases were unpacked, and it was near to every shop I needed within a very few minutes. No need for taxis now, but there always was the old hire car firm, Satchell, that I had used ever since my Rank days. They still functioned, and for those increasingly uneasy trips to Harley Street they were invaluable, and with Bob Pearson and Ron Jones, friends from long ago, unease was comforted and soothed.

Maude managed to find a lady to come and do the things I really couldn't do about the house, like ironing collars and much of the dismal work. She was a sullen Polish girl who, as she frequently reminded me in a growl, had been a student of something or other in Warsaw and now bitterly resented the fact that she was, as she called it, '*kneeing* always to rich people like a slave'. She was forced to accept any work she could while awaiting a visa for Canada, where, I was assured, there was a big, sympathetic, Polish community to which she knew she would be welcomed. She would never have to '*knee* to the rich' again. She was damned certain that she would knee as little as possible to me, and when I gave her a rise in salary (to Maude's indignation: 'You'll ruin the market. You pay her the fair price!'), to encourage her slothful efforts, she shrugged, stuffed the money in her bosom and said that as I was so rich I could have afforded more. I bought a whole bottle of whisky a week! *She* couldn't afford that! She really was rather disagreeable, but I was assured that she was honest. So I settled for Miss Warsaw, remembering, in flashes of memory, the noisy, laughing, weeping, angry, often joyous, always brave and affectionate 'Lady'.

However, it was essential that I had some assistance. I was

trying to write again, and had to be available to Forwood for the journeys to Harley Street, which seemed, gradually, to increase once we had, as it were, settled in London. He felt the need of medical reassurance at all times, so I saw rather more waiting-rooms and old copies of the *Field* and *Punch* than I ever wanted.

Then Bernard called one day to say that he had found a possible house; it was not yet on the open market but he knew that it was going up for sale. Could we meet by the flower stall outside St Mary Abbot's in High Street, Kensington? I said yes: my gut lurched with despair. 'I have a feeling this may be *exactly* what you want!' Bernard said, and I called for the hired car and we headed 'across the Park,'

Most of my adult life, and during all of my childhood, I had heard that to live north, 'across the Park', was considered to be rather a bad move. It was not quite acceptable, 'across the Park'. The people there were 'different' from those south of the Park. It frankly didn't bother me at all, from the point of view of snobbery, or inverted snobbery. I just didn't care for it. It was a different country, Kensington. Nothing to do with Chelsea. I knew Chelsea very well, its streets and squares, its mix of people. I was at home and secure there. Kensington was an alien land to me, full of people who were similar but subtly different from the gayer, casual, more bohemian Chelsea-ites. It was more forbidding, genteel, more Victorian, uglier, seedier even, less friendly and now fast becoming a mixed-race area of tatty bed-sits.

Crossing the Park from south to north had exactly the same effect on me emotionally as crossing the border from England to Scotland had all those years ago when I was sent off from Euston Station into sheer, unadulterated loneliness and misery. And school. Poor spoiled brat! And spoiled brat I suppose I was that day in the car driving to meet Mr Walsh. If he was right, and it *was* just the house we wanted, then I'd go ahead, if all things were to be agreed, and sever my safety cords of familiarity, warmth and security in Chelsea.

Desolation sang: but I didn't let it show. And no one heard it. It was the right house. At least it would have been, anywhere else but where it was. But that was set aside. Forwood was enraptured. A small early eighteenth-century house, beautifully maintained, light, elegant, set in a narrow street opposite the gardens of a large monastery. It had pleasing rooms, one on top of the other, five floors connected by a simple, elegant, very narrow staircase up which, I could instantly see, much of the stuff sitting presently in store in France would never find its way.

But suddenly Forwood was alive again, plans were being made as I wandered reluctantly about the pleasant rooms. I could hear him and Mr Walsh chattering away eagerly. There was no garden, merely what was euphemistically called a 'patio', exactly eight feet long by five wide, backed by a high wall smothered in a rampant Nelly Moser, with some terracotta pots crouching about the stone-paved floor stuffed with ferns: ferns because it was obvious that, even on a hot August day, the sun never glanced into this dark pit except, perhaps, for a fleeting second or two in the evening. However, it was exactly what the patient wanted, and the sudden gentle spurt of energy, the rousing of interest, the lifting of his sad spirit, made its purchase imperative.

Bernard was given instructions to start negotiations right away, which he did, while I contacted the firm in Cannes to release the stored furniture and send me a copy of the inventory (I had one which Forwood had compiled in France, but theirs was shorter for customs), and told them that I would advise them of the exact dates. They said it would be sent off immediately, but I had to contact the UK branch of XYZ who would be responsible for carting the stuff to Kensington, when the time was right. My heart plummeted at this news. XYZ was the same firm who had destroyed so much of my furniture and goods on the way out to France.

'I am certain', said the happy voice all the way from Cannes, 'that you will be *very* satisfied. We use them almost all the time and it is August, you know? Holidays?' Meaning, politely, accept.

So I just shut up. Even *I* couldn't quite believe that disaster could strike again. Which was daft.

Now the evenings in the Chelsea house were filled with conversation and plans were drawn, albeit with a shaky hand but still plans, and for three or four days we drove across the Park to measure up the rooms. One day we arrived to find a huge sofa sticking out of a great hole in the wall where the sitting-room, on the second floor, was. *I* now had a sofa, found by diligent Maude, which would have to travel into the same room very shortly by the same route. I grabbed the two toiling gentlemen, Frank and George, who were covered in brick dust and mortar, and kept them for myself. I was starting to become involved as well. I had not the least idea how to go about finding a replacement for Monsieur Rémy in the middle of Kensington. So these two were the birds in the hand and not in the bush. Some weeks later they swung my second-hand sofa through the same hole in the wall, re-bricked it, and stayed on to build bookcases and do whatever decorating was needed. Not much, but the bookcases were essential.

One hot day a bored voice called to say that all my worldly goods had arrived at their depot outside London. We were all together at last after a year, separated now by a short distance, but on the same island. Even I felt more cheerful, my slight worry about the new house merely being that the front door opened immediately on to the street, and that already someone had pushed a used condom through the letterbox. But this, after all, was London, not the hill. And lots of people's houses opened directly on to the street in London. I'd have to get used to it. I never, quite frankly, ever did.

There was a first, very unhappy visit to the XYZ depot outside London. No one was about; it was, I was informed by a lard-faced girl in glasses eating a Mars bar, the lunch break, but she showed me where the stuff would be. Huge warehouses set among acres of cracked concrete roads, threading through tufts of ugly weeds and bramble. Wire, rust, broken boxes, old crates, a forgotten mantelpiece lying among crushed tea-chests. Far up an alley between the warehouses I saw a group of men sitting around a big white table, in someone's armchairs. They were eating sandwiches and drinking from cans of beer. Closer I saw that it was my big white table from the terrace, and I was the someone in whose chairs they were sitting: the white armchairs in the Cogolin cotton from the Long Room.

They looked up, vaguely hostile, as I got nearer. 'You want something then?' I had interrupted a game of cards.

'Well, help, if possible?'

'Lunch break. Come back two-thirty.'

'You are sitting in my chairs. At my table. Could you tell me where the rest of my stuff is? Just so that I could check through. I did speak to your Mr Broad.'

'He's a fart, to begin with. Broad. These *your* chairs?'

'Yes. And the table. Sorry.'

A tall, red-headed man got up, wiped his hands on dirty overalls.

'You who I think you are?'

'I don't know who you think I am.'

'Bogarde. Dirk Bogarde. A film star? Right?'

'Years ago. No more. But I am Bogarde. Yes.'

'Shouldn't have put it on the pallets. Your name. That was barmy. On the papers, the invoice like, inventory, it's not that. It's Van der something . . .'

'That's my true name. The other is my stage name.'

'Well . . .' He sat down again. In my white chair. 'Mistake to put it on the pallets. Very tempting, that is. When they unloaded the stuff at Calais someone must have wrote your name in big letters all over them. Red chalk. Asking for it that was. Very naughty.'

I know that I stood perfectly still in shock. 'Unloaded the stuff. At *Calais*?'

Another man screwed up his sandwich wrapper, squashed a couple of beer cans in his fist. 'Yers. Reloaded on a British ferry. From the containers. Can't ship the containers. Your stuff's along there, down the left, shed 5. We'll be down there soon. Come on you lot, up!'

I went back to the car. Forwood was sitting on a box by the side of the pathway ticking things in his inventory. He looked up as I reached him.

'Found someone?'

'It's all been repacked. Our stuff. From the French containers. At Calais. Some of it's already been unpacked and being used. Give me your wallet, I've got to buy some goodwill, I fear.'

'Oh dear God! Not a repeat of last time?'

'Well, it's begun pretty grimly. If you have tears, as they say, prepare to shed them now.'

He handed me his wallet and I helped him to his feet.

Pretty funny, if you think about it.

Chapter 10

I have said that I am writing from memory, with no diaries or journals to aid me, but there *are*, however, a few odd pieces of stuff which have survived only because they originated here, in England, after the move from France. Not much, and nothing of value to me except perhaps the original inventory made by Forwood before we quit Le Pigeonnier. This he kept in a bright new school exercise book. He was using it on that wretched day at XYZ's storage depot, sitting on the box by the concrete road. The inventory itself is of no account: almost everything on it has been dispersed now. But, tucked away at the back, written much later (I can tell by his handwriting), is what appears to be the draft of a letter. It is unfinished, undated, and I can't guess to whom it was addressed, or even if it was ever sent. I reckon it was perhaps to someone in America, judging by one reference, but I can't really be sure. However, I only discovered it today, wondering how to start this chapter, and it seems to me that it fits quite well. Anyway, here it is as written.

> *I know you'll forgive the elegant writing paper. but* [*sic*] *you may not so cheerfully hack a path through the tangled Jungle* [*sic*] *that passes for handwriting. I'm simply not accustomed to writing without a machine. and in addition to that there is a tendency, if one has Parkinson-related problems, for one's handwriting to shoot suddenly up through the ceiling. and our three machines are in storage. isn't all that detail just fascinating? Anyway it was a joy to get your letters during a ratty Christmas, with D. slowly recuperat-*

ing and fighting off this December Bronch.[sic] Not very satisfactory it must be admitted; but half of the London population seems to be prey to it and the glories of Kensington High Street are heard as from a dog show. Yes, leaving Le Pigeonnier was dreadful, as we always knew it would be when the time should come. and it came, when it decided to, very suddenly. One minute we seemed to be on the terrace and a quarter of an hour afterwards we were ensconced in the Lancaster in Paris – another climate, another world. But Coward [Noël Coward] always said 'If you have to be ill be ill in English' and as usual he was right. I suppose. I'm on a course of a new Japanese invention, by which I mean just tablets, and I seem to feel certainly well on them. Of course neither D. nor I have any remote form of Health Insurance in this country, and between the two of us we could probably open our own clinic.

So now we are here, in a little early 18th century cottage in what might be called 'London's Little Montmartre'. I have no doubt that it is referred to in such terms and it certainly has qualities of Paris about it. And D. dislikes it intensely so I reckon we'll be on the move again ere long. In the meantime it really is rather attractive, but no-where to have a living in maid or man-servant. D. without his little studio up at Le Pigeonnier, has not found it possible to write, so he's fairly grotty. We were supposed to spend Christmas with David and Patsy Puttnam, but I really didn't feel quite up to it. They have a lovely house: in a mill in fact: in Berkshire. I think that David is returning to L.A. [Los Angeles] before packing up and quitting the place. I am sad about it – we all are – but I really never saw it coming to pass. I just do not see any major American Studio in the hands of a Limey.

And there it ends, unsigned. It is curious to read it now, not pleasant. It feels sneaky, reading someone else's letter behind, as it were, their back. I can't think to whom it was addressed. Someone in America? I don't think he'd ever have compared the house in Kensington, or its area, to Montmartre to anyone in France. But it does prove that he *did* like the house and that I disliked it.

I did my best never, I thought until this letter, to let it show. I suppose it sort of emanated from me or something? I didn't actively display my dislike, I was determined only that he should be comfortable. He hadn't much cared for the little Chelsea house because he thought it was 'too frilly and feminine' and found renting someone else's furniture and bedding 'unattractive'. He was at all times the most incredibly fastidious of men.

His reference to the Puttnams is interesting. He was devoted to them both, admiring David enormously for his vision, honesty and determination, and Patsy because he loved the look of her, her beauty and her solid-down-to-earth sense, and above all for her devotion to her husband. He considered Puttnam, rightly I believe, to be the only possible hope of a renaissance, if there ever could be one, in the British film industry. No one else had his audacity or courage. We dined together at Taillevant in Paris the night before they left for L.A. and his Columbia deal. It saddened Forwood that Britain should lose him. Saddened him deeply when it all turned to slander, pain and humiliation. But that evening at Taillevant he made a short-list for Patsy of his most cherished friends in L.A. whom, he knew, could help them both to settle in. Unhappily it didn't work out that way. They hardly had time to settle in before they were deliberately eased out.

I have said 'wretched' about the day up at the storage depot: that's precisely the word I have to use. Every pallet, the large chipboard containers in which all one's goods are packed, opened up to reveal heartbreak upon heartbreak. It was an exact repeat of the trip that they had made out to France. Even worse.

I moved tactfully about the card-playing group sitting at my terrace table that day pressing ten-pound notes into accepting hands as freely as communion wafers. Twenty, in the case of the red-haired gentleman who said that he was Ernie, who turned from truculence to infinite kindness once he discovered, for himself, just what a disastrous error it had been to have my name, my 'film star' name, scrawled across the chipboard walls. As one piece of ruined furniture followed another, as one broken frame, smashed mirror, torn and legless chair, splintered piece of rosewood, or canvas landscape thrust through by a marble lampbase made its appearance, Ernie muttered sadly, 'My word. They *have* done you over.' Presumably out of spite and, could it be, envy?

The only things which had survived more or less intact were those which had been packed in the cardboard boxes. Wrapped, as Elizabeth had said, in tissue paper, brown paper, and sealed all around with red and yellow sticky tape with the name of the packers in Cannes. Everything else, unwrapped on the dock side at Calais (Ernie had seen it all with his own eyes), was damaged almost beyond repair.

Worse even: some things had simply never arrived. Pictures, ornaments, a ravishing Capellio poster, life size, of Mistinguette, pots and jars, bedheads and footstools – all were apparently left behind on the dock. Because, as Ernie said, there wasn't room for them in the pallets. Naturally enough: slung into the things like skips, it was junk ready for the tip – there *would* be no room.

But the thing which was the most damning, when it came to lawyers and solicitors and all the rest, and of course it did, was the fact that the junk was wrapped roughly in sheets of newspaper. *English* newspapers. Of a date far later than the original date of the packing, which was October of the year before. Proving that all the care lavished on the stuff in France had been a waste of effort. Someone had unwrapped every individual piece and dumped the lot: hence the white armchairs, now covered in oil stains, and the terrace table plus four or five of its small tin chairs, being used by the firm's employees as a restful set-up for a game of poker and a few cans of Heineken. The one cheering thing was that almost all the large paintings from the Long Room had remained intact. Packed with meticulous care they had obviously escaped damage, probably because they were too difficult to unwrap, or rip off, due to their protective covering. Perhaps there was just not enough time to take a bash at them? Or because they could not be actually *seen* they did not incite destruction? Anyway, I could, more or less, judge which they were by their shapes, and rather like Helen Keller felt my way about and collected up five of the smaller ones (the Ben Nicholson among them) and stuffed them in the boot of the car.

Ron, our driver, was a little doubtful that this operation was 'quite all right'. They had to be checked out with the inventory? But Ernie turned a blind eye, said he 'hadn't seen nothing', and 'our Mr Broad', who apparently held the inventory, very wisely decided not to present himself. I saw him coming down the alley at one point, flourished a Queen Anne chair leg at him, which stopped him dead, and when I raised a splintered panel of satinwood in my other hand he turned back to the sanctuary of his office with the whey-faced Mars-bar-eater. We never set eyes on him again. Which, in a way, was sad, because I had a violent desire to ram his wire-rimmed glasses down his throat, but that would only have meant a charge of grievous bodily harm, which would have been the truth but more than I could handle just at that time, so I decided not to try and pursue him and got on with the miserable job in hand. I had witnesses in Ron and, indeed, in Ernie, who said that he would be happy to give evidence against 'our Mr Broad and the sodding firm'. Which is why he exists under a pseudonym here.

After a good deal of denial, then whining, and blustering, and frothy whinnying, XYZ, faced with lawyers and solicitors and the rest, grudgingly agreed to pay for 'restoration' without ever admitting that there might have been an error on their side. As before, years ago in France, they were terrified of publicity, and when I had suggested, pleasantly, that I could arrive at the depot with a representative and photographer from a tabloid newspaper, they rapidly caved in. 'Restoration' didn't amount to a fortune. It was the utter loss and destruction of things which saddened me. Some things which I had cherished for years were not restorable. And even if, as the disdainful little valuer from Monte Carlo once had said, the things were 'amusing' and of 'no intrinsic value', I had bought them and lived with them and loved them. Anyway, you can't fight an old-established firm.

Maude swung into action and came to my rescue. After pouring a good deal of Scotch down my throat – I was hoarse with woe and anger – she arranged for a friend of hers, a man of impeccable pedigree in the auction rooms, to remove all my pallets (I think there were twelve altogether) from the depot, plus the wreckage, and have the whole lot transferred to another depot in Fulham. Safer there and easier for me to go to from Kensington. I think this is what happened. It is hardly surprising that XYZ permitted this violation of their premises. Once the words 'press' and 'photographer' were mentioned they had withdrawn as swiftly as the snail into the shell. So I never got the chance to deal with 'our Mr Broad' – and I *did* mind that very much indeed.

The Kensington house began to take shape. Smaller by far than Le Pigeonnier, it required less furniture, which was just as well frankly, and most of the big pictures simply couldn't be got up the narrow staircase. So they had to be sent back to storage and the ones that fitted were the ones I had to accept. It was an imperative weeding out. Much of the furniture was equally restricted because it wouldn't go round the staircase bend. We couldn't go on banging holes in the walls and tearing out the windows to sling things in and out, even though Frank and George were willing and able.

So we settled for what would fit the Doll's House and then began the real unpacking. Elizabeth, Maude and Brock's wife, Kim, came to help unwrap pots and pans, cups and saucers, knives and forks, and various bits of china. The kitchen, in the basement with shadowy views of whitewashed walls on both sides, rang with happy cries of 'Where does this go?' or 'You'll never use this here!' or 'If you don't want it I'll take it, willingly . . .' and '*Three* saucepans! With buttercups on them. Anyone found the lids?'

It was happy confusion and the dustbins filled with paper and straw and the women looted joyously, because I chucked everything away that I couldn't immediately think of placing or, more important, using. As I could hardly crack an egg or boil water I didn't know what many things were for. I kept Forwood out of the way and made him fiddle about with his stereo equipment and Montserrat Caballé up in the sitting-room.

Eventually it all got sorted out, roughly, and the first month ended. We had a base at last, familiar things – those not being repaired, veneered, polished, screwed together – around us. Shirts, socks and vests were in most of our drawers. We were in.

I didn't hear the wind at first. Stuffed with sleeping-pills in my narrow bed up in the attic, I only really became aware of anything unusual when I opened doped eyes and saw, silhouetted against the landing light, the naked figure of Forwood holding his portable radio. The BBC news at three o'clock informed us, in a calm voice, that there was a hurricane blowing. I remember putting on a lamp, staggering towards the window which was slamming and crashing and trying to secure it with the belt of my dressing-gown. I got Forwood down the stairs back to his bed and we sat listening to the radio. No mistral this: a real, honest to God hurricane. And in three hours' time the car was due, and we were supposed to be in Pentonville Road, for the scanner.

I dressed and at four wandered out into the gusting dawn. Light was slowly leaking into the night. At the top of Church Street there was a double decker bus, all the lights blazing, abandoned in the street. Desolation. The canopy from the Indian corner shop bucketed and jigged down the hill, papers flew like demented gulls, bricks, slates, shards of chimney pots, slabs of shattered tile from somewhere formed a rockery of ruin all the way down the street. Only the traffic lights seemed to have retained their normal function: endlessly red, amber, green . . . A branch, hysterical with twisting leaves, sailed frantically away, eddied upwards, crashed into the doorway of the Pâtisserie Française.

I got back to the house, holding on to the railings and crawling on my knees when they petered out.

'It's pretty bad. I don't suppose the car will even get here. Wreckage all over the place.' Forwood had managed to dress, shaved himself, cut his face. A scrap of Kleenex wagged on his chin. 'I'll *have* to get to the scan. It's the most important one.'

I had made some tea, and we sat in the kitchen among half-emptied packing-cases and assorted casseroles. The car arrived, amazingly, on time at six o'clock. It was not Ron, this morning, but Tony: young, bearded, determined. I was grateful to him for his calm. No problem, he said, we'll get there. And we did, by driving through the Park across the grass, swerving past giant trees, scattered tooth-picks on a billiard table, across the branch-strewn sand of Rotten Row, dodging flailing boughs, bumping and bouncing. Holding on, spinning, sticking, revving, bursting free, we finally reached the gates by Marble Arch. It was fully light by now. Tony, I noticed with interest, had never lost his cockaded cap. 'I'll wait,' he said. 'I have a book. I hope they've got power in there, lots of lines are down.'

They had. It took a little time to get everything together, but eventually they came for him and I sat looking through a battered copy of *Woman and Beauty*. Wasn't a good scan. I got a feeling that it wouldn't be when a bespectacled man in a white coat passed me on my way to the scanning chamber. He touched my arm and said, '*Very* good luck.' I said thank you. But I knew, by his compassionate smile and the hand on my arm, that there was doubt. So does kindness betray us.

A pleasant Asian woman, crisp in white, a shining bun, smiling, arrived with Forwood. 'I'm afraid I peed myself.' He was bleakly apologetic. She shook her head, earrings swung. 'People nearly always do. We are quite used to that.' And to me she said, 'Mr Wrigley has your telephone number of course? He'll be sure to call you in a day or two.'

He did, one late afternoon. I was putting summer shirts and things away in a drawer in my attic; Forwood was down in the kitchen making himself some tea. I picked up the telephone instantly, before he would even reach it. Mr Wrigley said it was not good news, he was afraid. It was not a shadow. A tumour. I heard myself saying, 'Is it very big?', as if that would make any difference, and his reply, 'I'm not talking about a pea. I'm talking about three bloody centimetres . . .' When he rang off, seconds later, I heard the kitchen extension hang up.

The cornflower blue carpet up to Wrigley's office was always so fresh and clean, a yellowing monstera deliciosa in the corner of the stairs – I always thought it was a silly name, always wondered how many anxious and frightened feet had gone down the blue flight to Harley Street. Or up, for that matter.

Forwood wanted to know if he would be in pain and was assured that he would not be. Cancer of the liver was not painful. He refused, there and then, any vague possibility of chemotherapy. 'I'm too vain. I'm damned if I'm going to lose what hair I have; I've lost all my teeth already. Clackers. I'm not doing any more.'

Wrigley, a good man, accepted that, and said that there was a new pill on the market. Japanese. It had been unusually successful in a large number of cases there. Would he like to try them? He had a supply he'd brought from Tokyo and was willing to share them with accepting patients who would take the risk. Forwood took it. As he said, 'What else do I do?' It was agreed that the treatment would commence from the following Monday. I don't remember why.

Ron was driving that day. In the back we were both silent. When we turned into Oxford Street he began a long, jolly story about some competition in which he'd taken part on Tenerife: windsurfing. He'd won a cup and a free return first-class ticket on Iberian Airlines. Pretty good, wasn't it? At his age? After all, he pointed out with a deprecating cough, he was no chicken was he? At his age, pretty good, eh? Excellent.

Somehow, oddly enough, now that it had been spelled out, in large letters, now that the very worst was known, it felt not so bad. Apprehension, not being sure, the constant wear and tear of anxiety hidden, covered, fell away. There was no need to speak of the thing: it had been spoken of. There was always the chance that the Japanese pill might work, might, as Wrigley said, start to 'demolish' the tumour. Still there was hope. Not all was black and lost, there was plenty yet to work for and to fight for. We'd just, we agreed, shut up about it. Even Gareth, his son, was not to be told. No one should know. What on earth was the point of dragging others into the affair? It would only make it worse all round. So that was it. It was rather as if we were two dogs who had successfully swum a flood-raged river. Safely across, after great effort, we stood on the bank, shivering, trembling. Now we must shake off the water, roll ourselves dry, and run off once more to seek new adventures. Something like that.

At any rate, Frank and George had finished building two desks in a little room next to mine, with shelves and drawers all about, and Forwood was soon occupied carting books and papers and files carefully. To start up the new 'office'. I hung all the pictures which could be got to go up the staircase. It took quite a long time, clambering about with hammers, picture hooks and tape measures.

Forwood came down from his office to admire my efforts. 'Don't overdo things. Remember we're no chickens,' he said, remembering Ron.

'I've just finished. That's the last. *The Yellow Sea.* Like it there?'

'Fine. I'll go down and do some rice. A bit of rice and prawns for supper? Okay for you?'

'Okay. Need any help?'

'May spill a little. I think I can manage. I'll call.'

He went down the stairs to the kitchen. I poured my first whisky of the day, picked up *Exchange and Mart*, which I bought to see if I could find a second-hand carpet for the downstairs room, and instantly found myself, face crushed against the banisters, inelegantly lying head first down the stairs. I still remember the smell of the carpet. And my surprise.

It was a bit jokey.

Lying there I couldn't understand anything. I hadn't had a drink. Not a sip. My legs were twisted through the banisters. That was clever of them. The carpet was rough on my face. Like being pressed into corn stubble. I couldn't move. But I *could* speak. I yelled down the stairs, 'Stroke!', but Forwood was running water in the kitchen and didn't immediately hear. When he did he came up as quickly as he could, ashen-faced, tried to lug me off the floor. Mercifully my left arm seemed to work, and I managed to drag myself into a huddle, slumped hard against the sitting-room door, which was open, thank God, otherwise I would have crashed into it and knocked myself silly. I remember all this part quite clearly. The new coal gas fire was flickering away deceitfully in its Regency basket, my whisky stood, absolutely untouched, where I had left it, the *Exchange and Mart* had spewed over the floor at my side. Mockingly almost. I leant back and tried to lift my right leg with my working hand but it was far too heavy. Ever carried a human leg? In your arms? I had to once in Normandy, with help. I'm always amazed that the body can maintain two of them.

'A stroke, I fear,' I said.

Forwood sat in a chair by the fireplace. 'Right side. But you can speak. Can you see all right?'

'Yes. Listen, I'm not slurring, am I?'

He shook his head. We half laughed.

'Golly!' I said. 'We really *are* paying for those years on the hill, aren't we?'

'We are. I'll call the firm.' The firm were the doctors who were in charge of him. Mainly. 'I'll probably only get a recording. It's after office hours.'

'Well, before you do, I'll have to have a pee. I can't just lie here and stream away. New carpet too. Empty that Evian bottle and bring it over.' I thought it was a pretty rum thing to do, but there was no alternative at that moment. Anyway I did it, and an hour later, or about that time, Jonathan Hunt was beside me full of apologies because he'd been called out to deal with a madman. Real, mark you, not a druggie, just violently mad. Yes, indeed, I'd had a stroke. Mild, as far as he could see. He called an ambulance, a private firm. No lamps flashing, no sirens wailing. Discreet in the little 'Montmartre' street.

I heard him speak to Edward VII, and heard him say, 'He's on his way as soon as the ambulance arrives,' and sagged with relief. He'd got me in. The ambulance arrived about forty minutes later. I had Forwood's wallet in case tips were needed. And of course they were. Two pleasant men struggled me down the narrow staircase, the elegant banister wobbling and bending under their weight. I begged Forwood not to tell anyone except Maude, but to wait until morning to telephone the family. No point in screwing up their night. In the morning we'd know more about everything. Gave the two ambulance men twenty quid each – they had been very careful – and we drove away smoothly and silently. No one knew in Kensington. In the twilight of the ambulance they talked about someone who was playing someone at somewhere at football on the telly. They wondered who might have scored after they had had to leave to collect me? Through the windscreen ahead I saw the lights of a restaurant somewhere and two unaware people being shown to a table up on a balcony, a pink lamp on their table. They didn't know that I was watching them, stuck at traffic lights below, struck by a stroke. Lucky them.

This is the time when you find out that it is a bit too late to worry about the state of your underwear. Our nanny, Lally, always insisted that, as children, Elizabeth and I were immaculate in our garments whenever we went out. Lest we be hit by a motorcycle and sidecar or, worse even, an omnibus. She hadn't ever thought of a mild stroke. Anyway, it was too late to worry. I was almost there; and then *there*.

By which time I had mentally let go . . . I don't remember much of the rest of the evening. I gave in and let others, better equipped, deal with me. I remember a room, a ceiling, a bed; people in blue and white, a chink of instruments, and being rapidly undressed and wrapped in a kind of shroud. It tied at the neck, and a young man in a white coat took out his key-ring and rasped his car key up my instep. I was mildly interested. He said did I feel it? I said no. And he did it again but roughly, and I still said no. He said goodnight, and I asked if I'd sleep. He said someone would make sure of that, don't worry.

And I don't remember anything else until I opened my eyes in the gloom and saw my sister, Elizabeth, sitting beside my bed. She looked as if she had just come in from the garden. Which, as it transpired, was almost what she had done.

'Hullo,' I said. 'I told Forwood *not* to say anything.'

'He didn't. Until six o'clock this morning. You can speak all right? That's good.'

'How did you get here?'

'Mark [her son] drove me up. I came right away.'

'I really didn't want anyone worried. Until things were sorted out . . .'

'Thank God Tote did call. It's in all the papers. I'd have *died* if I'd read it.'

I tried, I remember, to struggle up. Failed. Fury, bewilderment, even rage couldn't get my body to behave. 'It *can't* be. No one knows. Dr Hunt, Tote, Maude, me – no one else.'

She named the paper. Huge headline: 'DIRK WILL NEVER WALK AGAIN?' – something like that.

'One of the nurses was reading it. She was livid. Just come

on duty and they're all hanging round the front door asking questions. Journalist people.'

'But *no one* knows! Unless the ambulancemen . . .'

'I've told the children, and our brother, I'll call Lally as soon as I get back. I'd better go now, they said two minutes. I've been two minutes, and I love you very much, and you'll just be fine. Gareth and Maude – is that her name? – are at your house now with Tote, so there's nothing to worry about.' She leant down and kissed me and I heard her shoes squeak away across the polished rubber of the floor.

I don't remember much about the first few days. I just lay about. People came and stuck thermometers down my throat, prodded things in my leg from time to time, went away again. I really didn't care. It was difficult, I found, to collect my thoughts. My head felt rather like a suitcase suddenly spilled in the street, things scattered everywhere. Unconnected, unlinked. Useless as they lay. I was unafraid, uncaring.

The first moment of clear thought that came drifting into the mess, the first tangible object from the scattered suitcase as it were, was the clear knowledge that I'd never now be able to return to France. Whatever the outcome of anything else might be (would be, truthfully), I was stuck. If I ever walked again I'd have to start out all over, and I couldn't do that on the hill, or anywhere else. The past had been severed by the fall downstairs. There was no going back. Period. End. Finish. Done.

I didn't think that there was enough, or indeed any, energy left to begin again from scratch, and I didn't very much care. I lay still and silent in my little grey room. Flowers began to arrive, letters, cables, cards. People had read the papers, someone said it was news on the BBC. Big deal.

The house in Kensington was running smoothly: Gareth (and indeed Maude) had taken control. Gareth got hold of Rupert and his wife Jacquie, to break off their first holiday in months to buttle and cook. I supposed that they all slept somewhere? In sleeping-bags all over the sitting-room? I knew he'd moved into my room.

Forwood came every day: weary, gaunt, valiant, refusing to start the Japanese course of pills until I was out. But when, I wondered, *would* I be out? Something rather odd had happened in my head. I suddenly didn't give a damn. My glass was empty. Not full, or half full. Dry. Clear. A void. I am not, and I never have been, a man prone to despair. It's not my thing at all. I had always faintly disapproved of those who did give in to it and crumpled. I always thought that one should fight it, beat it, deny it. And I was not in despair now. I know despair, I have been witness to it, seen the mark it has made on others, comforted those who suffered from it, but I have never felt it to be any part of my bodily, or for that matter, mental make-up. I managed to play characters in films, in the theatre, who were riven by despair simply because I had observed it closely, but had never given way to it. Therefore my judgement was clear, objective, uncluttered and I could replay it in a role convincingly. I don't really know where this all came from: something in childhood had forged a sort of strength . . . and my father's words, which always so alarmed, even distressed, strangers – 'We are not expected to fail in this family' – were a continual echo in my head. *Others* might fail, they could do what they wished, but I could not.

And yet, lying there in the shadowy grey room, it might

seem that I was just about to break the rule. That I was about to give up and let go of the reins of my life. Easy to do. Everything was well taken care of around me, there was no possible future ahead, as far as I could see. I had, I felt, done all that I could do, and now this was the way it would finish. I would just sleep to death. Painless, smooth, perfectly comfortable. I had absolutely no intention of going on with the fag-end of my life as a cripple. The fact that feeling had gradually returned to my hand and right arm didn't much mollify me. It made bed-life a little easier, but my leg was still a log. Introspection is what this was all about, and there was a mass of dead time in which to indulge in it, especially at night after we had been, as they said, 'put down' for sleep. One was undisturbed: a face might peer fleetingly at the little glass panel in the door, check that one was not on the floor or raving mad, and disappear. But the thoughts wouldn't go so fast. They grew darker with the night. And although despair never reached me, *hopelessness* did – a different thing.

In the blackest pit of night, that weary time about three o'clock, I rang my bell for the booster sleeping-pill which usually got me through until the morning. On swift and silent feet the pretty young night nurse was beside me, with a small paper cup containing the pill. She set it on the bedside table, out of reach; sat easily on the end of my bed, hands folded in her lap. Had I had a good day? People been to see me? I'd heard, of course, about the disaster at King's Cross underground station? They still weren't certain how many had perished. She used the word with pleasure, rolling it round her lips, making it sound rather like the rubber in a hot-water bottle or a bicycle tyre. *Perished.* Not merely dead. I had watched it on the television. It was dreadful, really appalling, but could I have my pill? I'd been awake for hours. She said it was right beside me, so I tried to reach for it with my now-active right arm, as she showed not the least inclination to assist me – testing me, I reckoned – but couldn't reach it. Can't reach it, she said? Well, get out of bed, it's only a step away. I was patient, explained that I couldn't walk. She knew that? Yes, oh yes, she said, she *did* know that. She also knew that I was behaving bloody badly. What on earth did she mean? Behaving bloody badly? Behaving disgracefully, a spoiled brat. Because you've been faced with a little set-back which you feel you can't lick. So you're giving up. You have no guts! You can walk if you want to. You can relearn easily, it's a *mild* stroke you had. You have speech, your arm works, right? How you *dare* throw it all up now, I don't know! You've given so many people such pleasure for so many years – you still can, you still *owe* it to them. You can't just throw in the towel and say, 'Enough!' I really thought you had a little more guts than that!

In my shamed silence she reached for the paper cup, handed it to me, and I took the pill and got wheeled down to physiotherapy the next morning, where an excessively bright, jolly female wrestler began to teach me how to walk in a complicated game which entailed the use of a great many walking-sticks spread along the floor. But I started up again. And I never stopped.

Some time ago the same nurse sent me a card to explain, and hoped that she 'hadn't gone too far? Trying to say to patients what will be helpful is difficult. Sometimes you get it right, sometimes you don't. I very much wanted to get it right for you . . .' She has my eternal gratitude. God knows, she got it right for me.

About three weeks later I was considered fit enough to relinquish my bed to a more deserving case, and got smuggled out by a secret door to avoid the ever-lurking photographers hiding behind parked cars. I managed to walk, almost on my own, to Ron and his car and then to the National Film Theatre, where some film of mine was being shown, and managed, without help, to walk on to the stage before a full house and confound the press. It was a very pleasant feeling, and one that I never again dared to lose.

In Kensington my brother Gareth had organized the house as he might have organized a frigate. My bed had been lugged down to Forwood's room, a mini-ward had been created, which made things easier for Jacquie, who took temperatures (of us both: Forwood was slowly becoming weaker) and brought up trays. She had been a SRN before marriage, so she knew the job. I managed to hop about from bed to bathroom, but did not yet attempt the stairs. I was determined now to become mobile. Forwood's pale, haggard face forced me. He had finally started the Japanese pills. We waited with patience to see if they might have some effect. He was not bed-ridden, and managed to haul himself down to the sitting-room or the kitchen (miles down below in the basement) for meals.

One evening, when everyone was having supper and I forked listlessly through a congealing bowl of pasta which Rupert had brought to my bed, I suddenly set everything aside, dressed, as best I could, hanging on to the bedpost with one hand, pulling things over my head, determined to go down to the kitchen and show them just what I was made of. I'd bump down on my backside, however long it took, and get to my feet at the kitchen door. Surprise! Surprise! *What* a clever fellow!

Well, I did all that: inched down – it took hours – and reached the closed door into the kitchen. Pulled myself up by the banister rail. Stood teetering, and composing myself for my grand entrance. Vague muffled voices came from the table, chink of cutlery, a tap running, a chair dragged across the tiled floor, a burst of laughter and then, just as I was about to launch myself into the room: ' . . . *can't leave the family all on their own much longer* . . .' I stopped. The tap was turned off. '. . . *It's a bit hard on that bloody floor every night* . . .' A saucepan was scraped busily. '. . . *Of course, until you can manage again, we could try and get you into a decent place. Residential* . . .' I stood frozen. '*I know of a jolly nice place outside Henley. Lawns down to the river* . . . *Expensive, but very good, you could have your own furniture* . . .' I turned away from the door as Jacquie's voice called out happily, '*Anyone want some more Parmesan?*'

I got up the stairs rather more quickly than I got down. Never eavesdrop on other people's conversation: you may just hear the truth. The next morning I was up, shaved, dressed, and hauled myself down the stairs into the sitting-room. Everyone was surprised and delighted. Patted my head. The clever dog had learned his tricks. A few days later Maude sent a faintly fey lady over to start work on my leg. She'd cure me in a 'couple of weeks', she said, pressing folded hands hard on the top of my head. Did I not feel the hot electrical flow emanating from her into me? All I could truthfully feel were a pair of clammy little hands squashing my skull as if it was a grapefruit. Hot indeed they were, healing not at all. I needed something a bit more than simple faith now that I had managed to pick up the reins.

★

There was a Christmas and I had bronchitis again. Jacquie brought over a small tree, insisted on decorating it, and covered it in flashing lights which wouldn't stop winking unless the plug was removed. There was the sudden surge of spring. Birds were singing in the gardens opposite, there were daffodils in pots on people's windowsills. Kathleen Tynan found me a splendid lady, Mrs Pink, who came across the Park with a box of electrical things which slowly began to bring my slightly withered leg back into use. Clumsily, uneasily, but at last I managed one day to walk unaided to the end of the street; later, *much* later, limped to the Indian shop on the corner for boil-in-the-bag things; eventually I was able to get as far as High Street, Kensington, and all the glittering magic and mysteries of Boots and Marks and Spencer's. I had a working household again – wobbly, uncertain, easily stalled, but managing, at last, for itself.

The Japanese pills didn't seem to have much effect really. Warning lights went on. Making tea one day for Frank and George, who were installing bookcases, Forwood poured the milk into the teapot and spooned the tea into the kettle. It got sorted out; we all laughed. But it wasn't comfortable.

'Have you got the soup on?'

He was reading and didn't look up when he said, 'Yes. Probably boiling away by now. Better lower the gas.'

I went down and saw it was on the stove. But not boiling. There was no gas. The sealed tins lay in an empty saucepan.

It was too difficult now for him to carry things up from the kitchen. So he had to have his tea every day, as normal, at five, sitting at the round table. I got him a cake of some kind from the French baker at the corner. It was important for me to use my leg as much as possible. I sat with him for company while he got his mug up to his lips, tried, and usually succeeded, in eating some of his cake.

One day I was filling a jar with water at the sink. My back was to him and he said, 'If things don't work just as Peter Wrigley said, about pain, I mean, you'd help me out? Wouldn't you?'

I assured him that I would and put the jar of freesias on the table. 'It's lunatic to think like that. You haven't given the pills time, really.'

He was silently unconvinced. I crushed the little cardboard box the cake had been carried in, stuck it into the pedal-bin. 'The stuff you would need', he said, carefully pressing a shaking finger on some crumbs on the table, 'is in my tartan washbag. Patrick gave them to me. Ages ago. Just make certain they haven't got stale. I've had them ages.'

I was busy doing something, trying to be brisk, dragging about as if there was a definite point to what I was doing. 'You are talking rubbish. I know it's going to work. In my bones.'

'I'd be perfectly all right,' he said evenly, 'if I was at home. When do you think you'll be fit enough to go?'

Chapter 11

The spring which had surged so promisingly, birds singing all over the gardens of the monastery, daffodils tall on window-sills, gradually buckled down to wretchedness. The sun might shine outside, the birds sing, blossoms bloom in gardens, but within the walls of the elegant little Doll's House things were getting pretty grim.

It was not for desperate want of trying to enliven things in this brilliant spring; one did one's very best. Wallflowers and little pink daisies were thriving in the window-box over the pit-patio. I filled the rooms with cut flowers, threw wide all the windows, I even sang; and Maria, the 'daily' (another discovery of Maude's) moved about the place as stately and as broad in the beam as a galleon, with all her pennants flying. Maria was, as Forwood had told me in hospital, from Colombia, a very black lady dressed in vibrating colours. A tropical Matisse, without a reasonable word of English. But she was *very* affectionate and a fiend with Flash and Sanilav. So that was all right. She was also very nice and jolly. But even her vivid cotton skirts, the glitter of gold and ruby glass, the violent carmines and yellows of her ample blouses couldn't lift the general atmosphere of increasing unease.

To begin with, the Japanese pills suddenly gave out; and the anxiety of the waiting for the next allocation from Tokyo was almost impossible to conceal. No one, really, had any idea if they *were* doing the tumour any harm. Which is what was longed for. One recent visit to Harley Street seemed to confirm that they had. A little. Triumph? But there had been so many false triumphs and dented hopes that no one actually opened champagne and sprayed it round the place like racing drivers. We meekly accepted the possibility and went on crossing our fingers. And then the beastly things ran out. As, indeed, they were bound to one day. We had to try and contain ourselves until the next lot came in.

Meanwhile I now took to walking in front of Forwood on his increasingly rare walks round the block, in front so that I could advise him of cracks, dog turds, kerbs and misplaced pavings. A lot of them around the Kensington area. This ploy didn't always work. There were ugly falls, which were distressing and often embarrassing but caused no cuts or serious bruising.

Until the one 'adventure', final as it turned out, when he insisted on going as far as the High Street to have a look at something. I forget now what it was. The crowds were thick, a tube had just vomited its load from the depths and blind, vacant-eyed people struggled like elvers along the jammed street. Somehow they got between him and myself, we lost contact for a moment, and he fell sickeningly, with his full weight on a pile of paving-stones ready for re-laying. He had had his hands in his anorak pockets. Thus, unable to save himself, he just crashed on his face. Blood poured, he lay like a fallen pillar, the streaming crowd of elver-humans split up round his head, one line to the right, the other to the left, and went on their anguished, sightless way. No one looked, stopped, even turned a head. I got him to his feet, eased his hands out of the pockets, found a handkerchief and tried to staunch the blood, without much success.

Standing there, swaying, locked together in the swarm of blank-eyed shop assistants, typists and bank clerks, or whatever they were, I wished very much that we had decided to stay on the hill after all. If he'd fallen in Saint-Sulpice, in the market, on Rue d'Antibes, it would have been a very different matter. There is more compassion in the country, I suppose? In the cities one becomes inured to violence.

As we started to shuffle up to the crossing by the lights, a young woman, carrying a giant floral display in a Cellophane tent, *did* stop. Her pale face creased with concern. 'Is he all right? I could fetch a policeman, somebody . . .', but I led him on, thanking her. We got to the lights and stood there until they flicked to green. I suppose we must have presented an odd sight? A tall, pale, ageing man streaming with blood from a wide gash, blood spattering his anorak, spilling on my hands which supported him, in a crowd of people all steadily watching the traffic lights, ready for the signal to swarm across to Church Street. Not a single person among the lot looked anywhere else but ahead. I'd forgotten, of course, that in England it is impolite to stare and that one should not draw attention to anything unpleasant. You could, happily, if it was funny or amusing. Not otherwise. And dangerous, of course, to become 'involved'.

At the firm, Dr Peter Wheeler stitched him up. 'I'm rather good at sewing. They won't show. Not a stitch!' As if it mattered really. But it was kind, comforting, and Ron drove back very slowly, so as not to jolt the patient, across the Park.

It seemed to me, that morning, that every kind of wretched thing had been slung his way since we had reached the UK and crossed that benighted stretch of deck-chaired grass. A perfectly unreasonable piece of reckoning, I agree. But I was not in a reasonable frame of mind. It didn't end there either, with a simple fall outside Barker's in High Street, Kensington.

Fate had more wooden balls to chuck at the coconuts. The punishment increased, gradually, but relentlessly.

One evening Forwood decided to go up to his bed. No supper, didn't finish his drink, excused himself to the two valiant ladies who had come to join us for a packet of Marks and Sparks heat-up. Supper was cancelled.

'I don't feel frightfully good. Sorry,' he said and I took his temperature.

A few days later a day nurse and a night nurse, Natalie and Anna, both Australians, young and pretty, arrived at the Doll's House. 'Why do we need them?' he asked. I told him that he had a 'slight urinary infection'. (Which is what I was told. Tactfully.) And that I couldn't now manage quite on my own. Of course, he didn't believe me. He appeared satisfied with my excuse, but his ingrained good manners and sense of good behaviour would never permit him to behave otherwise. He knew bloody well that a 'slight urinary infection' was a euphemism for something far uglier, but he was not about to distress others – or himself. Let it lie. So be it.

'You remember what you promised? That afternoon?' he whispered one day before his voice completely failed. 'In my tartan washbag?'

I was giving him his Bloody Mary; it was the lunchtime drink he always preferred, usually in a tall glass, this time on a pad of cotton wool pressed to his dried lips. He could no longer swallow much more than saliva. He was also almost completely paralysed.

'Of course. I remember. I've checked them. They are okay. But you *aren't* in pain? Are you?'

He gently shook his head from side to side, smiling, made

a sign with his eyes for another taste of his Bloody. 'I must look like one of those money boxes? No teeth, big grin?'

Sometimes I sat with him while Natalie or Anna sat glued to the TV downstairs watching *Neighbours*. They swooned with nostalgia for Australia as I dealt with urine bottles, shifted bedpans and eased pillows. It was only on twice, as far as I remember, a day, and it really did cheer them up tremendously.

Finally there were no more visitors. They were stopped. There never were many: he felt too weary and far too vain, as he confessed. He didn't look very good. So eventually visiting was limited only to Mary Dodd, his cousin, whom he loved very much, and Betty (Lauren) Bacall, who made him laugh and bashed away with enormous brio and affection, as if nothing whatever was wrong. She was the force of life for him.

Brock was allowed once, Maude, and Rosalind and Nicholas, I remember, but even his son Gareth and his grandson Thomas were finally forbidden. It was useless to have visitors, he said once (by this time I had to put my head to his chest to 'read' the vibrations: he no longer had a voice), because even though he had asked them much earlier on, and even though the ones he asked to see *all* had a car, none of them would agree to take him home. He knew that *I* wouldn't take him home. *I* kept telling him that he was *at* home . . . There was a small hand-grip for a change of underwear, and he would be able to direct them once they got to Avignon.

One night, helping Anna to turn him, he made signs that he wanted to speak, and when I pressed my face to his chest it was to say that if we had done such a thing to a dog we'd have been arrested. He so longed to 'go home' that one night he started to dress himself. Pulled on a jacket, his overcoat. Anna had left the room for a moment. When she came back he was sitting on the edge of the bed, trying to get on a shoe. A long shoe-horn in his hand. He shouted angrily at her, with full, amazing voice. I heard him in my room above and rushed down in time to duck and weave away from the furious, flailing shoe-horn, wielded like a baseball bat. Anna had a cut cheek. I tried to make him get back to bed, he raged about going home. He *had* to go home! He was needed there! He had a meeting with Monsieur Rémy. I *must* let him go. *Must!*

Jonathan arrived, rumpled, weary, called from his bed to give him a sedative.

'They try to stop me going home!' The voice was frail now. The power had gone, the final burst of furious strength ebbed away. He never spoke again.

He slept all the next day, slipped into a coma. I sat at his bedside looking silently at the dreadful demolition job being wrought on a good, kind, gentle man. It was quite enough to make anyone question any possible belief in God. Sometime in the early hours of the morning Anna shook me awake. He was very ill, breathing badly. Come down. He was quite still, eyes shut, lying on his left-hand side. I took his hand in mine. He whispered a soft, imperceptible almost, sigh and then was still. 'I think he's gone,' I said. Anna burst into tears, covered her face with her hands, head bowed. A replay of Christine on the terrace long ago.

I gently put his hand under the bed covers. In case it got cold? Touched Anna's shoulder, gave her a kiss, went down to the sitting-room to telephone his family. It was 2.15 a.m.

*

And what happened then? After this length of time I'm not absolutely sure of the sequence of events. It's the 'engraved goblet' business again: vision through space to vision. If you watch, with a steady gaze, fifty years of your life being carefully negotiated down a too-narrow staircase in a plastic body-bag you do rather come to a full stop. It is a dulling sensation. Numbing.

I watched through a crack in the door-hinge, feeling it wiser, after past treachery, to keep out of the way. So his son put on a black tie and did all that was necessary for the final untidiness of death.

As soon as he and the undertakers had moved off into the dawn light of Kensington I remember wandering over to the window. Opposite, in the monastery garden, an elderly monk was removing side-shoots from sweet peas, a prayer book in his hand, sandals on bare feet, his lips moving. Who was he praying for, I wondered. Himself? Or just cursing the green-fly? I wasn't really interested.

The house was very still now. No crackle of crisp white overalls, no clattering of kettles and cups, no sickly theme tune from *Neighbours*. Nothing. It wasn't Maria's cleaning day. The air was still. Dense as fluff. I could hear the cistern filling up in one of the bathrooms. A bubbling sound. It stopped and the monk opposite opened his prayer book and continued his morning wander. Anna had left earlier, after a two-hour doze on the settee, face creased with weary sleep, a small grip in her hand. She said she'd write to me from Cannes. She was going to do the South of France after her next job. Mr Forwood loved Cannes, didn't he? Not all that much really, but I didn't say so. She gave me a kiss, told me to look after myself now and left. Then it was all silent again.

I stood motionless at the window until the milk-cart purred to a stop and I went down and paid a bill that I owed and got some milk. We were short of milk. The nurses drank coffee endlessly. I was short of everything. Direction mainly. What on earth to do? It was the suitcase metaphor again. Pieces scattered everywhere, bits lying around. Unconnected. Unfamiliar suddenly. And I had not the least notion of how to start repacking. What to keep, what to leave out. I realized fully just how bloody useless I was on my own. There was absolutely no need for anything that I might do now. No morale to boost, no tray to set up, no sandwiches or take-aways for nurses. No Bloody Marys to soak in the cotton wool. No work. No future. Bewilderment all round. My carousel had ground to a halt. I had no idea how to restart it.

I was spoiled rotten, unequipped to deal with my own life. I had always known, or at least known for a long time, that one day I'd have to come to terms with the finality of death. That I'd have to deal with myself. But I had made no kind of preparation. For fifty years I had had a manager who had, actually, *managed* me. He had seen me working in a small repertory company. I was considered to have some sort of 'quality and potential': he was not certain what it was or how much of it I actually possessed. We signed a contract by hand-shake and, apart from the war years, he took charge.

My first job in the West End was his work. My first movie after the war, my first break at the BBC. Set me on course, you could say. And you'd be right. Every legal problem, every contract, scenario, script, all the solicitors, accountants, lawyers, bank managers were his concern, never mine. Brilliantly he erected a protective wall round me, formed by good manners, politeness, immense calm and a very shrewd understanding of his subject (myself). Most important of all was his impeccable behaviour and breeding set against the uglier elements, and God knows there were enough of them, of the cinema and (less so) the theatre. He dealt with them all, defusing anger, charming mistrust, thus allowing me, finally, to present myself as a man of infinite courtesy, always amenable, usually 'charming', to one and all. It was his hard work which had been done to smooth the path for me, to clip the thorns, remove the rocks, fill in the little craters, make everything look simple. All that *I* had to do was deliver the performances uncluttered by any anxieties or vexations.

Now, at the window watching a contented monk wandering about in prayer, I felt more alone than I had ever felt in my life before. As a child, at school, banished to Scotland, in the Army, I had never been *alone*. Solitary, yes, often. But not absolutely isolated, lost, bewildered and, suddenly, quite hopeless. The hermit crab shell-less. I felt exactly how it must be to appear without warning stark naked in some vast cathedral at Evensong, or High Mass. What on earth should I do? There was no possibility of returning to France. A dragging limp and the constant underlying fear that there could be another stroke lurking about put paid to that idea. 'Be ill in your own language.' I'd had quite enough of doctors and clinics and things to last me a considerable time.

That morning I telephoned everyone who might have been able to help me. I suppose I could have made some sense? Anyway, things began to move, banks, solicitors, accountants, all slowly set things in motion. I would now remain in the UK. They would work out a plan for my future life.

The first essential was to get out of the Doll's House with

its panelled walls and pit-patio. I had always hated it, and now more than ever. Bernard Walsh was advised. As soon as possible you must find me a flat? One floor, no steps, or stairs, south-facing with a terrace or garden. Impossible he thought. Try, I suggested. Then money. What to do for money as I had none? My bank account was in Cannes and the Crédit Lyonnais in Le Pré. What to do? Sell the Ben Nicholson, bought as an investment: now was the time of greatest need. After the brutality of something called Capital Gains Tax and the giant commission paid to the gallery, there was not a great deal left. But enough to keep me solvent, in beer and sandwiches for a time. It was blindingly obvious that I would now have to start up again and try to earn a living. Books didn't make you a fortune, and they took a long time to write, but in my case they had supplemented the olive crop handsomely. Alas! It was cheaper, *by far*, living on the hill.

My solicitor, Lawrence Harbottle, who had looked after me from the start of my film career, loaned me a very brisk and competent lady called Barbara Peerless whose sole job now was to sit up in the new little office in the attic and destroy the contents of some thirty box files kept over the years by Forwood: paper upon paper, documents, statements, estimates, tax returns, contracts. He appeared to have kept a copy of every transaction he had ever made, going back to the dawn of mankind. It was a lengthy, tiring task.

One day, skipping through a bundle of photocopies which didn't seem to be related to anything else, she realized that perhaps they were mine, and should not be 'shredded' without my agreement. The bundle was four chapters of an abandoned novel called *Jericho* and half a manuscript of an edited collection of letters, untitled. Barbara didn't know it then, and neither did I, but my future was in those pages. How they came to be where they were I do not know. I was certain that Elizabeth and I had burned almost all my stuff by the pond on the hill. Obviously he had kept the copies. Madame Pasquini had long ago insisted that I copy everything I ever mailed to my publishers, which of course I did. Sometimes there would be a spare copy; these were they.

This was not the only stroke of good fortune. In the dark days, just when the nurses had first arrived and the future dared not be considered, a pleasant young man had arrived at the house for a drink one evening. Would I consider reviewing some books for him? He was presently the literary editor of the *Daily Telegraph*. The suggestion was so unexpected, the whole meeting in the unhappy house so bizarre, that I accepted. Why not? I *had* to pretend that life would continue. All was really quite normal, there was no one in the room above fighting for life. Nicholas Shakespeare didn't know it, but he was the person who chucked a plank across the ravine for me. I felt a mild glow of hope. I'd manage somehow. After all, you didn't need two legs to write. You could do it all sitting down.

A package of books arrived one morning as I was making some tea. About 750 words? By the 27th? Whichever book I preferred. I had a job to do! I didn't know if I *could* review a book. I hadn't written anything for three years. Had rather crash-stopped as soon as it was apparent that Le Pigeonnier had to be sold. I had tried to batter away up in the new little office, but it was hopeless. Worry intruded, my ear was constantly on alert for sounds other than the clacking of a typewriter or the mumbled whispers of an excruciatingly reluctant muse. But now I had no real excuses. A book to review. Money had to be earned. Up in the little office, among the pillaged files, I sat down to write to Mr Shakespeare.

In a corner, filled with crumpled past efforts, lay the large cardboard box with 'JAFFA ORANGES' on its side. We'd had desperate need of Madame Bruna's laundered sheets during the last few weeks. The fresh, familiar scent of them, unpacked for the first time since their arrival at the Lancaster, very nearly unmanned me. Red dust under bare feet. The scent of cut hay hot in the sun, of the cypress bleeding gum down its scaly bark, the twitter and cheep of budgerigars outside the Mandelli front door, the rustle and tremble of soft June air down by the pond, arum lilies bejewelled with pulsing emerald tree frogs – all came back, flicking visions, in a furious rush of memory. An ache of sadness in the barren, ship-tidy little office whose window looked blindly at the yellow brick wall opposite. I'd never feel, hear or see those things again, in the same way that I'd never say some of the silly phrases again. I doodled them on the paper before me: 'Ratty! Where's Ratty! Seek Ratty!' and 'Who wants dinners! Eh! Dinner time!' I'd never call that again, never see the tree rats. Never shout 'Bendo!' 'Labo!' or 'Daisy!' Never yell, 'Walkies?' No more baby language. Words of affection to dogs. Why do we? Talk to them like that? Anyone overhearing such idiocy would consider one pretty daft. One was, joyfully.

All quite pointless nostalgia, the elderly person's overt vice. There was no point in trying to indulge oneself in yesterday, for that was what it was. Past. Done. Over. The undertakers had driven discreetly, smoothly, away carrying off their empty husk. Very soon afterwards, in the still, sunny, deserted street, the milk-float had purred up to the door. Clink of bottles. Snatch of some song whistled. Ring of the bell. 'Morning!' Life, normal life, resumed. Familiar patterns, for a few hours scattered, reassembled like the twisting of a kaleidoscope.

Before me now on the hastily put-together desk in the little office was my old typewriter, paper inserted, waiting. Beside it two glossy books. Which one to choose? Both now read: so decide! A or B? Decisions, *decisions*! A pulse began. I started to type my letter with two hesitant fingers: 'Dear Nicholas Shakespeare, I have decided on . . .'

Maria was singing a Spanish song down in the kitchen far away. The carousel was creaking, starting to move, inching round with a throb of its engine, shuddering into motion, beginning to turn. The horses, the pigs, striding ostriches, the symbols of up and down, joy or sadness, slowly shuddered into life once more. I had made a firm decision when I blundered on to the stage of the National Film Theatre, unaided, that I *could* do it. *Would* do it. By myself if need be. I *had* done it once, that day. It was a pleasant feeling. I wasn't altogether certain just how things would work out now, but I'd try. I was not about to cower on my backside, a can of beer in my hand, in this empty house listening to the cistern refill. Sod that.

In the grocer's shop which I knew very well, near the little rented Chelsea house before the days of sandwiches and boil-in-the-bag rubbish, Mrs Bott, the lady boss, plump, jolly, in glasses and a white blouse and skirt, called to me across a table stacked high with boxes of *marron glacé*.

'Hello, sir! Where did you come from? How lovely to see you.'

'I've come shopping. Been for a haircut, and come to see you all.'

'All the way from Kensington! Fancy! You're not supposed to be here, you know?'

'Where am I supposed to be, then?'

'Lying in a dark room, inconsolable, drinking four bottles of Scotch a day. Didn't you know?'

'Who said?'

'Oh. A Sunday paper. Big piece. Gone into seclusion, you have. A recluse. It says. The awful lies they tell. *And* get away with!'

'Now where did you see this, Mrs Bott?'

For a second only Mrs Bott looked concerned, put a hand on my arm, lowered her voice. 'Mr Forwood has died? Hasn't he?'

'He has. Yes. The other side of the Park . . .'

'I *am* sorry. Really. It said at St Stephen's. You should sue! Really you should.'

'He died in his own bed. I was with him . . .'

'Poor man, he did look so dreadfully poorly, didn't he? I am so sorry.'

'What is St Stephen's?'

'A hospital. Poor fellow. Don't you worry now. It's lovely to see you again . . .' She went off to attend to someone at the check-out. I think I got some cheese, a bit of cold something to eat, I can't remember now what. I do remember I got a baguette and some Coleman's mustard.

In the car I asked Ron if he'd seen any Sunday paper? Anything about Mr F. and a hospital? He said oh, yes. He had. What is St Stephen's Hospital? Should I know about it? Is it for cancer? A specialist place? Oh no, sir, said Ron, it's not for cancer so much as for people with AIDS. We turned left and headed for the gates to the Park. Why didn't you tell me, Ron? If you saw it? I didn't know . . . Ron looked at me in the driving-mirror. Well, he said, it wasn't true, was it? Spiteful rubbish. No point in distressing you. Wicked. I thanked him, looked out in shaken disbelief at the Park. Ordinary things out there. People walking, laughing, sitting on the grass, running, rowing on the lake; alive.

After the years of anxiety, fear, apprehension, the slow and agonizing decline into gradual ruin and distress; the loss of pride, the utter humility of trembling hands, shaking legs, cruel falls, and the scan which showed not a pea but a three-centimetre tumour, the death knell overheard on the kitchen extension; Anna weeping silently – after all that, this then for an 'obituary'? A journey of high courage rubbished by a cheap tabloid. Friends protested violently and traced the journalist, who admitted it was untrue, but they were told the paper had already gone to press and it was too late to stop.

'You can't afford to take legal action,' Lawrence said. 'It would take at least two years to bring them to court, and you just frankly haven't got the money to fight them. Let it die away.'

The anger never died. I remembered that Pa, a journalist all his life, had eventually removed 'Occupation' from his passport, in the later years of his life, as a modest form of protest at the fouling, as he said, of his profession. I'd always wondered why, honestly. But not now.

There were some timid achievements in the weeks which followed. My typing got marginally better, I began to rejig the edited letters which Barbara had found, wrote an Author's Note and an Epilogue. It was really only half a book. It had been chucked by Norah Smallwood. 'You've done a lot of work. But no one wants to read letters. And *not* letters to an elderly woman in America. Get on with a novel.' So I did. But these seemed to have matured a little with time. I sent them off to Pat Kavanagh, and we had lunch. I think I must have taken her out to eat. I can't remember ever feeding her a packet of spaghetti bolognese in the underground kitchen. She said yes, with the little drawings, they make a modest book. A start. Viking agreed. I was accepted and I had work in hand. It was a good feeling.

One afternoon a letter arrived from Thomas, an important letter which he had taken time to compose. Would I, he asked, 'take over' from his grandfather? Carry on as he would have done? He had one grandfather in France, he'd very much like to have one in England; after all, I had known him since before he was born. In Forwood's will, when it was released, it appeared that I was to be given power of attorney over the money which he had left to his grandson, but which Thomas could not touch until he was twenty-five. So it fitted extremely well, and I accepted Thomas's suggestion. It was exactly the responsibility, small as it was perhaps, that I needed at that moment. I had a book ready for publication, collected a grandson, and had put on a terrific amount of weight since giving up smoking. I had a face like a melon, a beer gut, from far too much beer, and tits like Dolly Parton. I was altogether disgusting. The beer was entirely my own fault. I started early now. There was no one to stop me. About ten-thirty seemed the right time of day to begin. Maude telephoned one day to ask me out to lunch.

'Just opened my first beer of the day.'

'At *this* time?'

'Is there a selected time? For beer?'

'No. Not if you need it. Up to you.'

But I knew there was disapproval in her voice. Unstated, but none the less there. I was drinking too much. Solitude. I made it the excuse. Beer dulled the dislike of the house, the long solitary hours. Especially in the evenings. That was the worst. The summer evening sunlight was not for me. It never actually got to the pit and there is something singularly depressing about sitting in the dark, as opposed to shade, in a brick-lined pit with a wide blue sky far above.

I had been assured that, after a couple of years, I'd return to my original weight. Meanwhile the clothes I possessed no longer fitted anywhere, and I didn't feel that I could hang on to them for two years more. So, a grey suit for lunch, a dark suit for supper, a sports jacket and flannels. That was my limit: off the peg and 'all right', all supplied by the sale of the Ben Nicholson.

I was still under the concerned care of Mrs Pink: 'You must not use a stick! Ever! You'll become dependent on it.' My limp was still quite a limp, and even though I was confident enough to get down to the High Street and push a trolley round Marks and Spencer (very early, to avoid the continual '*Weren't* you Dirk Bogarde? A long time ago?' questioning at the check-outs), I funked anything more taxing.

So I refused a great many invitations to things which might have alleviated the solitariness of life, too scared that I'd one day fall over (visions of past falls flew before my eyes). I didn't want that, and even though I'd put my name and address in my wallet I was terrified that one day I'd end up in casualty somewhere with a line of curious walking wounded asking for autographs. Because, even though I'd been away for so many years and had only made one unremarked and unremarkable film for television in the UK in twenty years, I was, to my consternation, recognized continually in the street. It was flattering but unnerving. In France I had never been accosted, except with a slight salute, a smile, a nod.

Limping about in a grubby anorak, in cheap trainers, and Marks and Spencer's jeans ('You don't have to try them on in the shop! They'll change them. Just keep the receipt,' said Elizabeth), was not the way I truthfully wanted audiences to remember me. Especially with a beer gut, a plum-pudding face and Dolly Parton's bust. I simply didn't feel up to close scrutiny. Or distant, come to that. Vanity is a killer, but it didn't stop me drinking beer. The new suits, of course, were extremely useful now that I had to accompany Bernard Walsh on our visits to try to find a suitable flat. I couldn't go around the area in which I wished to spend the next year or two left to me dressed like a derelict (I'd decided that about *two* years would be as much as I could cope with: if I reached seventy that would see me out). I had kept Mr Walsh to a strict area bounded by the Kings Road, Brompton Road, Pont Street and Eaton Terrace. Anything beyond those confines was out. Unless there was something ravishing on the river. I was told that unless I was extremely rich I hadn't a hope. But he'd keep looking, and he did.

I was becoming absolutely desperate now to leave the Doll's House. I'd clear out and go to an hotel rather than stay there after the summer. I couldn't face a long dark English winter there on my own, so I began to make cautious arrangements once more to store the furniture and clear off. Room service would be more attractive than these continual heat-ups in the kitchen.

Bernard called one day to say that he had had an offer for the house, but could I be out by the end of July? I could. Shaking with excitement every time the telephone rang, I found it hard to contain my impatience. The house was sold, at a profit: a great deal of work had been done to it by Frank and George. The paperwork and contracts took ages to settle – there was a Bank Holiday – but finally all was well except that I had nowhere to go. An hotel seemed inevitable until the indefatigable Mr Walsh proffered a glossy bunch of 'final possibilities', one of which, with only two modest bedrooms, did seem possible *except* there was no room for an office in which to set up a desk and typewriter. Now that my living had to be by writing (I now had a contract with the *Daily Telegraph*, much to my surprise), it was essential that I had a workplace. The possible flat was almost exactly what I wanted, and located where I wished to live. As I had given myself a lifespan of about, give or take a month or so, two years, I reckoned I could splash out a bit financially: I wouldn't be around to worry for long.

But the lack of one bedroom for an office did bother me idiotically until Molly (Lady Daubeny) telephoned on the very evening of the day on which I'd seen the place. We were old friends: I'd first met her when she had just arrived from South Africa, bright and starry-eyed, in 1947. She married Sir Peter Daubeny, the impresario who had had the brilliant foresight to bring a play in which I was appearing in Notting Hill Gate into a West End theatre. The sad fact that *Oklahoma!* opened in the same week, at the Theatre Royal opposite in Drury Lane, made us a certain disaster area, and we closed within a month. But Molly and I remained friends.

Now, so many years later, and widowed, she was the

'friend in need', a meal, a drink, a shoulder to weep on. This time we were talking flats; she had just moved into one herself, and I found her extremely useful to check prices, leases, freeholds and things.

She asked, suddenly, if I knew the works of Saki? I said yes, years ago, hadn't read him in yonks. Well, did I know that on November the 17th it would be the seventy-fifth anniversary of his death in action? In the First War? No, I did not. What, I wondered, was she talking about? Why Saki? Well, she had a perfectly thrilling idea that they should do some kind of concert thing on that date to commemorate his life. And death. Some readings of his works. Did I follow?

Uneasily, with a gradual build of inner panic, I did begin to follow. I was, somehow or another, going to be dragged in and involved in this Saki business. She came quickly to the point. Would I consider reading some of his stories? Perhaps just five or six. The funniest ones? I could choose them myself. At the National Theatre? Perhaps the Olivier, or the Lyttleton? Terribly thrilling, she thought. She felt almost certain that she could get one of the theatres for a platform performance. A frightfully nice person, Amanda Saunders, would perhaps help. Would I do it? They'd be certain to agree if *I* would agree? I said that the idea simply appalled me. I hadn't been on a stage for thirty years, I had a severe limp, as she knew, and couldn't walk far, let alone stand about on a stage reading. I'd never read before in my life. The very thought of being *near* a stage, at the National of all places, filled me with terror and I had no desire whatsoever to attract the press, who filled me with equal terror. I was, I said, hand on heart, terribly sorry but *no*. So she said that she was sorry too. It would have been thrilling, but anyway it was such a *long* time ahead. Perhaps I'd just think about it? Keep it in my mind? She thought I had *exactly* the right voice for reading Saki. Would I think about it? November?

So I said yes. To shut her up really, for I was far more exercised by my own immediate problems. My house was sold, I told her, I was technically homeless, the only flat which was exactly what I wanted was too small – no room for an office – and, in any case, I only had until noon of the next day to decide because after noon it would be put on the open market.

Molly's voice, on the telephone, was as light, high, and joyous as that of a lark ascending. 'Darling! If it's *exactly* what you want, just put a desk in the second bedroom and have that as your office! Simple!'

'But there might be people staying. My sister. Thomas. The children. Someone . . .'

'A desk, with a bed. Why not? It would be only for a night or two presumably, and if it's family they wouldn't mind a scrap. I mean, darling! You aren't *entertaining* now, are you? Your office is far more important. You'd be mad to let it go if you like it, just because it's one room short of perfection.'

Of course, she was right. The flat was exactly that. Perfection, but one room short. It had everything I needed: a terrace – I suppose you might call it a roof garden in estate agent speak – or correctly a wide balcony, a sitting-room of good size, two bedrooms, very small, two bathrooms to go with them, and a kitchen which was of such modest proportions that, should you stand dead-centre and spread your arms wide, you could, with a slight list to either side, touch the walls. A place to boil an egg rather than roast a sheep. The whole would have fitted into the Long Room. From the terrace (which I shall call it), great trees and green leaves; distant roofs, chimney stacks, more trees. Above all, the wide, cathedral-high canopy of the sky. Most important, perhaps, it was all on one floor, one level: no stairs. If I had another stroke I could, just possibly, drag myself to the telephone. Things like that had now to be seriously considered.

Bernard Walsh and I had, once again, trailed from one unsuitable place to another, he always brimming with optimism, I awash with sickening apprehension. I had never lived in a flat in my life. Never had neighbours above, below and all around. I really found it difficult to believe that people could actually exist in some of the fearful places into which we had to venture to see, simply, if they'd 'do': Adam-green walls, pale watercolours in huge mounts and thin gold frames, brass chandeliers too high on the ceiling, kitchens sticky with frying-fat, bedrooms sagging with candlewick bedspreads and oval mirrors, bathrooms clogged with hair-combings and stained Kleenex tissues, views across dark wells into other people's rooms, dingy through the filtered light from dusty net curtains. Some places, of course, were much better than that: but this was the average. The next morning, very early, Mr Walsh collected me for another viewing.

'Now, this is a *marvellous* block. I think you'll like this one. Princess Diana had a flat here once . . .'

We were driving wearily to yet another address; at least, I was. 'Does that make it so different from the other places?'

'Well, she's a Princess. You know, Spencers, wonderful family . . .'

Bernard was determined to see hope in everything, even in a hideous block of apartments, one of which had once been occupied by the Princess and a slew of chalet girls and Knightsbridge au pairs. But it had a pub on one corner, so that settled that. I insisted we drive on without even entering the place. He looked crestfallen, so I suggested that we might return, immediately, to the flat on the roof short of one bedroom.

'You *did* say it was too small, Dirk?'

But we got there and he produced the keys again and we went up. He tactfully wandered out on to the terrace, left me to look round once more, without distraction. I could easily get a small desk, and a bed, into the little bedroom. It faced north through a tiny attic window. A view of a gable and racks of chimney pots. Writers must work in peace with no visual distractions. I was told. In the little hall the lift opened directly into a sort of closet. A shaft of brilliant August sunlight flooded straight into the sitting-room. Mr Walsh stepped in from the terrace, a last glossy brochure in one hand, jingling keys in the other.

'We really *ought* to be moving on to Pont Street? I said ten-thirty and it's nearly eleven-fifteen after this diversion.'

I said, don't let's bother with Pont Street. I'll settle for this place. It was really all I needed. He started to remind me of its faults: only two small bedrooms, right up on the roof, very exposed, a school playground just below.

'Would that matter?' I was looking at the awfulness of white wrought iron and glass-topped tables which surrounded us. Far worse than school playgrounds.

He shrugged. 'Children screaming? Little ones. Difficult to control, all that energy to let loose. Of course they *do* have *tremendously* long holidays . . . And you are entitled to the use of the private gardens below. I know you are a country boy at heart . . . Near the shops, of course: chemist, grocer . . . And the balcony would be a temptation for you. In summer?'

In summer. Pots and tubs, nicotianas, hostas, aquilegias, foxgloves, a rose or two? Why not? I was leaning over the low brick wall of the terrace, looking down on trees, smooth lawns, a pair of magpies strutting arrogantly.

'We really ought to be moving, Dirk. The car is on a yellow line . . .'

I rolled a gob of spittle on to my tongue, let it fall with a silent splatter into the cherry tree below. 'Don't let's bother, Bernard. I'll settle for this. What's the lease again?'

'Sixty-two years.'

'Lud! That'll see me out. The telephone, I think, is in the hall. Would you call and clinch things?'

Chapter 12

Standing on the cliff top looking out over the immensity of the ocean, it is perfectly apparent that the tide has turned, come racing in, and swirled all your petty endeavours away. The sea frills, swells, surges and scallops along the edge of the cliff far below. Gulls mew and wheel against the sky, dipping low in great swooping glides across the sparkling water. The waves, or wavelets in truth, suck and smack against the rocks, claw graspingly across the pebbles, and then, almost as you watch, they begin to ebb and turn, the tide pulls away, swirling, moon-dragged, towards the distant line which marks infinity or just the usual old horizon. Once again, lying there before you, stretched wide and glistening in the sunlight is that enormous expanse of sea-washed sand. Corrugations of ripples and little ridges, shallow puddles of left-behind water, sparkling shards of broken mirror, trapping tiny crabs, darting shrimp, ribbons of torn weed. All new, pristine, waiting for bare feet to come down and plash and splash, for the little red spade, and work to start on the foundations of another fort.

No matter that the tide will turn once again and destroy all that you will build (and that in the depths of your soul you know that this will happen), you thrust the spade in the hard-packed rippled sand, outline the beginning of a moat. Soon a fort will arise, decorated all about, once again, with shells and weed, with towers and turrets, arches and a drawbridge, each turret capped with a conical limpet shell. As glorious as the first one ever was, probably even better from the experience gained by its destruction, and every bit as impermanent.

The flat was my new fort. I preferred to consider my three rooms and balcony as a house, for no other reason than that I had never before lived in a flat, and the word 'house' came more readily to my lips. The small lift compounded my illusion by opening not into a hallway and a row of numbered doors, but immediately into my own hall so that when it whispered down I felt that I was inhabiting a wholly secret and private place high on the roof. There were neighbours, of course, but only below me. No one above or to left or right, so it was, almost, a house. Anyway, I preferred the name, and the fact that I could smell what everyone was cooking in each apartment in the block didn't, after a time, trouble me. The scents of roasting meats, over-garlicked stews and fried fish which spewed up from the central well were almost constant reminders of the life around me, but apart from two apparently maniacal sisters who once practised on grand pianos for twelve hours at a stretch, and the greasy odours, I might just as well have been back on the hill, as far as silence and peace were concerned.

To be fair, after a disgraceful effort on my part to break down the sisters' front door with my feet and fists (I was hysterical, you might gather, after a twelve-hour session of 'Breeee – brrrop – brungg!' and lost my head completely), they kindly consented to stick foam-rubber under the keys and peace, more or less, returned. I was rebuked by another resident of the block for complaining. 'After all,' she said at a tenants' meeting, 'you are *new* here. No one else *ever* complained.' I did not point out that I lived *above*, and that the sound of two grand pianos in full spate raged up the chimney. I just accepted my reprimand but never attended another tenants' meeting. Best avoided at all costs. Very like a WI meeting in Blakes Cross or Lacey Magna without lottery tickets, jars of pickled beetroot, coffee and biscuits, or appeals for Bulgarian babies.

Otherwise, amazingly, one almost never sees anyone at all. I never know quite how Fate, or whatever it is, arranges the timing. But whoever it was, or is, I am grateful.

Elizabeth, Frank and George moved me from the Doll's House one hot September morning. The van which brought my worldly goods was so modest that it almost took up no more room than a large Honda motorbike in the street below. A far cry from the twelve pallets at the XYZ depot. I kept only the things I needed: bed, chairs, particular pictures, chest of drawers and so on. All the rest was handed over to Maude's impeccable friend, who valued it, carted it about, stored it, and, finally, sent it off to auction. What Alain and Christine did not buy, what I did not keep, Kensington, Knightsbridge, Fulham, and assorted dealers bid for. I later saw a painting which cost me five pounds in a junk shop in Cookham, and which had always hung in every house I'd owned (it was too large for the staircase at the Doll's House), going for £85,000 in a shop in Walton Street. I got £2,000. My bad luck. But it would never have fitted into my new scheme of things.

Life was altogether simpler, I saved only the bits and pieces with which I'd always lived, some from my early days in a rented house in Chester Row and the carved stone figure of Bacchus who had always guarded the front door of Le Pigeonnier and who now stands sentinel on the balcony, staring blindly into the trees. He proves a comforting link with what was. Once speckled by the shade from the vine, he burns in the thin London sun or dribbles sorrowfully in the grey rain, but is staunchly my friend and familiar.

At first it was all a bit bewildering and difficult. I had given myself two years to continue, so it seemed wise to stop sitting on the balcony in the late sunshine (it was a wonderful summer that year) drinking whisky and watching the kestrel in the big plane tree and the silence of evening descend on my part of London. I had no incentive. Without that I knew that I would perish, to use the word the night nurse had used to me in the Hospital, rapidly. I'd just swig away at the whisky in the evenings – I was getting through a third of a bottle a night – and bash at the Heineken in the day. Otherwise, apart from a slightly hung-over drift to the grocer to get something cold (that is to say something that did not require cooking) to eat, or a visit to the chemist, or (very daring this) to look at the books in John Sandoe's bookshop, I did nothing whatsoever. All day. I couldn't possibly continue like this, even though I rather enjoyed it, because at the rate I was going I'd not last a year, let alone the two I had so generously allotted myself.

So, I bought some pots and tubs, some sacks of compost, and began to make a modest garden on the roof. Then I bought a paperback cookery book and learned, painfully, how to make corned-beef hash. I was so impressed by my work that I cooked and ate it every day for a week. Then, wearying slightly, I tried a packet of spaghetti and a bottle of vicious acidic red sauce. Pretty awful, but far better than squashed sandwiches soggy with mayonnaise and old avocado dip, and better by far than boil-in-the-bags. I knew the taste of them *all*. And the unrelenting flavour of monosodium glutamate had practically taken the roof off my mouth and blunted any tastebuds I might once have had. But I *had* spent time cooking. The most important thing was that I was 'creating' something. Learning again. Even if it was something as humdrum as just cooking, it was a start. A reawakening from the immensity of loss.

Pots full of compost and some instant-gardening plants like asters and geraniums on the balcony, a cookery book and saucepans in the kitchen and, very gradually, a return to the typewriter to fulfil my duty for Mr Shakespeare – it was a cautious return to life. The press had seen to it that old friends knew that I had come back to the UK. I was, at first, in demand as a spare pair of trousers at many a dinner party, but that pretty soon wore off. I had been away and out of touch for far too long and simply couldn't hold my own at anyone's supper, or luncheon, table. I was as entertaining and fascinating as a pair of wet gloves.

Incentive gradually returned with Molly's extraordinary idea about an evening event to celebrate Saki. With the help of Amanda Saunders of the National, and three splendid volunteers to help me, Tim Piggot-Smith, Barbara Leigh Hunt and Zoë Wannamaker, I once again found myself in rehearsal for a stage performance and, after thirty years, standing stage-right before a full house at the Olivier. Hideous fear dried my mouth to pumice dust, made tremble my 'wonky' leg, misted my glasses, and sent my voice ranging between basso profundo and high treble. But I did it. We were a success, and we all trolled off together to other dates.

Suddenly I was modestly back in the stream again, confidence so badly dented and dulled began to gleam. I almost enjoyed myself, even managed to stand up straight and stop the apologetic stoop which I had adopted since I returned to the UK – a useless form of concealment which never worked anyway. There were offers to take the show on tour: to America, to Australia, around Britain. But I was not absolutely certain that trailing about doing exactly the same thing every night was really what I wanted to do with my life. But at least I was considering a future. It was a great deal better than sitting in stately solitude waiting for death, more or less. And the feeling of restlessness now engendered was rather exciting.

I decided to extend my expectations of life a little bit longer; there were obviously things to do, and things which I *could* do. All that was necessary was to branch out and try something absolutely on my own. Just to see if I could?

The chance came when Bea Gilbert, a friend of years, suddenly, literally out of the blue, telephoned to ask me for the private telephone number of Mr XYZ, an extremely famous actor. I refused: private is private. She found my pompous refusal irritating. Why, I asked, did she want this hallowed number? Well, Bertrand Tavernier, the French director, was about to make a new film and wanted to get hold of Mr XYZ. It was, she said, just in passing, a script which I had been offered years ago and turned down. *What* script? And when she told me I remembered instantly. I wasn't mad about it and it had arrived on one of the wretched days at Le Pigeonnier when Patrick was looking worried and anxious. The script was about a dying man so I had rejected it out of hand. Now I rather cunningly suggested that if it was *true* that Tavernier was going to direct it (he had not been associated with it before), and if he would consider me, I'd like to do it now. Bea said crossly that she was 'not a bloody agent, you know' and three days later Tavernier, whom I so greatly admired, was sitting with a cup of coffee before me in my own sitting-room. He said he was 'absolutely delighted' that I would work for him. Shooting would commence in September.

This was the test. The biggest I had had to face on my own for years. Could I make it? All alone? Would I have lost my touch? Did I remember my French? It was all to be made in the South, only three characters, a not-quite-right script. But it offered me the chance to stand on my own two feet, to work with a brilliant director, and to try, finally, to eradicate the acute distress of the last two films I had made, I thought, for ever. I really didn't *want* to end a fair career with a dud routine war epic and a hacked-about movie called *Despair*. Give it one more try? Just one? I had gingerly inched back to the theatre with the Saki evening, now I must lay old ghosts, try again, see if I could cope.

I bought, for the first time since I burned everything by the pond on the hill, a diary at W.H. Smith's to record this singular event day by day.

Tuesday, 12th September

Airborne for Paris and the Hotel Lancaster, where we shall have the script conferences, wardrobe fittings, make-up. The first will be enormous, the second easy (I have all my old gear in the baggage compartment), the final nil. I never wear make-up, and as a 'dying old man' won't need to. I'm ready as I am for the camera. Up here, crossing the Channel, I realize, with a start, that this is my first movie for over twelve years. I hadn't realized it was so long. Supposing I can't do it now? I may not just be dusty. Merely out of touch, out of date. Have I lost the trick? I'm playing a retired English (useful for my forgotten French) commercial traveller for Yardley's who has just had a double by-pass. All jolly fun. Most of it will be in French. The fun ends there. Tavernier awaits me for luncheon at the hotel. Maybe I've bitten off a bit more than I can, actually, chew. Over Dieppe now. Too late to turn back.

Evening, 12th
Hotel Lancaster

Why did I think that he would look like Truffaut? Neat, agile, dark, intense. Until he arrived at the flat I had this vivid, inaccurate picture of him in my mind. At lunch today he was suddenly very tall, white-haired, eyes laughing behind thick glasses, perfect English and an hysterical laugh. He loves his food and wine. Very much his own master and knows it, expects one to know it too. I do, anyway. We have an instant bonding. My heart soars, fear almost lifts but the not-very-good script remains. A worry. Dinner tonight at Le Val d'Isère.

'A little late to say you don't like it! Why?' Pouring his Sauvignon liberally.

'Well, Bertrand. It's a bit, sort of, well . . . yucky. Sweet. Whimsy. You know?'

'Not at all. My ex-wife wrote it. She is very *clever. Irish. I* adore it.'

I mentally ducked, and suggested that we'd all get it right during the playing. Somehow. We went on eating our *fruits de mer*. Jane Birkin was my 'daughter' and Odette Laure, from the theatre, my 'wife'. They were both adorable. Thank God.

Night, 19th
Hotel Lancaster

Just we three in a small villa in Cinemascope. Rather amazing. They usually use that for battle scenes and disaster movies.

Tavernier grins at my surprise, waves hands exuberantly. That *is why! He chooses Cinemascope because it will be such a challenge composing three people in such a wide area. 'Composing for the big screen will mean you will have to be very patient,' he says. I promise faithfully. This is obviously not going to be small-screen stuff, all of us jammed together in a row. Certainly not television. Tomorrow we leave for Bandol in the South.*

The Lancaster held no ghosts for me. It was odd. Everything was just as it had always been: the red-lacquer lift, the blue carpets, marble floors, flowers, and the familiar and attentive staff. All as before. I even had my usual wing-armchair in the bar. The monkeys were still stealing fruit on the murals. That morning, on the way to pay my bill, two laughing women came out of the old suite. I passed them in the corridor, a haze of Shalimar, very chic, a good deal of gold. Clattering the brass key. Were the curtains still rife with parakeets and twirling ribbons? Anyway, no ghosts, no shades anywhere. It was exactly as if a slate had been wiped clean, leaving not a wrack of memory behind. I was setting off again. Amazed how I had managed to get myself to Paris all on my own, with baggage, tickets, travellers' cheques, passport. Never done that before. Well, not for over thirty years. Never had a cheque book, credit cards, carried money. You have to relearn everything. But I was most surprised by the lack of hurt. The Lancaster was simply an hotel. I had only ever been a client. It was all finished.

Thursday, 28th
Toulon. Rest Room

Flat on my back. No pillow, of course. Intensive-care ward in huge, new heart hospital. Glittering, vast, efficient, gigantic, terrifying.

Makes most London hospitals look like garden sheds, and this is in 'the sticks'. Drip-feed, tubes of blood, a catheter (thank God! unattached), oxygen cylinder, mass of plastic writhing about me make me feel like Gulliver. Helpless. Fear catches my bladder, nags away. Do I, don't I? If I do want to pee the nurses (real, crisp, efficient) will take half an hour to unlace me and release me from this transparent spaghetti jungle. I lie still, dousing panic, trying to remember my first line in French in the script. 'I'm going to die, aren't I?' Just how I feel.

Sunday, 1st
Bandol. Hotel Pullman

In my room here. A concrete slab of a place. Cardiff and the Holiday Inn again but with a glorious view across the sea. Fin de saison, so it's empty except for me, three waiters and a vaguely hostile woman in reception who won't smile. Rest of crew in humbler accommodation or have rented flats or little villas. Sensible. Lonely as hell up here. Now I do know what loneliness means. Now it hurts. Only a 40 watt bulb in the bedside lamp. Wrestle with the 'cuteness' of the script, trying to eliminate the 'Daddykins' and 'Pussykins'. French to English is hard. We do not speak the same language. No French word for 'naughty', no English word for 'merde'. Bertrand has closed the set up the hill, thank God, so no press or idiot interviews while you try to work and create a new world . . . I am beginning to enjoy myself, except on Sundays like today. No work. The crew off to the sea or beach, Jane with her children somewhere and I can't get the BBC World Service on my little tin transistor. Still, I'm beginning to like this . . .

Tuesday, 10th October
Bandol

Jane, Bertrand and I worked after dinner at the script. Hacking away. Looks are more useful than words. The cinema is a visual medium. One brilliantly exchanged look between two people is worth far more than two paragraphs of sweet polemic. Yesterday Bertrand patted my head, kissed Jane. We felt like teacher's pets and liked it. I wrote him a letter last night to tell him just how amazing he is, if I simply said *it he'd forget it in half an hour. I want him to remember. So I write it down. The written words linger. Spoken they evaporate.*

Saturday, 14th
Bandol

A weekend. Alone. Oh well. Many stage actors insist that cinema work is not acting at all. Dead easy, boring. All that waiting about. You can do it reading the small ads in the Evening Standard. *That's why, I suppose, they are seldom any good on the big screen but make it on TV? Every character actor becomes a star on the small screen. For a little time. Bertrand works in ten- to twelve-minute takes. A whole magazine. Exciting for theatre-trained players. Tough on the others. Exhausting but nerve-wracking if one makes a titchy error. All that work over again, and Jane and I overlap and ad-lib a lot. A luxury in which I revel. Forbidden in my early days in the British cinema. The script was always sacrosanct. And inevitably stilted. Mostly they were written by elderly ladies of both genders. Disasters all.*

Brock, amazingly, has just called to say that he and Kimbo are to make me a great-uncle! Do I mind? Wow! Great!

Wednesday, 11th
Bandol

Shooting in the dreary bar of a closed-up hotel. Jane leads me with amazed joy into an even drearier little room adjoining, which contains a plaque stating that Katherine Mansfield wrote two novels here. I wonder if she died here too? It's so depressing and dark. Perhaps in her day Bandol was glorious? Now, like so much along the coast, it has all gone. A vast marina full of hideous yachts bobbing and swaying, gladioli in jars on all the cockpit tables. The standard yachting decoration. High-rise flats where the pines once were. The present inhabitants, anyway at this time of year, all over sixty, in floral prints, sagging shorts, 'cardies', both sexes, hillocked with varicose veins. I trudge through this lot every evening to the harbour to try and get an English paper. Only the Financial Times *or the* Mirror. *Both useless. Take* Newsweek *at vast expense. Hobble back here in the fading evening. Walking still tiring, breathing pretty breathy. I'll manage.*

Tuesday, 17th
Bandol

The location, an empty hotel up the hill, is hellish to get to. I drag up each day on foot. It's only minutes from my hotel but might be at the end of the earth. Leg bloody painful. So have to rest every twenty yards or so. Feel so silly just standing in the gutter resting my slightly withered 'relic'. And I gasp like a fish out of water. I now understand absolutely what the phrase means. My French, however, after three years in England, is coming back at last. A great joy. The kindness of the crew almost makes me blub, if I were the blubbing kind. Tonight they have all gone off to the dailies. I never do. Never have. The feeling on set is pretty good; we manage to work about sixteen hours a day with no draining tea-breaks. Jane and I share one room in the empty hotel to dress in, there is a single working loo, no seat or bolt on the door. Otherwise it's into the pines. Wouldn't do for some. The single loo is for us all, crew included. So it does get rather 'noisy'. I can't imagine any of the bruvvers in the UK accepting this deal.

Bertrand works very much like Visconti; he is the nearest director I have come to who has that kind of magic with his players. A complete understanding of the mind at work. I really am beginning to enjoy this. Thank God, or Fate, that Bea made that daft telephone call for Mr XYZ's number. The thaw has started. I really do believe.

Friday, 20th
Bandol

Last night Bertrand sent me a 'love letter'. Slipped it under my door when I was down at dinner. 'You made me weep during the dailies tonight. I do not do that.' I was touched and very happy. However, the dailies are screened in a clapped-out little flea-pit in the next town. The sound is out of sync, the picture bleeds across the proscenium curtains and the walls. It only has a regular screen, and the colour is a washed out navy blue and yellow. So how can he tell? Maybe that *is what made him weep? Lab reports from Paris, however, are excellent and full of praise for us all. So that's all right. Perhaps?*

Thursday, 26th
Bandol

A difficult day today: we are getting tired. Ton-Ton, the sound engineer, can't speak a word of English but knows instinctively when a scene has been right. He just sticks up a thumb high above his head, earphones clapped to his ears. Jane and I play some of our scenes in English only. Ton-Ton has a desperate job on this location. Gulls screaming continuously, ring-doves cooing in the trees all round the place. They have colonized the woods. A half-hourly ferry chugging slowly *across the bay to the islands, motor-bikes of yobbos who rev up just to infuriate him and screw up a take. Plus helicopters and Mirage jets from the base at Toulon! It plays hell with intimate scenes. Ton-Ton fires a vast gun into the air in fury. This scatters the birds and sends the gulls into a frenzy because they fear that one of their number has been killed. Peace until the next ferry; we try to grab a scene of 'heart-breaking intensity', or something, but the gulls return in a dreadful squadron and dive-bomb us with rage. It's all tremendous fun. But a great deal better than sitting alone in my room. Life is a cabaret, they say . . . Never been a truer phrase.*

Friday, 27th
Bandol

The last day, apart from one day in Cannes next week, arrives. They usually do. Chaotic, grabbing bits and pieces, extra lines to record for voice-overs, we all do everything we can except actually say 'Goodbye' or 'That's a wrap.' It isn't anyway, but only a token crew will come to Cannes. So it is *the end for most, and it has been intensely happy. We have been a family for weeks. Now there is nothing left to do but start wrecking the sets and packing. Tavernier wandered away, alone, down the dusty lane to his hotel. I called out after him and he stopped and we embraced in silence. Very firmly. I watched until he was out of sight hidden by the oleanders and pine trees, walking alone down to the sea. It has been a wonderful, healing time for me. Now it's all over. Funny way to earn a living, I reckon. Filming. And this is the very last I'll ever make. It's a splendid way to finish.*

I abandoned the Smith's diary about then, just entered dates and times and things, so I rather flounder now, relying on my memory – not awfully good at the best of times. I do remember that the last day of work was on the terrace of the Carlton Hotel in Cannes at dawn, to avoid the traffic noises and crowds, and that we played a key scene, Jane and I, in the half-light of the morning, clutching our buttocks with apprehension while someone held up the traffic on the Croisette.

And then it really was all over, and we all peeled off and I wandered off to find a chemist I had known for years, and a bookshop-newsagent I always went to when Forwood and I came down into town to the bank or to get haircuts. They had both gone. Wrecked. Holes in the ground, like the old Palais de Festival which had held so many memories. But it was useless to even think of memories now, no good looking for the past, it wasn't there any more. Time, even a meagre three years, had cleared away so many things and places I once knew.

Back at the hotel I lay in splendour on my company paid-for bed and dialled Madame Bruna up the hill. A sharp cry of delight. *Quel plaisir!* Why and where? Was I well? Yes, all was *d'accord* with her. Marie-Thérèse had another child, Gilles might have gone off for good, she wasn't certain at the moment. He was a very sensitive boy. Did I know about Etienne Ranchett? Dead? Poor Florette, *quelle catastrophe!* He died in the Peugeot of Monsieur Forwood. Bought it from the *garagiste* in Saint-Sulpice who had bought it from us. He was so thrilled because it was all electric. And air-conditioned! Perfect for him when he went on safari to kill birds and deer and all the other animals in Senegal. He *always* went to Senegal, did I recall? To kill *innocent* creatures. And died in the Peugeot because, in the middle of a sand storm, the electric circuit failed. The windows wouldn't open, the air conditioning seized up and he died, roasted to death from a heart attack in his oven! Wasn't that *incroyable? Et vous, cher Monsieur*, vous *etês coupable!* Delighted laughter.

But all was otherwise very well. Madame Pasquini? Ah, she had been moved to Le Foux now, there was a new person at the *bureau de poste*; and a terrible Club Méditerranée, with 2,000 beds, had been built up on the hill behind Sainte-Anne-le-Forêt, the lights on all night, six tennis courts! And boom, boom, boom from the disco until dawn. *Ah si, si!* I left just in time, the whole region was becoming ruined. Germans, Dutch, Americans and Belgians. Yes, yes, *bien sûr*, Monsieur Rémy was well, and very occupied with all the new properties being built. Monsieur Danté had retired. He had dislocated his back and finished work. Now he just sits in the bar at Le Pré. Oh! She was *so* happy to hear me. There had been a photo of me in *Nice Matin* last week. Did I see it? Should she find it for me? It was very good, I looked so well and happy, it was in colour, and my French was *much* better now than it had been when I lived there. How strange! I said it was perhaps because I was no longer 'timid', and she laughed a good deal and we blew kisses and I sent messages of love to everyone, and that was that.

The next morning I got the first flight out for London. Nice airport, once so cruelly familiar, was still the same airport. The palms were the same palms, the newspaper stall still the same stall and in the same place. Monique, behind the till, recognized me after a moment of considered doubt and exclaimed with pleasure. We kept a line of irritated passengers waiting to pay for their journals and cigarettes while we discussed who had left and what had happened to Dominique. Did I know that she had married a boy from Villeneuve Loubet and was now working as a waitress at Le Coin Joli? People got restless. I paid for my two cigarette lighters, one for me, one for Brock. Mine had 'I Love Cannes' on it. Monique and her friend, plain as an old galosh, had always kept the Sunday papers for me under the counter. If Monique or Dominique were on duty we had a luxurious evening up on the hill. If not, well we might have to just rely on *Nice Matin* or *Figaro*, but she always did her best.

In the Pullman Bar, on the observation floor, it was just as it always had been over the years. The same chairs and tables, the same Muzak tape gently soothing the nervous traveller with 'Strangers in the Night' and 'Autumn Leaves', the same hideous murals, the same affectionate waiters: Bernard, Jules. *Ah, Monsieur! Mais Monsieur Forwood? Hélas, il est mort, Jules. Ah. Quel dommage, un vrai 'gentleman', eh? Un vrai.*

On the flight I didn't look out of the window, I never said farewell to anything. I never had and now never would. Over the Alps I looked vaguely down into snow, felt the gentle bumping in the currents of air, sipped an altogether too early glass of champagne. I'd always insisted before that you could drink champagne for breakfast. And that's exactly what I was doing. I had no sadness, no regret, just a feeling of quiet surprise that I'd managed the trip and the film all by myself. Proving once and for all that I could manage on my own if I had to. I'd just been too bloody lazy. Protected. I must confess that I was pleased with myself. It seemed to me, sitting in my seat high above Grenoble, that somewhere along the way down my corridor, which had grown pretty dark for a time, after the slamming of a door, I had seen a very thin crack of light far ahead. It was not all Stygian dark and gloom. A slight push at the door marked 'Saki' had been rewarded. Behind the door there was a glorious ball going on to which I had been invited. I had accepted the invitation.

I remember, ages ago, saying to Forwood when things had got really wrought, that if he desperately wanted me to rummage in the tartan wash-bag I would do so. He had thanked me and told me that the time had not yet come. He would still try to hang on. I remember saying then that I would get the last brick off the top of the chimney for him, if I had to, but if he felt he *could* manage that he should. He said that he would manage, for as long as he could. He was not frightened, just, as he said, 'bloody angry, there is so *much* I still want to do'.

Looking down across the snow-capped peaks sliding slowly below, I decided to put my self-administered *fatwa* on hold. I had learned my lesson, there was still so much that *I* wanted to do now, and, as far as I was aware, I was being permitted to do those things. The first mission had been accomplished.

And then we were over Kew Gardens, belts were fastened, last cigarettes stubbed out, the pagoda swung into view, the Palm House, the coiling loops of the river swung away. I was back again. I felt a drift of pleasure when I thought of the fort waiting for me and, if I was very lucky, Maria. It was a Wednesday, her day to clean things. And then all at once there was Ron, leaning over the rail at Immigration, taking my luggage. All well? A good flight? All well, this end, thank you, sir. No news, not to speak of anyway, and yourself? I looked very well. Brown. Good weather? The trivia of pleasant small talk as we drove through the grey light up the Cromwell Road.

Maria was there, smiling, dressed moderately today: no longer the florid colours of Colombia, now the more sober greys and browns of Kentish Town. I had bought her a glittering bird of paradise brooch in red, green and blue glass. It weighed a ton and looked a little out of place on her in London. It had seemed perfectly all right in the sunlight of Bandol. Typical. But she liked it and showed me, with enormous pride, the clean ticking cover on the settee. 'I wash. In machine. But is now more *small*.' It *was* 'more small'. But I didn't really give a fig. I was home. I remember that I said that aloud to Maria, '*I am home*' and she laughed with relief and said that I wouldn't notice the cover really because she had found 'string and needle. I put all right. You see.' It looked very like an overweight man in a too-tight suit. Gaps and bulges. I gave her a kiss and told her to go away, I'd see her on Friday. The fort, the flat, house, whatever, looked sparkling and bright. She'd polished every piece of wood, every bit of glass, washed every bit of porcelain. They all looked welcoming, familiar, cherished, in place. Well, she had had weeks in which to do it all.

I unpacked, suddenly felt dreadfully flat and weary. A fine rain spilled down the windows. On the terrace the pots and tubs were draggled and sere with the last of the summer. I'd deal with all that later. Now to walk. I remember I wanted air. Even London air would do, the aircraft smells of paraffin and stewed coffee lingered.

Maria had not spared my little office: clinically neat, pens all in rows, books on the shelves according to height, not title. I'd never be able to find anything ever again. Three piles of mail stacked according to the postage: first, second, foreign. Perhaps she'd been a shelf-stacker in Colombia. Beside my shrouded typewriter, a pile of tidy paper: 'JERICHO.' DO NOT SHRED – the stuff which Barbara had saved. Who were these odd people? *William, James, Helen?* I had three chapters here of an unremembered novel. What was the idea? The idea was to write to deflect apprehension, waiting for X-Rays, scanners. Abandoned when darkness fell. Who were they all? And *Florence*? I had no recall. Perhaps I could rejig the stuff? It seemed to be set in Provence. I'd been in Provence only four or five hours ago; while it was still vibrant in my mind perhaps I'd better start to think about these people again? I'd think about them later.

I shouldered into the old anorak, felt for my keys, and clattered down in the lift to the street. I walked up under the dripping trees to the square, the damp cold biting through the anorak, misty rain on my face, my leg dragging a bit, but better after its ten-week exercising; I even managed to breathe fairly easily. I'd go up to the top, turn right, come down into the square, that would be enough. Managed to weave my way through a crocodile of squealing, laughing, punching schoolboys on their way to somewhere. So much life ahead of them! So many things to do, so many pits and traps before them. And they hadn't the least idea. Yet. As it should be: ignorance can be bliss.

However, I knew, more or less, what was ahead for me. I was back after a long time away. Now it was a return to work. A new phase was starting up. I turned right at the top of the square and headed home.

But no dogs leaping in idiot welcome, no scent of freshly cut hay, no scuttering lizards on the stone walls, no quick 'plops!' from suddenly disturbed fish in the pond. No pond. No voice from the terrace calling, 'Were the London papers in yet?'

Emptiness sighs. Perfectly all right. No problem.

Offenbach said, in one of his lyrics, 'When you can't have what you love, you must love what you have.'

Fine. I'll go along with that.

Why not?

London
4.2.93